YOUR HEALING MIND

YOUR HEALING MIND

Reed C. Moskowitz, M.D.

AVON BOOKS ◆ NEW YORK

AVON BOOKS
A division of
The Hearst Corporation
1350 Avenue of the Americas
New York, New York 10019

Published in hardcover by William Morrow and Company, Inc.; for information address Permissions Department, William Morrow and Company, Inc., 1350 Avenue of the Americas, New York, New York 10019.

The William Morrow and Company edition contains the following Library of Congress Cataloging in Publication Data:

Moskowitz, Reed C.
  Your healing mind / Reed C. Moskowitz.
    p. cm.
  1. Stress management. 2. Medicine and psychology. 3. Health behavior. 4. Mental health. I. Title.
RA785.M68 1992
616'.001'9—dc20   91-27490 CIP

First Avon Books Trade Printing: April 1993

AVON TRADEMARK REG. U.S. PAT. OFF. AND IN OTHER COUNTRIES, MARCA REGIS-TRADA, HECHO EN U.S.A.

Printed in the U.S.A.

OPM 10 9 8 7 6 5 4 3 2 1

To my loving wife, Debra,
and our beautiful baby, Marissa—
living proof of the effectiveness of these
mind-body methods in overcoming infertility
and achieving happiness

Contents

Part III
Healing: Restoring Your Physical Well-Being
199

Foreword

Scientific understanding of how our mind affects our body has expanded rapidly in recent years. As executive director of the Institute for the Advancement of Health, I worked directly with the leaders in this emerging field to educate the health care community and the public about how our thoughts and emotions effect often dramatic changes in our physical health.

To facilitate this education process the Institute published a journal called *Advances, the Journal of Mind-Body Health,* and a newsletter, *The Mind-Body Health Digest.* It created a scientific advisory council to guide the publications and other education programs so they met the strict criteria of scientifically reliable information. This council was guided by physicians and scientists from leading medical schools, including Harvard, Johns Hopkins, and Stanford, and from internationally renowned health centers, including The Rockefeller University and Memorial Sloan-Kettering Cancer Center. The scientific advisory board included leaders in the field who have published landmark books for the public, such as Dean Ornish, M.D., author of *Dr. Dean Ornish's Program for Reversing Heart Disease;* Steven Locke, M.D., author of *The Healer Within;* and Norman Cousins, author of *Anatomy of an Illness.*

It became apparent that while great progress had occurred in the scientific understanding of mind-body healing, these treatment methods needed to reach a wider audience both in the public and the health care community. We contacted Dr. Reed Moskowitz, who had been helping patients to heal with those mind-body techniques for over fifteen years.

In an important article for *Advances,* Dr. Moskowitz discussed the clinical progress in utilizing mind-body methods to treat such disorders as vascular, migraine, and tension headaches; high blood pressure; back pain; irritable bowel syndrome; and bruxism.

In *Your Healing Mind,* Dr. Moskowitz breaks ground by showing how mind-body methods can be used further in treating such serious medical conditions as infertility, heart disease, eating disorders, chronic fatigue, multiple chemical sensitivities, sexual dysfunction, high cholesterol, and severe allergies.

In 1989 the Institute saw the need for a forum in which people could learn mind-body techniques and where an individual's questions about specific health problems could be answered. We planned a full-day workshop that included a lecture by Norman Cousins, an Institute trustee and one of the driving forces in bringing to public awareness the importance of our emotions to our health. Dr. Moskowitz, whose own work coincided with the pioneering achievements of Dr. Cousins, was the workshop leader.

At the workshop, I watched Dr. Moskowitz wonderfully capture the attention of the participants, teaching them the mind-body techniques he offers you in this book. The same caring and helpful personal response to people's questions is evident here as Dr. Moskowitz takes you into the actual process of healing to show you how you can become an active particpant in regaining and maintaining your own health and well-being.

—ALLAN LUKS

Acknowledgments

First and foremost, I want to thank Dr. Linda Carter and Arthur Carter, whose belief in the importance of this work reaching a wide audience has been absolutely essential to the publication of this book. I will be forever grateful for their crucial, generous, and unselfish support.

I have been blessed with good friends who have been helpful during the writing of this book. Among those who reviewed my manuscript with critical eye, but loving heart, Lisa Schwarz deserves special mention for her tireless efforts and invaluable insights. In addition, I want to thank Andrea Pratt Gross and Elizabeth Hirky for their useful ideas. Susan Frank, board member of Resolve NYC, has been particularly helpful in reviewing the section on infertility. Gerrie Rahey Clark has been essential to the preparation of the manuscript. Her intelligent suggestions have aided me throughout. Lloyd Merrill, Peter Seiden, and Michael Danchak have been sources of strength and encouragement as well as valuable reviewers of my work. I am fortunate to have had good counsel to guide me through this experience in the world of publishing. Special thanks go to Stu Goldberg and David Lubell for their wisdom and excellent advice.

I deeply appreciate the vital support of the mind-body program provided by Robert Cancro, M.D., professor and chairman of the department of psychiatry at New York University Medical Center. I am also fortunate to have benefited from my interaction with Dr. Dan Baker of Canyon Ranch, Mary Begen, Mary Fanning, Elliot Fineman, Susan Fisher, Neil Hirschfeld, Dr. Richard Kavner, Lisa Lang, Peter Landis, and Kevin O'Donoghue. All of them have been of help to me in innumerable ways, as have Edwin and Clara Aaron.

I want to thank the people at Hearst, Morrow, and Avon, whose collaboration has made this publication possible. I am particularly appreciative of the support and guidance of Howard Kaminsky, Hearst Trade Book Group president and chief executive officer; Adrian Zackheim, executive editor at Morrow, and his assistants, David Madole and Suzanne Oaks; Judith Riven, former executive editor at Avon; Scott Manning, publicity director; Phyllis Heller, publicist; Linda Kosarin, former jacket-art director, Bob Aulicino, jacket-art director, Barbara Levine, assistant to the art director; and Robbie Capp, copy editor.

Finally, on a personal note, the memory of the love and devotion of both my late parents, Edward and Sylvia, and my Aunt Estelle, continue to be a source of strength for me.

Introduction and Overview

At festive occasions, we frequently raise our glasses and toast one another, wishing for "health and happiness." The common belief is that only the lucky ones can have such a wish come true. Most of us expect that our lives will not be so blessed.

Recent advances in medical knowledge show that we can make a big difference in achieving our own health and happiness. We can influence major areas of our life that directly affect our well-being.

A Personal Note

A few years ago, in the middle of the night, I was suddenly awakened by an excruciating pain in my stomach. The pain came in waves and literally left me doubled up in agony. My wife rushed me to the emergency room of Columbia Presbyterian, a world-renowned medical center in New York City. I was a member of their teaching facility as well as having gone there for my medical-school training. I was treated by one of the world's leading surgeons, who is also a warm, caring personal friend and very conservative physician.

I was diagnosed as suffering from an acute obstruction of my intestines. Bed rest in the hospital relieved the immediate crisis. However, this was not the first episode I had suffered. I was born with a nearly fatal intestinal obstruction. Within twenty-four hours of my birth, I had to have major surgery to survive. Ever since then, my intestines have been my Achilles' heel. My friend explained to me that surgery was indicated to prevent further obstructions, which could be life-threatening.

I told him that I had been under a lot of stress recently and I felt that my tension was the precipitating factor in my illness. I pointed out that stress might be causing involuntary muscle contractions and obstructing the passage of food through my intestines. He acknowledged that stress might be the culprit, but noted that there was no known method, short of surgery, of preventing future obstructions. I proceeded to explain to him how I was working with new mind-body techniques that relieved such stress-related disorders as muscle tension, headaches, and back spasms. I said I'd like to try these methods as a way of preventing intestinal obstruction.

He was skeptical. He stated that the intestinal musculature was considered to function automatically, outside of our conscious influence. He pointed out how different that was from the voluntary muscles involved in headache or back pain.

While I acknowledged that the reigning scientific wisdom of the day did consider such differences to be crucial and absolute, I requested his support in trying an experiment on myself. I asked for a two-week grace period to see if I could use my methods to significantly open up my intestinal passage, so that surgery might be avoided.

We agreed that two weeks later I would undergo a GI series. At that time, I would swallow contrast medium and have its passage through my digestive track monitored by X rays and motion pictures. He was sure that a fundamental narrowing of my digestive tube would still be present and would require surgery.

During the next two weeks, I practiced the mind-body techniques described in this book and asked God for His help in my healing. On the day of my test, I focused on keeping my muscles relaxed and doing slow, deep breathing. I knew I had done my best and felt at inner peace.

My surgeon was totally surprised by the test result: a completely normal intestinal tract! He told me he still couldn't understand how what I had accomplished was medically possible. He congratulated me on my self-healing, but remained skeptical that it would last. He let me know he was still ready to help with surgery if things didn't go well during the next few months. Well, that was in February 1983. I've never needed to call him. I've maintained the gains on my own, with the help of simple and effective mind-body techniques.

While this is my personal story of success, as meaningful as it is to me, more important is my belief that each individual has the potential to experience his or her own success with mind-body methods.

The Method: Refined Over Years

As a physician, over the last fifteen years I have been helping people regain their spiritual and physical health. During this time, on countless occasions I have had the opportunity to witness the process of healing. Each individual's journey back to health has had its own unique twists and turns. However, over the years, I began to observe that certain elements are crucial to success.

Typically, I am called by a person in a state of desperation. Often, years of pain and suffering, innumerable visits to doctors, and the complete run-through of every test, procedure, and treatment known to traditional medicine have preceded my involvement. My first visit is usually with someone who feels like a hopeless, helpless victim—with his life totally out of his own control. Yet, often within ten visits, a seemingly miraculous transformation occurs. Not only does the pain and suffering subside, but what's more, a hopeful, optimistic, self-confident person emerges "reborn" and feeling in control of his life. The treatment does not involve any drugs or surgery, yet patients are able to maintain their gains on their own without further visits.

The changes are real and based on clinically established techniques. The premise of the cure is to enable individuals to marshal their own inner healing powers. From my years of work, I have been able to refine the essential change-producing steps. I am convinced that you can use this approach to help develop your own natural healing processes. I have written this book to share with you my clinical experience and the rapidly growing body of medical research that supports our understanding of these miraculous phenomena.

Love Heals

The treatment approach I have developed focuses on the growth of the self and the spirit. The techniques foster the emergence of factors crucial to healing. The most important is love. The healing power of love has been noted throughout history by philosophers, religious leaders, and through common folklore. Now, as I will discuss in this book, science is beginning to understand how this miraculous phenomenon promotes healing. Love heals in so many ways. When we love someone we extend ourselves, we grow.

Love involves caring and consideration and its reciprocity by the one we love. We all have firsthand experience with the power of love. Our mother's love enabled us to grow and develop and thrive as infants. The lack of adequate mother love leads to failure to grow, and illness, even death. If you can't recall your own earliest experiences with your mother, just look around you at all the new mothers and their babies. The warmth, the smiles, the hugs, all promote trust in the infant that the world is a safe place. The trust that develops out of the maternal bond enables growing children to begin to experiment with the world and develop their own sense of self. In an optimal environment, this growing self-confidence leads to an increasing sense of self-worth and self-esteem. The growing child feels he or she is important and in control of his or her world. Through learning at school and enjoying playing with friends, healthy growth of the spirit, mind, and body proceeds. Children develop the faith and belief that they can cope with difficulties themselves, knowing that the loving support of their parents is there if needed.

But this optimal environment does not always exist and that's why the depletion of our spirit and physical health occurs. The world is often less than perfect. In fact, the stresses today are greater than ever before because there are so many crises that have no resolution. The media bombard us constantly with information about disasters, violence, drugs—seemingly endless tragedies that we feel helpless to do anything about. This leaves us with a sense of hopelessness and despair about the world as a frightening, dangerous place. With the breakdown of traditional values of home, family, and community, life loses positive meaning. Desperately, many seek to be numbed out of this painful existence through drugs and alcohol.

The good news is that we can start all over again. We can be reborn in a second-chance family. We can learn to heal the wounds of spirit and body. As a physician, I have been granted the privilege of employing many powerful techniques for healing. However, the most powerful force supersedes all these techniques and gives them their vital energy. It is the force of a warm, loving, caring therapeutic relationship marked by openness, honesty, and sharing.

In effect, it is a second-chance family in which the healer is the good mother encouraging the growth and spirit of the self of the patient. Once "reborn," the new loving self can both care for itself and share the lessons learned with their loved ones.

Taking Control of Your Life

Millions of Americans are becoming actively involved in directing their own healing processes. Many are creating new working partnerships with their physicians. As in the past, these people are using their doctors for the best that medical science has to offer. But now, they are insisting on being treated as fully participating human beings, not just diseases. They are asking questions and seeking ways to help themselves. Medical doctors who choose to work with these people share their attitude. These physicians know that it is most important to take the time to listen to and talk with the person who has the illness. They seek to understand the values and belief system of the individual to facilitate communication. These doctors see their primary role as helping patients to tap into their own inner resources for healing.

The benefits in health and well-being that result from this new healing partnership more than justify the time and effort spent by both patient and physician. People experience changes for the better in their lives. Some outcomes are dramatic and lifesaving. Individuals have triumphed over such feared killers as heart disease and cancer. Many are learning how to cope with the daily stress in their lives. In so doing, they are finding relief from within for the everyday pain and suffering of anxiety and depression. Others are using simple and effective techniques to decrease their muscle tension and stop the aching in their head or back or stomach.

The New Model of Health

These positive developments stem from advances in medical knowledge about how the mind and body work together. Recent scientific discoveries have been demonstrating the links between our mind, nerves, hormones, and immune system. This exciting new field called psychoneuroimmunology (PNI) holds the promise of revealing even greater healing possibilities for the future.

In years past, medicine ignored our unique individuality. Our bodies were treated like machinery, needing repairs only after breaking down. It was like going to the body shop to fix your car, as though hearts were like engines.

This "biological" model, used alone, was very successful against infectious diseases. However, the diseases of civilization from which we suffer have multiple causes that need to be addressed. This shift to a more inclusive model has occurred previously in other areas of science. In physics, discoveries in the twentieth century have enabled major advances from the more limited, mechanical model of Isaac Newton. We are able to harness the power of forces that we can't directly see or touch, and powerfully transform our world. The same kind of advances are happening now in medicine. We are learning how to tap the vast powers of the mind to heal the body.

We Hold the Key in "Who We Are"

Each of us has our own unique personality. Certain personality types are at risk for serious illnesses. For example, studies show that hostility is a key trait that puts the "Type A" personality at risk of an early heart attack. The gifted actor Martin Sheen has spoken about his heart attack at the age of thirty-seven during the filming of *Apocalypse Now*. To help others learn from his experience, he revealed how his personality intensified the stress he was under. He said he gave himself the heart attack.

At the core of our personality is our sense of self, our sense of who we are. When we say, "I am" or "I want" or "This is mine," we express our sense of self. Martin Sheen described his sense of self before his heart attack in terms of feeling driven to make a success of the film without regard for personal cost. His brush with death dramatically changed his sense of self by changing his outlook on what is important in life. He now appears vigorous, happy, and in robust health more than a decade after his own personal apocalypse. We can make a huge difference in our health and well-being by learning how to change parts of our personality that are harmful to ourselves.

Our values and beliefs are important in getting and staying well. Our spiritual well-being is crucial to our physical well-being. Faith and hope can give new meaning to life and help reverse disease processes. Laughter can indeed be the best medicine.

Negative emotions such as chronic rage, hostility, and anger can contribute to such serious problems as heart disease. It's important that we can learn how to turn off these negative feelings and eliminate their harmful effects on our body.

The stress response is a final common pathway by which negative thoughts and feelings from the mind cause harmful damage to the body.

The Stress of Modern Times

Hasn't there always been stress, you may ask? The answer is that the nature of stress has changed dramatically, while our bodies are the same as our ancestors' in prehistoric times.

Imagine, for a moment, that you are one of our caveman forefathers living in the jungle. Life is harsh, brutal, and short. In a typical life span of approximately twenty years, the dangers are acute and physical. A wild animal comes into view. An emergency response is triggered. On seeing the danger, a lifesaving "fight or flight" response occurs. Your pupils dilate as you become wide-eyed with fear. Adrenaline pours into your body. Your hair stands on end and goose bumps appear on your flesh in anticipation of the struggle ahead. Your blood is shunted to the muscles of your arms and legs to prepare for battle or running away. The surging blood comes from the abdomen, which tenses, and digestion is abruptly halted. You can feel your heart pumping rapidly and loudly. Your blood pressure soars, forcing blood to the parts of your body that need it. Your breathing speeds up and your chest heaves as you strive to get more oxygen to the needed muscles. Sweat pours off you, which cools your body and enables it to burn more energy. Sugar and fats pour into the blood to provide fuel for quick energy. Temporarily, you achieve a strength and endurance that surprises you. Within half an hour the danger is over. If you have survived, your body goes into a deep state of relaxation and returns to normal physiological functioning.

Now bring your focus back to life in our modern, fast-paced, technological era. The contrast couldn't be more striking. Instead of acute, physical dangers, you face continual psychological and social stresses in your sedentary life-style. The phone doesn't stop ringing, the papers pile up on your desk, your boss wants five different things as of yesterday, your spouse wants more than you have the energy to give, and the bills mount up, as do problems with the kids. We're chronically triggering the stress response which was passed on to us from our ancestors.

We owe our lives to the fight-or-flight response, but the world is drastically different today. We live in a time of accelerating change. Everything is happening at an even faster pace. Instant communication from television and telephones bombard our nervous system relentlessly. We go from crisis to crisis personally, environmentally, globally. Our bodies are prepared to fight, but we don't, and thus, we never reach the aftermath of a state of relaxation. The body has difficulty returning to normal physiological functioning.

How This Book Can Help You Cope

As a clinical assistant professor at New York University Medical Center, I developed the "Stress Disorders Medical Services" program.

I have created a new short-term, effective program from my years of experience as both a physician and psychiatrist. This ten-session program shows us how to tap into our own healing system by treating the mind and body together.

Each of us carries our own unique emotional baggage. Working with this program, you can quickly learn to let go of the heavy emotional burdens of your past and free yourself to enjoy the present. This release of positive energy can be harnessed to achieve personal renewal.

Despite the fact that we can't eliminate the stresses in our lives, we can learn how to turn off the stress response. By changing basic body functions previously thought to be beyond our will, we can train ourselves to alter our heart rate, blood pressure, muscle tension, and breathing pattern.

Easily learned methods such as muscle relaxation, abdominal breathing, and biofeedback help us to achieve voluntary control over these basic body mechanisms and turn off the harmful effects of stress to our system. We can slow down our racing heart, lower our blood pressure, decrease our muscle tension, and increase the oxygen going to our brain. By doing this, we trigger the relaxation response. This is the body's natural alternative to the stress response. In the process of shifting gears, we turn off the excess adrenaline. We bring our nervous and hormone system back to normal levels. The increased oxygen going to the brain enables us to think more clearly and make better decisions. Many people hear the word *relaxation* and assume that the mind is out to lunch. A typical initial reaction from many people goes something like this: "Doc, I can't relax at work. I'm being paid to stay alert and do a job." The reality is that our mind functions better when our body is in a state of relaxation. Instead of the rushed, panicked attempts at thinking that occur under stress, we can more rationally and logically think when we are more calm. The relaxation response promotes mental awareness.

Learning how to shift gears and turn off the stress response is a necessary step to getting back in control of your health. However, we often have emotions such as anxiety, depression, and anger that continually trigger the stress response. It's like being in a leaky boat. You can bail out the water to avoid sinking. At some point you need to plug the hole in the boat. Otherwise, you will eventually get exhausted just trying to keep up with the water rushing in. Plugging that hole—turning off the stress component caused by the mind—requires other techniques. Your doctor can help you learn effective ways to turn off these negative emotions and achieve peace of mind and body.

Treating Stress-Related Disorders

Medical care is broadening its scope and empowering the patient to take an active part in healing. Great progress has been made in treating the chronic stress-related illnesses of modern life.

As a pioneer in the treatment of complicated mind-body problems, I present in this book the methods I have developed to deal with a number of different disorders: infertility, sexual dysfunction, high cholesterol, heart disease, high blood pressure, eating disorders, chronic fatigue, severe allergies, and multiple chemical sensitivities [M.C.S.]). Although each of these is a distinct problem, requiring its own specific modifications of the mind-body approach, they all provide examples to help us explore how we can more fully use the new and powerful mind-body methods to renew ourselves.

Each of these disorders requires an emphasis in working on the mind side of the mind-body approach. I have used the case study method to reflect the process of how treatment works in curing each of these disorders. These cases show that there is a specific approach to each of these complicated problems. There are specific issues and particular ways of addressing them, unique to each illness, just as there are specific medical treatment protocols for ailments such as heart disease or cancer.

As in treating any serious disorders, there is no simple cookbook, no how-to recipe. Each disorder requires both a treatment protocol and engaging the healing mind of the patient. Throughout these studies, I have noted how this works in the treatment process. The approach and the results are reproducible, not magical.

Infertility and Sexual Dysfunction

In Part I, Happiness, we see how, step by step, the couple Laura and Rick overcome both infertility and sexual dysfunction with these methods. The science of fertility has made enormous advances in helping couples have a child. Coordinating my efforts with those of fertility specialists, we have seen remarkable results. We learn what to look for in a "stress" doctor and how to maximize our benefits from working with such a specialist.

Heart Disease and High Cholesterol

These well-documented short-term methods can actually reverse existing, severe heart disease, without the use of medication or surgery. Later, in the Healing section (Part III) of this book, we will explore in detail how Steve, a man with a "hostile" heart, learned to curb his self-defeating rage. In chapter 8, we will see how people have dramatically lowered their cholesterol by using their own healing powers.

High Blood Pressure

High blood pressure, the "silent killer," can also be reversed with this new branch of healing, known as behavioral medicine. The solid scientific and clinical evidence for this, as well as how to lower our own blood pressure, is presented in the Heart Disease chapter. (In the initial section, Happiness, Rick becomes impotent from using antihypertension medication, an unfortunate common side effect of such drugs. With these techniques, Rick was able to fully restore his potency.)

Eating Disorders, Chronic Fatigue, Severe Allergies, and Multiple Chemical Sensitivities (M.C.S.)

These disorders can be life-threatening. Concluding Part III, the Healing section of this book, I discuss in detail the treatment of a young woman, Susan, who was suffering from many serious problems. She was literally starving to death when she first called me. In addition, she was chronically exhausted and highly sensitive to common chemicals, such as ammonia in cleaning fluid. How she cured herself with these new mind-body methods is an inspiration to us all, and a testament to the power of self-healing.

How to Help Yourself

Part II of this book, Health—Taking Charge of Your Life, presents scientific and clinical evidence underlying the new behavioral medicine. Chapter 5, Stress and Our Health, provides a deeper understanding of the role we can play in healing ourselves. A useful guide to the information is provided by subheadings such as:

How You React is the Key

Our Personality Shapes Our Perceptions

Helping Yourself

The Brain Connects Our Thoughts and Feelings and Our Physical Health

To help you see if you are in danger of suffering from a stress-related disorder, the following subheadings in Chapter 5 provide a list of things to look for:

The Signs and Symptoms of Stress

Mental Symptoms of Stress

Behavioral Symptoms

Physical Symptoms

Stress-Related Illnesses

Chapter 6, Coping with Stress—Regaining Control, describes how to use the mind-and-body techniques. The first part of the chapter focuses on practical mental approaches as detailed under the following subheadings:

Reframing and the "Worst Case" Scenario

Problem-Solving Replaces Fear

Calculated Risks

What Is Control?

Look Inside Yourself

Understanding

Unconscious Conflicts
Mental Defense Mechanisms
Discovering the Motivation to Change
The "Good Mother" and the "Second-Chance Family"
How We Learn to Be Our Own "Good Mother"
Using Visualization
Calling on Your "Good Mother"
Self-Respect Is Not Selfishness!
Love Is Not Self-Sacrifice
Self-Respect and Relaxation: Changing Your Cholesterol Level

The final part of the chapter shows how to use simple and effective body techniques under the following subheadings:

Where to Begin Proper Breathing
How to Learn Belly Breathing Quickly
Biofeedback
Learning How to Do It Yourself
Taking the Training into Daily Life
Making a Choice: Good Health or Cigarettes
Help through Hypnosis
Doing Self-Hypnosis

We can use these methods to find relief from the pain and suffering of everyday problems. Tension, anxiety, headache, backache, and upset stomach are just a handful of common stress problems that can be solved with the new mind-body methods.

The Health section of this book also serves as a guide to help us determine what we can do on our own, and when we need to work with a professional. This part of the book also describes the general mind-body format as well as the specific techniques I use in helping people. This is analogous to the general format and the specific techniques a physician uses to treat our ailments. A doctor, while working within the framework of his specific medical skills, will work with one approach to treat a cold and a different approach to treat an upset stomach.

Similar variations in approach occur in treating different types of stress-related disorders. For example, the treatment of back pain will be somewhat different from the treatment of migraine headaches. However, the variations in treatment plans will be within the framework of the mind-body approach. More specifically, in treating back pain, the focus is on muscle relaxation techniques, whereas migraines require attention to blood flow and hand temperature monitoring.

Chapter 8, Heart Disease—Treatment and Prevention, provides information you can use to help yourself. Some of the topics covered are indicated by the following subheadings:

The Role of Stress and Personality

Cholesterol

Type-A Personality

Hostility

High Blood Pressure—the Silent Killer

Learning How to Lower Your Blood Pressure

Controlling Hypertension Without Drugs

Heart Disease—Often Silent Until Fatal

How to Deal with Chest Pain

Reversing Heart Disease Without Surgery

Preventing a Second Heart Attack

The Success Stories: People Like Us

Most of this book is devoted to a step-by-step account of how people suffering from a severe stress-related disorder can help themselves get back to health and happiness. Their stories are both real and inspirational. Most important, they illustrate how we can do the same for ourselves.

My hope is that you will not be suffering from as severe a set of problems as these people, and your task will be easier. However, even if you are suffering from a serious or life-threatening illness, their examples can show you that you can make the difference in your own recovery of health and happiness.

Using your healing mind is ultimately both an art as well as a science. This book is written to give you a picture of what is possible today and where we are headed. It is meant as a guide to empower you with information and help you make intelligent choices in working with a stress specialist.

Part I

Happiness: Rediscovering Joy in Living—
Laura and Rick's Story

In writing this book, I want to stimulate a chain of hope—and healing—to help you to reestablish a sense of self-control over your life. The people discussed in this book have taken charge of their health and happiness. You, too, can take an active role in making life work for you.

How people grow and change is often shrouded in mystery. This section of the book is designed to reveal how the process of renewal occurs.

Stress affects each of us differently. We all have our own Achilles' heel. One person may get headaches, another backaches, a third may be most vulnerable to upset stomach.

Some of us need a doctor's help to diagnose and treat complex and serious problems. Laura and Rick did. Some of us know the changes we need to make in our lives. The difficulty is getting started and staying on track to complete the job. Often, the help of a trusted guide can make it easier to deal successfully with the pitfalls along the way.

Whatever situation you may find yourself in, reading the following story will show you how you can work with your doctor to solve your problems and create positive changes in your life.

Chapter 1

Infertility—The Gift
of Life Restored

"It's a girl!"

What joy I heard in those words.

"I'm so happy. I'm here at the hospital holding my very own baby. After all these years, my dream has come true. You're the first person I've called. Rick and I feel so grateful to you for helping us to become parents," Laura said.

"I'm thrilled for you," I replied. I could feel her joy, and a big smile spread over my face. "We all worked so well together as a team, I feel privileged to have been able to help you reach this blessed day."

"I'm so happy, I'm going to cry," Laura said. "*You* know, more than anyone, how much this means to me. She's so cute. We can't wait for you to see her."

We spoke a little longer and made plans for the proud parents to show me their bundle of joy. As I sat in my office, I recalled the first call I received from Laura a little more than a year earlier.

"Hello, I'm Laura Thomas. May I speak to Dr. Moskowitz, please?"

"Yes, this is Dr. Moskowitz. How can I help you?"

"I didn't expect you to answer the phone. I thought I'd get a secretary or an answering machine. I heard your talk about stress and infertility and read your article in the Resolve newsletter. I'm calling to find out if you can help me. My husband and I have been trying to get pregnant for five years. We're both at the end of our rope. We've been through every test and procedure imaginable. None of the doctors can explain why I haven't gotten pregnant. Everything appears normal. We switched to a different fertility specialist. He found an antibody problem, but isn't sure if that's causing me not to get pregnant. I've been in psychotherapy for years, and analyzed everything six ways to Sunday. Yet, I'm constantly physically tense and on a monthly emotional roller coaster. Can you help me?"

"Yes," I answered, "I think I can." "It is universally accepted that infertility causes stress. The constant assault on mind and body caused by infertility wears down our coping abilities. We approach burnout, the exhaustion of our strength. Psychotherapy alone is often insufficient to help us to cope. Mind-body skills can turn off the stress response and trigger a return to inner peace and calm. In working with my short-term mind-body stress-reduction training, I have observed some exciting results. A high percentage of so-called 'normal' infertiles such as yourself have become pregnant when learning to achieve voluntary control over turning off their physiological stress response. Researchers at Harvard Medical School have been achieving similar results in a study they are doing. Other basic research has been showing the likelihood of links between stress and such reproductive functions as ovulation, tubal pickup and transport of the egg, and placental implantation."

Facilitating Function—Not Finding Fault

"I have mixed feelings in listening to what you are saying," Laura replied. "I'm eager to learn any coping techniques to help reduce my stress. It makes me feel better to hear that women like me have gotten pregnant. But if stress is causing my infertility, aren't you saying the problem is my fault? I've already spent years in psychotherapy working through guilt, thinking it was my fault."

"You're bringing up a very important issue," I replied. "Most definitely, it is not your fault. It only adds insult to injury to falsely blame the victim for infertility. It is as awful as blaming a rape victim for being raped. Twenty years ago, scientific knowledge about the physical processes involved in creating a baby was still in the Dark Ages. Very little was known and even less could be done to help infertile women. Uncomfortable with their own ineffectiveness, doctors would often say such things as, 'Well, I've done every test possible, and they have all come out normal. There is nothing physically wrong with you. You do seem tense and anxious. You just need to relax. Go on vacation.' Some might even directly suggest that the problem in conceiving was in the woman's head and suggest that she see a therapist.

"The message given by such statements is false and often tragically causes more needless pain and suffering. Countless women were blamed for their infertility problems. Understandably, being told that the problems were not physical, but in their heads, many women underwent years of psychotherapy. They would look in vain for some unconscious conflict about becoming a mother. When this proved fruitless, they were often left feeling that it was their fault that the therapy was unsuccessful as well.

"In recent years, many new physiological causes for infertility have been discovered. Now, over ninety percent of cases have a known physical cause. Twenty years ago, a physical cause was known in only about sixty percent of infertility cases. Thus, almost one third of the women being treated were wrongly told that it was just in their heads. We now know that the problem is not in some deep unconscious conflict, nor is it in the woman's imagination. The problem is at some biochemical level that we don't fully understand yet. Perhaps there is a slight imbalance in the delicate orchestration of hormones and enzymes. Perhaps there is reduced local blood flow at a critical time period between fertilization and implantation of the embryo in the uterus. The plain fact is we don't yet know all of the physical causes. What we do know is that there are techniques you can learn quickly to control your body's stress response to affect blood flow, hormone levels, immune responses, and a host of other measurable physiological parameters. I believe that one or more of these physiological changes that result from using the body-stress techniques account for the surprisingly high number of pregnancies. My sense is that in turning off the chronic-stress response, the woman's body returns to a physiological balance and harmony consistent with being able to conceive.

"Medical progress often occurs in this way. First, a doctor observes that a certain treatment approach gets some surprising results. Typically, it takes a longer time to understand fully the details of the physiological and biochemical mechanisms involved. For example, penicillin was accidentally discovered to be able to kill certain bacteria. This important observation occurred before our scientific understanding of how penicillin actually works."

"I'm relieved to hear you say that," Laura replied. "I'm tired of feeling it's my fault. I can see that reactions can take place in my body that are beyond my control and willpower. My infertility has clearly shown me that. If I can learn ways to affect my body for the better, I'm all for it."

"Yes, you can," I replied. "The techniques are safe and effective. There are no drugs, needles, or invasive procedures. You learn to tap into your own capacities to change your physical responses. It's one of those rare situations in medical care, where there are really no negative side effects. You can certainly learn ways to feel better by reducing stress. If you also get pregnant, that's an extra bonus."

"Sounds like it's worth a try. Let's make an appointment," Laura said.

Developing the "Good Mother" Within

After the phone call, I made a note for myself about the significant way in which treatment had begun. Laura had been in conflict about making an initial appointment. While she was eager for help, she was understandably concerned about unfairly being blamed for her infertility problem. Talking directly about this issue was essential to help reduce her stress. I like to spend ten to fifteen minutes with an initial caller to establish a human connection. For me, the most important ingredient in healing is developing a strong working alliance with the patient. A bond of trust is essential to enable individuals to become active on their own behalf. Immediately, I begin to establish a relationship by focusing on what I refer to as the "good mother" within each of us. As I look to encourage and work with a patient as an ideal mother would, I begin to open the doors of understanding for the person to treat herself or himself in a similar fashion. I offer support, understanding, encouragement to develop one's own potential, and comfort in the face of fear— the qualities a good mother would offer her child. By visualizing this good mother, the patient develops a basis for healing to occur.

A Second-Chance Family

We all know that real mothers and fathers are human, not ideal. We have all had to deal with the shortcomings of our parents. It's part of assuming the responsibility of becoming an adult. However, we may find that although we accept responsibility as adults, we often know there is something that is right for us, but hard to do. It may be losing weight, quitting smoking, or not getting so angry at everything. Sure, we try. But we often lose patience with ourselves, avoid making the changes, or just give up hope that anything can be different.

The biggest challenge I face is to get patients to see that they can make a difference by trying again. Their sense of despair is understandable. They have tried many things, seen many doctors, undergone many tests and procedures, taken many prescriptions. Still, they are suffering. Many have reached a point of desperation. They fear things can only get worse. Many have lost hope that there are any answers to their troubles. Often, they have lost faith in their being able to find relief inside themselves, from doctors, or even from faith.

Right from the start, my task is to help revive faith and the hope that things can get better. Motivation needs to be rekindled to develop the courage to try again.

When I started doing this work almost twenty years ago, I thought that learning specific physical techniques, such as proper breathing and muscle relaxation, would be sufficient to promote healing. I soon discovered, however, that the most important part of successful treatment involved something far more human than mastering specific techniques. The capacity to create a human bond of trust was the essential precondition for successful learning and change to occur. I have come to think of this process of developing a trusting bond as being like creating a second-chance family. All of us have experienced our first-chance family through growing up in the family created by our parents. While I choose to talk about good mothering, the process is similar in good fathering, good friendship, good coaching, and good teaching. They all are based on human bonds of trust.

As children, our parents served as role models. We learned by imitating them. We did things the way they did. We learned habits of thinking, feeling, and coping from observing them. The degree of love, trust, confidence, and respect our parents showed us became the foundation for our own inner sense of love, trust, self-confidence, and self-respect.

The paradox of being in a crisis—at a turning point—is that, as the word's definition indicates, there is both danger and opportunity. In a crisis, we are more open, more vulnerable. We can reconnect more easily to a good mothering figure. We can absorb those qualities for ourselves. This process of internalization is the same natural way we, as children, took in our parents' qualities. Being vulnerable again is very scary. Therefore, above all else, I will continue to remain sensitive in my interactions with Laura, to stay in touch with my own reactions, as well as look for cues from her about the atmosphere we are working in. I will try to foster the development of the good mother within her. The goal for Laura is to progress rapidly in our work, and more important, to be able to maintain the gains on her own at the end of our brief working relationship. That's the real test. As anyone who has tried to lose weight can tell you, losing the weight is the easy part. Keeping the weight off is the real challenge!

Face-to-Face

Laura arrived a few minutes late for our first meeting. "Hello, I'm sorry I'm a little late, but my boss is working on a deadline, and wouldn't let me go until I finished taking some dictation from him."

As I was listening, I noticed her appearance. Indeed, she looked like she had just rushed over from work. She was conservatively dressed in a round neck, powder blue, short-sleeved cotton blouse tucked into a navy blue, mid-calf length, pleated skirt. She wore a plain gold wedding band on her left hand. Beige stockings and navy blue pumps completed her outfit. Laura looked about 5 feet 4 inches, and her slim frame was topped off by a pert round face. She wore her light brown hair shoulder length, with bangs over her forehead. It was a warm summer's day, and her mascara and eye liner looked a little smudged around her hazel eyes. Despite looking a little frazzled, Laura radiated a bright energy.

As we entered my office, I suggested that Laura make herself comfortable on the big leather couch. I sat in my leather chair placed about five feet away. I have found that this seating arrangement creates a comfortable balance between a conversational zone and enough extra distance for patients to feel they also have their own space. Long ago I put my desk in a corner of the room. I had found that sitting behind a desk created a communication barrier between doctor and patient, with the doctor appearing as an authority figure, dictating to the patient as passive supplicant. My experience has been that by literally moving to the other side of the desk and talking face-to-face, without any furniture in between, an atmosphere is created for real dialogue between two people working together.

"You gave me a brief summary of your infertility treatment when we spoke on the phone," I began. "I'd like to hear about your experiences in more detail. Your thoughts and feelings are as important to me as the medical data. Describing them will help in understanding the stresses you're experiencing and how you're coping."

"I can give you a more detailed history," Laura said, "but why are you interested in my thoughts and feelings about it? On the phone you told me the problem wasn't in my head. Anyway, I'm still working with my psychotherapist on my thoughts and feelings."

"You're bringing up some important points," I replied. "I'm glad you're confronting me with your concerns, so I can respond to them. I did say that the stress response involves changes in body function—heart rate, blood pressure, muscle tension, hormone, immune, and nervous systems. The stress response occurs when our body reacts as we prepare ourselves to meet a perceived threat. Feelings and thoughts can trigger the stress response. We can learn how to turn off the stress response by learning how to cope better with negative thoughts and feelings. The focus will be on pragmatic, here-and-now ways to develop more positive mental habits that enable our body to function in harmony and balance. This approach is not in competition with traditional psychotherapy. Rather, it is complementary. Traditional therapy probes more deeply into the past and subconscious motivations. I work with many people who are involved in more traditional psychotherapy at the same time. Actually, getting relief from symptoms of stress frees up energy that can be used with your therapist. However, years of unsuccessful psychotherapy could result in the patient being charged with resistance to treatment, adding continual anxiety to the problem."

Sexual Dysfunction

Laura and women like her are not alone in being criticized when they are seeking a cure for their problems. As women have endured mistreatment in the area of infertility, thousands of men suffering from impotence and premature ejaculation have had to endure a similar mistreatment approach. They might spend years in psychoanalysis being urged to get in touch with such alleged causes of their problem as unconscious negative feelings toward women and repressed homosexuality.

Finally, Masters and Johnson developed their revolutionary breakthrough. The cure they developed involved easily learned physical techniques combined with a positive approach to changing negative thoughts and feelings. Learning ways to turn off fear and anxiety during sex enables the mind to experience the natural physical pleasure of sexual stimulation. Using this mind-body approach, men can quickly regain voluntary control over erection and orgasm.

Masters and Johnson's work was initially very controversial. Orthodox psychoanalysts claimed that the cure would be temporary. These analysts clung to the doctrine that the problem was still in the unconscious. They declared that curing one symptom, such as impotence, would merely result in the substitution of another, such as premature ejaculation. Well, that didn't happen. There was no symptom substitution. The problem was not in the man's head in the sense of being in his imagination or in an unconscious conflict. The part of the problem that was in his mind related to feelings of fear and anxiety as they interfaced with current, here-and-now performance. Negative thoughts were instrumental in that they could trigger here-and-now fear and anxiety.

The Connecting Link

We now know that particular locations in the brain are responsible for transforming such emotions as fear and anxiety into chemical messengers that affect body functions such as erection and orgasm. So there is a direct link between the mind, which is the subjective experience of thoughts and feelings, and functions of the body. The new mind-body techniques enable us to voluntarily influence bodily processes previously thought to be totally automatic. We have come a long way from the old false notions that mind meant imaginary, not real. It is also clear now that problems in the mind that need to be dealt with when there are physical problems are not deep unconscious conflicts. Thus, there is no justification for finding fault, seeking blame, or experiencing guilt in dealing with these types of problems. We are not dealing with a failure to resolve mental conflict. We are not dealing with a specific personality type being responsible for problems of the body. We are simply dealing with learning how to influence ongoing body processes by using some easily learned techniques.

Stress and Conception

Our new understanding is consistent with some long-observed facts. Women with all different types of personalities get pregnant. Some women who appear anxious and as though they were undergoing a lot of stress get pregnant, while others don't. What accounts for the difference? In terms of body function, the effect of stress depends on a balance of forces. We all have different natural capacities to buffer the physiological effects of stress on our bodies. Everyday experience teaches us that if two people undergo exactly the same stress, the effects will be different, since each has different innate capacities to buffer the stress. However, we can learn ways to improve our coping abilities. Thus, we can tip the balance of forces back in our favor. We can take an active part in restoring natural balance and harmony to our body systems in the face of stress.

Ongoing stress can create a vicious cycle of functional impairment resulting in more stress, leading to a worsening of function. Such a downward spiral may be at work in stress-related infertility. The standard definition of infertility involves at least one year of trying to get pregnant. Just as a matter of nature, a certain percentage of women will take longer than others to conceive. As time goes by, not getting pregnant causes stress. We are dealing with delicately balanced biological and biochemical forces. For some women, the increasing stress associated with what may have started out as a normal variation in taking longer to get pregnant, may affect the delicate orchestration of events needed to conceive. Links have been shown between stress and ovulation, as well as between stress and the fallopian tube picking up and transporting the fertilized egg, and the process of placental implantation. These are specific body processes. Learning to decrease the bodily effects of stress may put the biochemical balance of forces back on track.

Making a Commitment to Change

After offering this information to Laura, she took a deep breath and began, "All right, I'll give it a try. I'm thirty-nine years old now. Rick and I have been married six years. A year after we got married, we decided we were ready to start our family. I stopped taking birth control pills. My gynecologist was very encouraging. He said I should be a mother within a year. I've been healthy all my life and I never expected to have any problem getting pregnant. I never even thought about the possibility, because I always took good care of my body. If you would have asked me at that time who would have trouble getting pregnant, I would have thought about women I knew whom I thought had too many boyfriends before getting married or experimented with grass or other drugs. I never did any of that. I was a good girl. Not only have I never used pot, I was a virgin when I met Rick in my late twenties. I only started sleeping with him after we were engaged. It seems so ironic to me that I postponed sex to do the right thing, then used birth control pills to wait until the right time to start a family—only to find out that I couldn't get pregnant even if I tried!

"For almost a year of trying, I was sure that each month would be the month for me to get pregnant. My gynecologist told me that he didn't expect any problems and I didn't either. By the end of that year,

I made an appointment to see him to find out if there might be something simple that we weren't doing right. He said he thought I was being overanxious and gave me a thorough physical exam, which was completely normal. He told me to start charting my basal temperature to help determine exactly when I was ovulating. Then he made an attempt at humor, saying maybe our timing was off and the chart would help us get it right. At the time, I felt reassured that he didn't think any serious problem existed. Later, I became very angry about the way he treated me, as if I were a little girl and he was telling me everything would be all right, when he had no basis for saying that."

Sex on a Schedule

Laura continued, "People talk about the joy of sex. They must never have spoken to any couple keeping a daily temperature chart! That charting was the beginning of the end of sex as Rick and I had known it. Before the tyranny of the thermometer, we had fun when we felt like it. Then the passion, the tenderness, got lost in the routine and sex became work. Doing a job on a precise time schedule to turn out a product—a baby, which, on top of it all, never got produced. Right from the start, the thermometer upset routines I had never even thought about. Just getting up in the morning became a chore! As my doctor told me, *basal* means the temperature of the body at complete rest. I couldn't even go to the bathroom until I had taken my temperature. I had to watch out for anything that might affect my waking temperature. Did I get up later than usual? Did I have trouble sleeping during the night? Had I too much to drink the night before? Was I feeling ill? Let me tell you, I was feeling sick about all this!"

Laura paused for a moment and I asked, "How long did this charting go on? Didn't your doctor tell you that after a few months, you should have an understanding of your individual pattern? After the pattern is known, charting usually can stop. Then you can just have sex on alternate nights around your expected ovulation."

"No," Laura replied. "That's what got me so angry at him. After six months of charting, he was still reassuring me to have patience. By that time, I had done some reading on my own and realized I was going nowhere. He really didn't work with infertility patients. I guess I should have been seeing a specialist right from the start. One of the books mentioned a national organization for infertile people—Resolve. I joined and they helped me get to a fertility specialist. Their newsletters and support groups have helped me cope through this unending crisis."

"Yes," I said, "Resolve's many dedicated women and men know first-hand about infertility. They provide invaluable service to those finding themselves facing this struggle. What happened when you finally got to a infertility specialist?"

Experiences with the Infertility Specialist

Laura replied, "He was very thorough. His nurse drew blood for every possible test imaginable that could relate to infertility. I'll never forget the pain she caused me. I have difficult veins to find in the first place. After sticking me in a number of spots, she finally got it right. After filling up endless tubes, she ripped the needle out of my vein. She pulled straight up vertically, instead of easing it out the way she had put it in."

"How did you react?" I asked.

"I didn't say anything. I was afraid to complain. I felt if I criticized her, she might drop all the tubes, and have to start all over again. And I remember his pelvic exam was really awkward, too. The doctor told me I have tense muscles, which I know is true. I can recall how uncomfortable the internal was."

"How do you know you have tense muscles? Can you describe for me what you experience and where?" I asked.

"I often feel a tightness in my gut area. My stomach gets upset easily, too."

"What gives you relief?"

"Sometimes medication helps," Laura answered. "Now that I'm on so many different fertility drugs I don't like to take muscle relaxants. Also, they tend to make me feel tired."

Muscle Relaxation Exercises

"This is a good point," I said, "at which to tell you about how you can relieve the muscle tension without taking drugs. I would like to suggest that in the beginning, you practice with the tape I'm giving you. Each side is about twenty minutes. The first side is called active or progressive muscle relaxation. You sit in a comfortable chair and alternately tense and then relax all your muscles, starting from your toes and moving up to your forehead. My voice on the tape will guide you each step of the way. Many of us are not aware of the amount of tension we carry with us. This tape will help you to learn to differentiate tension levels as well as to reduce them.

"The second side of the tape is called passive relaxation," I explained. "The focus is more on your breathing and learning how to relax your body continually, without any alternate clenching or tensing of muscles. Achieving deeper levels of relaxation involves changing your breathing pattern. Relaxed breathing is called diaphragmatic or abdominal breathing. It involves taking slower, deeper breaths. As you inhale you will notice your abdominal area expand like a balloon does when it fills with air. Thus, this is also known as 'belly' breathing. Practicing this side of the tape helps you to turn off the stress response to your body even more effectively and trigger your own natural state of calm. When doing the tape, remember, this is an experiential exercise. By that, I mean you want to look for two things in particular. First, a letting go of tension in the different muscles in your body. Some people describe it as feeling themselves melt into the chair. Others talk about feeling a looseness where there was formerly a knot of tension. The second change I want you to look for as you scan your body with your mind is an increased sense of warmth, particularly in your extremities. Your hands and feet may feel a pleasant warmth or tingling sensation. This is a sign that your blood flow is going back to a normal pattern throughout all your body— characteristic of a mentally alert, but bodily relaxed, state. At the same time, more blood flow will go to the gut and pelvic areas, helping to decrease physiological stress there."

I continued, "The stress, or emergency fight-flight, response shifts blood flow away from the gut and extremities and to the major muscle groups of the arms and legs, and to the heart to prepare the body for the battle ahead. These, and other exercises I'll be showing you, restore the normal baseline physiology to your body, as you turn off the stress response.

"Each side of the tape is about twenty minutes, because it takes about that amount of time to shift gears from stress to calm. After you've done the active side of the tape a few times and feel that you've mastered the sense of difference in tension states in the range from clenched to relaxed, then just use the second side. This passive relaxation exercise lets you get to deeper levels of calm. Doing the tape in the morning and again early in the evening helps both to start the day right in the morning and to rid the body of accumulated stress from the day during the evening. If you find thoughts going through your mind as you listen to the tape, don't be disturbed. Just let the thoughts pass through and refocus on the exercise. If you find yourself dozing off during the tape, it just means that you're letting go of so much tension so quickly that you're going right to sleep! While there's nothing wrong with that, we are trying to train our bodies to get to a relaxed state while we are still awake. Do the tape a little earlier in the evening or sit in a less comfortable chair to help stay awake."

Laura asked, "How long do I have to listen to this tape?"

I answered, "The goal with all these exercises is to make the calming response an automatic part of your coping skills. How long this takes varies with each person, but we're talking about weeks, not months. You will know you're 'getting it' as you experience deeper levels of muscle relaxation and warming of the extremities. As in learning any skill or sport, the more you practice, the more proficient you become and the more automatic the response. The goal here is to shift the daily balance of forces in your life from stress-inducing to calm-restoring. After a few weeks, you will be able to trigger the muscle relaxation yourself without the tape. Some people create their own relaxation tape in their mind. As you become more skilled, you will be able to notice when you're stressed at an earlier stage, and take a few seconds to calm your system down."

A Variety of Stress Reducers

"How many different types of exercises are there?" Laura asked.

"In addition to muscle-relaxation training," I began, "you can learn to turn off stress by methods such as abdominal breathing, biofeedback, meditating, prayer, autogenic training, visualization, imagery, hypnosis, behavioral modification, emotional restructuring, and cognitive-perceptual change—to name a few. Every person finds the combination of possible approaches that works best for them. Nobody needs to use them all to conquer stress and restore inner peace. I'll be showing you how to use some of these other methods as we progress. From working with people with stress-related disorders for a long time, I've created a structure for this training that seems to get the best results in the shortest period of time. With this format, it usually takes a person about ten sessions to master the skills and find relief that can be maintained on one's own."

I continued giving Laura background information. "We know now that almost every illness has a stress-related component. The American Medical Association and health insurance companies recognize the value of this treatment for a wide range of disorders, including high blood pressure, headaches, irritable bowel, back pain, and other pain syndromes. Some doctors use just one approach, such as biofeedback. Others see the patient just once, and have all the treatment done by a technician. While some people achieve gains by this approach, I have discovered that healing can be better facilitated in the context of a therapeutic alliance between doctor and patient."

Focusing on Laura's program I said, "Today's meeting between us will run about an hour and a half. That's typical for an initial session with me. You need time to practice the skills you're learning, so treatments are scheduled a week or two apart. In your next visit, you will begin working with the biofeedback equipment and practicing proper breathing techniques with a specially trained nurse-clinician. From the third session on, each visit has two parts. First, we'll meet for three quarters of an hour to review your progress, focusing on the trouble spots. We'll look at your coping style, how you handle stress. We'll work to help you to deal with your emotions, perceptions, and behavior under stress. The second part of the session, also lasting about three quarters of an hour, will involve further training in mastering the body techniques for turning off stress. I have found that combining mind and body techniques is the most effective way of conquering stress. I often think that effective coping with stress is similar to dealing with a leaky boat in water. Bailing out the water provides quick, short-term relief—as does body techniques, such as muscle relaxation. However, you have to seal off the hole in the boat to maintain long-term relief—as in changing your perceptions, emotions, and behavior." I concluded, "We've covered a lot of ground today. Do you have any questions for me?"

"Not right now," Laura replied. "You've answered the ones I had earlier."

I added, "Call me at any time between sessions if you have any questions or problems with doing the techniques. It may take a little time at first, but you will master them. A difficult part is maintaining the motivation to do what we know is right for us. An important part of our work will be to focus on ways to help you find the 'good mother' within to guide you to do the right thing for yourself."

What to Expect from an Initial Visit

I had a good feeling about our first session. I believe that the main goal of the initial meeting is to start the process of working together. The key to developing a therapeutic alliance is trust. Trust takes time to develop fully.

An initial interview is a two-way street. Too often, both doctor and patient approach their interaction as though it were a sophisticated game of twenty questions. Typically, the doctor fires a series of questions and lab tests at the patient. The answer to each narrows the field of inquiry further. This method of diagnosis by exclusion continues until ultimately the answer is supposed to be revealed by "ruling out" everything else. This approach may work for identifying acute infections or anatomical disease. Nowadays, however, over three quarters of the visits to the doctor are for the type of vague, chronic, multisystem and life-style problems that come under the general category of stress-related disorders.

Dealing with these types of problems requires a return to the old-fashioned art in medical care—taking the time needed to understand the symptoms in the context of the patient, not just identifying a disease entity. This step is essential, because the doctor needs to help motivate the patient to make necessary changes in his or her life to achieve healing. Exclusively focusing on high technology to the exclusion of the individual does not offer healing for a person with a stress-related disorder. As a matter of fact, all the patients I see have been frustrated by the lack of healing that traditional medicine has offered them.

What to Look For in a Doctor

So what should you look for in a doctor you're seeing for a stress-related problem? Some of the same old-fashioned qualities that doctors used to have in the days when the local general practitioner made house calls: caring enough to take the time to listen to you in a nonjudgmental manner so that you can really open up about what troubles you; having the capacity to communicate with you in a way that makes you confident that the doctor both understands what is wrong and can help you make changes to set things right.

Trust is earned. Test your doctor, as Laura did both in her initial phone call and our first meeting. If you're concerned about something, say so—as Laura did when she asked if looking at thoughts and feelings would result in "blaming the victim." You have the right to a response from your doctor that makes sense to you and eases your concern.

You may be saying to yourself, "I couldn't be that assertive." Well, you can with time and practice. Obviously, Laura wasn't assertive either, earlier in her fertility ordeal. Remember her not saying anything when the nurse hurt her drawing blood? Laura was afraid of the repercussions if she complained. But over the years, her frustration led her to be motivated to change. Laura learned to be more healthily assertive, as evidenced by the way she questioned me.

The fact that Laura was able to change on her own and become more assertive with doctors brings up another important issue. Our ways of reacting can change. While personality and character reflect habitual ways of doing things, we *can* change our behavior. You can learn to be more assertive with doctors, your spouse, parents, friends, or employer.

People are complex, and not reducible to pat formulas or stereotypes. That is why all the attempts to find an "infertility personality" are forever doomed to failure. There is no such thing. Obviously, women with all sorts of personalities both give birth and are infertile.

To facilitate healing, it is necessary to examine whether thoughts, feelings, behavior, and reactions are promoting the stress response or the relaxation response. We can then learn how to adjust to promote inner peace and calm. This restores natural balances and harmony to our interrelating body systems.

Many times we are told by others, or tell ourselves, "We just need to relax." But this old bromide to "relax" is worse than useless. When you are tense and worried, being told to relax makes you more tense and worried. Relaxing is not a mental act of will. Relaxation is a physiological, body reaction involving changes in heart rate, blood pressure, breathing patterns, muscle tension, hormone, immune, and nervous-system functioning. We can measure some of these changes. This is the value of biofeedback. We can learn to trigger the relaxation response. We can learn to create the physiological state of being relaxed.

I have worked with people who appear to be under no stress at all. They don't feel anxious nor do they appear so. Yet, they carry the stress in their body—in headaches, backaches, upset stomachs. With biofeedback instruments we can now detect a body's specific stress and monitor its return to normal physiology as the relaxation techniques are employed.

Laura spoke about her experiences of body tension. She talked of often feeling tightness in her gut. She recalled her tense muscles during an exam by her infertility doctor. When I greeted her at the beginning of the sessions, I shook hands with her. Her hand was cold. She was under physiological stress, although she appeared calm and sounded assertive.

Becoming an Active Participant

Before ending the initial session, I had to make sure that Laura had begun to be brought into the treatment process as an active participant.

The first step in accomplishing this was to make sure that Laura understood the treatment approach and that she had the opportunity to ask questions. The second step involved giving Laura the muscle relaxation tape, which gave her meaningful homework to do. Learning, growing, and changing all require effort in mastering new skills. Practicing the tape twice a day not only relieved stress, it also involved Laura in making a voluntary commitment to play a responsible role in her own healing. Instead of feeling out of control, Laura would begin to see that she could regain control of herself. This engages the process of self-motivation. Most people working with the tape find it a pleasant way to begin. Practicing every day is relaxing. Feeling better even for a short time creates an enormous positive incentive to help maintain motivation and make more changes.

Almost everyone experiences some level of muscle relaxation doing the tape. By telling Laura that she could call me if there were any problems in doing the tape, I provided a fail-safe mechanism. If, as rarely happens, Laura had some negative feelings about the tape, we could discuss them and I would make some suggestions to help things work better. For example, some people find playing soft music, along with my voice on the tape, makes the relaxation exercise easier to do.

Chapter 2

Sexuality—
Mending a Marriage

Laura was visibly tense as she arrived for her first hour of training with the biofeedback equipment. Despite the summer heat, her hands were cold, a sure sign that she was under stress. The temperature biofeedback recorded 74.2 degrees in the right hand and 74.4 degrees in the left hand at the start of the session. During the training, Laura tried to focus on relaxing her muscles and doing abdominal breathing. It was visibly clear that she was having trouble relaxing. The biofeedback instrument confirmed this. She was barely able to raise her hand temperature to 77 degrees. She was obviously preoccupied. However, all inquiries were met with, "I'm fine." Laura doggedly continued with the session, without either relaxing or being able to talk about what was troubling her. Her wish to keep things to herself was respected, as it became evident that all attempts at encouraging her to talk were met with visible agitation as well as the repeated protestations that she was OK. At the end of this session, Laura was asked to think about the dilemma we faced. Clearly, she wanted help and was working hard. Yet, something was troubling her. I hoped she could think about things before our next meeting. Perhaps exploring what was bothering her might help her to be able to turn off her stress response.

The Loss of Intimacy

"I know you're going to be upset with me," Laura began our next session.

Seeing the worry in her face, I reassured her. "No, I'm not going to be upset with you. I am sincerely concerned about you. You are obviously troubled about something. Perhaps it will help if we can look at the situation together."

Avoiding my gaze, Laura said, "I haven't been able to sit down and work with the tape. I keep putting it off."

"What's your sense of why you haven't?" I asked. "Remember, I'm not interested in blame, I'm interested in how we can work together to help you with your problems. Something must be getting in the way. You're obviously determined enough to come back here, even though things aren't going smoothly."

After a long pause, Laura said, "Well, it's a very personal type of problem. It took a long time for me to talk about it with my therapist. I finally did, but that hasn't helped. Talking about it hasn't changed anything. Not only is the problem getting worse, I'm finding that talking about it just gets me depressed. It seems so hopeless. The less I think about it, the better I feel."

I had tried to prepare mentally for this reluctance of Laura to talk about what was troubling her. Her obvious preoccupation had prevented her from turning off her stress response during her initial biofeedback session. After that session, I reviewed my notes about our initial phone call and face-to-face meeting to look for clues to where the problem might be. I remembered that I was somewhat surprised that right at the start of her describing her fertility history, she spoke about sex. Her two statements were both filled with irony. The first about being a virgin and postponing sex only to find herself infertile. The second about the lack of enjoyment of sex during the temperature-charting phase of her fertility workup. Infertility patients don't usually bring up sexual issues at the start of their describing the history of their problem, but usually focus exclusively on the medical tests and procedures they went through and their emotional reactions to realizing they were not getting pregnant.

"Perhaps this mind-body approach," I began, "can be of help with this problem. Even if it can't cure the difficulty, learning to create a state of calm within your body will help lead you to a better resolution of your feelings."

"I see what you're saying," Laura replied. "Either way, I can benefit.

I guess it's the old guilt thing again. I've been so caught up in 'who's to blame' in my therapy. That just makes it feel worse to discuss the situation."

"Here, we will take a problem-solving, not a fault-finding, approach," I replied. "The important issue is how to deal better in the here and now—not to find some justification in your unconscious for your suffering."

"All right, I guess I have nothing to lose at this point. Even if we can't cure the problem, at least I can learn to live with it better and be able to stop beating myself up for it," Laura said, in a voice that showed she was trying to convince herself as she spoke. "Well, here goes," she continued, after a brief pause.

Life Without Sex

"We don't have a sex life anymore," Laura blurted out, and burst into tears. While dabbing her cheeks with a tissue, she continued, "It's so bad, we're afraid even to try anymore. That's why I was so upset the other day at the biofeedback session. The night before, we tried to make love for the first time in a long time. Once again, it was a failure. Rick can't make love to me anymore," Laura said, bursting into tears again. After trying to compose herself again, she remained quiet. She glanced up at me, her eyes looking for some comment.

"I can appreciate both how painful the situation is for you and how difficult it is to talk about," I began. "Very often the stress of an infertility problem creates severe strains on a marriage. Sexual problems commonly develop as a consequence of the emotional pressures and the treatment process. Many of these difficulties can be resolved. Could you tell me more about the nature of your sexual problems with Rick?"

"It's gotten so complicated, I don't even know where to begin," Laura replied.

I suggested, "Perhaps a good place to continue from is where you left off in our first meeting. You spoke about the 'tyranny of temperature charting' and how that interfered with your sex life. What happened after that?"

"Yes, the chart was the start of our sexual problems," Laura explained. "After a number of months, my chart showed that I was ovulating at slightly different times each month. My cycle has never been an absolute twenty-eight-day process. I can get my period anytime between twenty-six and thirty-two days after the last one. As I learned, ovulation occurs fourteen days before the onset of the next period. Obviously, I don't know in advance if my period is going to be day twenty-six, day thirty-two, or a day in between, until I get the period. So, without some means of testing, I don't know if I'm ovulating on day twelve or day eighteen of my cycle or on a day in between twelve to eighteen."

"How did the charting affect you and Rick?" I asked.

Laura paused for a moment, a wistful look on her face. "You know, it seems so long ago. Before the charting began, Rick and I had a great sex life. We had fun. We were spontaneous. There were no pressures, no dos and don'ts. We just went with our feelings, when we wanted to. The charting brought too much planning, too much calculation, just too much thinking about our sex life. It no longer seemed like making love. It became work. Doing a job at an assigned time. The whole tone of our intimacy changed so gradually that it's difficult to pick a specific turning point. At first, we were confident that we could have a baby when we desired. Even when we started with the charting, we were still optimistic. We initially looked at the thermometer as the answer. It was going to tell us exactly when to do it, and presto, I'd get pregnant. After a half year of disappointment, our attitude had changed. The thermometer became a daily reminder of our humiliating failure to become parents. I was the only one who had to submit to this daily thermometer ritual. That made it feel like it was *my* fault that things weren't happening right. You know, the 'sick patient' is the one who gets her temperature taken every morning. In addition to that guilt, I began to feel like a nag. After getting a temperature reading indicating ovulation, I had to tell Rick that we had to have sex, so we wouldn't miss the day when the egg was supposed to be traveling down my tube."

Laura paused and looked at me for my reaction. I wanted both to acknowledge her ordeal and also to try to lighten her mood a little, so I said, "I can imagine that after a while, the whole thing began to feel like the countdown at Cape Canaveral before a rocket launch. You were monitoring the atmospheric conditions to determine the exact best time for the space shot. A mechanical, precisely timed process replaced what used to be fun."

Laura smiled briefly at my analogy. "Yes," she said. "I began finding myself watching the clock, anxiously waiting for him to come. I felt so restrained. We had to do it exclusively in the missionary position to maximize our chances. Then I had to lie on my back with a pillow underneath me for twenty minutes, to help the sperm to swim in the right direction! Pretty soon, an emotionally exhausting monthly cycle took hold. Starting about day ten of my cycle, I would anxiously await the rise in my temperature indicating ovulation. Then, after our perfectly timed sex, I would fantasize that this was it, that we had succeeded. Near the end of my cycle, I'd become anxious about whether I'd get my period. Then, the depression would hit when I would start to bleed. My life became a monthly emotional roller coaster of anxiety, hope, and despair. I began to feel angry at my body for not working the way I wanted it to. The disappointment, guilt, and anger took its toll on my desire for sex during the rest of the month, when we didn't have a command performance. Every period hit me like a rock. My body had failed me again and I just couldn't immediately shift gears and take pleasure from it."

Laura paused and then continued her account. "Eventually, the repeated pressures of our monthly sex got to both of us. We began playing games to avoid doing the job. I would get caught up in reading the latest romance novel and say I just needed to finish the chapter. Rick would find that he just had to see the late-night movie on TV. Sometimes our delaying tactics worked in the sense that one of us would become too tired or just plain fall asleep before we could have sex. That would just create more guilt, however. I knew things had to change when I found myself falsifying my monthly chart. You know, you make an X on the chart on the days you have sex. I felt embarrassed showing my doctor a chart with so few X's. So, I'd cheat. I'd pencil in a few more. That's when I realized I needed a new doctor. I just couldn't talk with him. He just set up all these rules that didn't work for Rick and me. I felt like I was back in school. Handing in my monthly chart assignment and being judged a failure by the teacher. He never had any new ideas about how to make things work. He made me feel it was all my fault. That's when I started to do some reading, joined a group through Resolve, and found someone who really specialized in infertility."

Impotence

As Laura settled back in her chair I began, "I have a very clear picture now of how—starting with the charting—the infertility began to take its toll on your emotions and love life. The whole situation can be such an isolating experience, especially if you can't talk with your doctor. I'm sure since joining a group through Resolve, you have found that many other people are also going through this struggle. I know that there is a lot more for you to tell me. I would like to get an idea now of your current difficulties with Rick, since it seems to be interfering with your relaxation training as well as causing you emotional pain."

Laura responded, "As I said before, we don't have a sex life anymore. Rick just can't make love to me. He can't maintain an erection. If he gets one, it's weak, and he quickly loses it. This really became a serious problem this past year. Rick has been under a lot of stress, both at his job, and with our fertility problem. He seemed basically OK physically. However, during a regular check-up, our local doctor noticed that Rick's blood pressure was above normal. Rick wasn't having any symptoms, but the high blood pressure continued. Rick's a little overweight and can't seem to change that. His father has had high blood pressure and heart problems. Since Rick just turned forty, our doctor felt it was a good idea to put him on medication to get his blood pressure down to normal. Well, he succeeded in doing that, but ever since Rick has been having trouble getting and keeping erections. He still wants to make love. He just isn't able to. I was so upset at the biofeedback session, because we had tried again the night before." Tears start trickling down Laura's face and her voice was choked with emotion. "It just seems so hopeless."

"No, it's not hopeless," I responded. "This is a common problem for men in Rick's situation. They need to bring their blood pressure down to avoid a heart attack or stroke. Yet, the medication often has the devastating side effect of rendering them impotent. This is because the process of erection involves maintaining an adequate blood pressure in the penis. Unfortunately, the medication lowers blood pressure throughout the body. The solution is for Rick to lower his blood pressure without the use of drugs. Rick can learn to do this using the same mind-body techniques you are learning. While it will still be important for him to have his blood pressure periodically monitored, it is possible that the medication can be eliminated or drastically reduced so as to not be a problem."

A look of relief brightened Laura's face. "That's great! It almost sounds too good to be true. Why does lowering blood pressure this way not interfere with erections?"

I replied, "The difference seems to be that by turning off the stress response you are not only lowering blood pressure throughout the body, but you are channeling blood flow back to the gut and pelvic area. This permits adequate blood pressure in the penis for normal erections."

Monitoring Your Own Stress Level

Laura's body and face showed that the return of hope was having a calming effect. Her initial hand-temperature readings in this session were 80.3 degrees in her right hand and 80.1 degrees in her left hand. She found it easier this time to focus on her belly breathing and muscle relaxation. During the training, her hand temperature rose to 85 degrees. Thus, both her initial readings and her highest level were significantly better than in her prior session. Laura was making progress now that some hope had been restored. She still had a way to go.

Hand temperatures between 80 degrees and 85 degrees still indicate a moderate stress response. Ranges between 85 degrees and 90 degrees show mild stress. Between 90 degrees and 95 degrees are within everyday normal functional range. In treating many stress-related disorders, achieving hand temperatures between 95 degrees and normal core body temperature of 98.6 degrees is often desirable.

These numbers are useful guidelines for monitoring ongoing stress levels. As with any individual test result, hand temperature needs to be evaluated in the context of the specific person's complaints and level of functioning. People vary in their capacity to handle ongoing stress. Good medical care always focuses on the person, not just treating a specific test result.

How Much Stress Can One Man Take?

"Hello, I'm Rick Thomas," the caller said, in an agitated voice.

"Hello, Rick. I'm glad you called," I responded.

"Laura said you thought you could help. I'm willing to try anything at this point. But I have to tell you, I'm not sure if some of the cures you doctors prescribe are not worse than the problem itself. It seems that Laura and I are going through one unending ordeal after another. Each new proposed remedy seems to create more problems than it solves. I guess I've become somewhat cynical about what the medical profession has to offer."

In listening to Rick, I was struck by the pain and despair just under the surface. "You have every right to feel frustrated about what has happened. I can understand from speaking with Laura that although you've been through a lot, it feels like nothing's been accomplished."

"I'm relieved to hear you say that," Rick replied. "It's the first time a doctor has acknowledged that reality. Some of the doctors I've seen act as though they are God. They announce a specific approach that I must follow. If things don't get better, it's supposed to be all my fault. They have no other alternatives to offer. Let me tell you, I'm in computer software sales. If I acted that way, I'd have no clients," Rick continued somewhat defensively.

"Rick, I certainly don't have all the answers," I said. "However, I have seen men learn how to lower their own blood pressure enough to avoid the devastating side effects of medication that you are suffering with. I can promise you that I'll work together with you in a problem-solving manner. If we run into difficulties, I'll try different strategies to get things moving in the right direction."

"That sounds fair," Rick replied, his voice brightening for the first time. "As I said, I know I could use some help."

After the phone call, I thought about the difficulties Rick was facing. The long, frustrating infertility, the loss of his own capacity to perform as a man sexually, and his health problems. How much stress can one man take?

Then my thoughts shifted to the challenges I faced in trying to help this couple. The most immediate task was to begin to help Rick restore his own confidence that he could make a difference in improving his situation. If he could make some progress in restoring his damaged masculinity, it could generate some positive energy to help heal the marital crisis. A renewed vitality in their marriage would give them both the energy to deal with their infertility.

Appropriate Humor Can Help

As he walked into my office, Rick extended his hand in greeting me. Through the firm grip, I felt the moisture in his cold hand that showed the stress in his body. Standing almost six feet tall, he had a big frame that made me think he had been active in sports in his younger days. His light-blue seersucker suit seemed a little rumpled. Laura had told me he was having some problems with his weight. This was clearly visible, as his belly protruded out a bit over his belt. His neck also bulged out slightly over his white shirt and solid-red tie. His full face was topped by a head of curly black hair. His sideburns and neckline indicated that he was slightly overdue for a trim. His soft-brown eyes tended to get lost in the fullness of his cheeks.

"Well, Doc, where should I start?" he began after we sat down.

"Let's start with your blood pressure and what the medication is doing to you," I replied.

"It's awful. Those pills make it impossible for me to have a sex life. I don't know what to do. I'm at my wits' end. I've been told that if I don't take the pills, I run the risk of a heart attack or stroke. So far, I've been following the doctor's orders. Laura says it's more important to her that I'm alive and healthy. But I can't go on this way forever. I don't feel like I'm living. The doctor feels that the medication is working, but I'm not," Rick said in a voice heavy with despair.

As in my phone call with him, I wanted to let Rick know that I could identify with his pain, while also lifting his spirits a bit. Acknowledging the awful dilemma he was experiencing, I said, "I appreciate the cruel irony of your situation. You're like the patient in the story about the surgeon who announces that the surgery was a success but, unfortunately, the patient died."

Rick smiled briefly and replied, "I like your ability to get me to step back a little and laugh at the absurdity of my situation. It's helped me look at things with a new perspective. Honestly, I'm surprised. I didn't think shrinks had a sense of humor. I thought all you guys do is somberly analyze the patient's words for hidden meanings. That's the sense I get from Laura's experience with therapy. She feels it helps to talk about everything. Maybe it helps her, but I can't see it for myself. I find it more painful to talk about things that I can't change. I just get all worked up and even more frustrated."

Everyone Can Use a Good Coach

"I agree with your focus on wanting to do something about your problems. That's my approach, also," I replied. "The way I work is like being a coach. Did you play any team sports in school?" I asked.

"Yes, in high school I was on both the basketball and swim teams."

"How did your coaches help you?" I asked.

"They taught us how to do things the correct way and helped motivate each of us individually as well as creating a team spirit."

"Right," I agreed, "a good coach shows you how to improve your play and helps you to concentrate your mental and physical energies on the task at hand. Even the best players, the individual superstars, have coaches today. In living life, a good coach is just as helpful in bringing out your best. We learn by trial and error. My job is to help you to take some calculated risks to change your life and your health for the better."

"I like that approach," Rick said. "I know that worked for me in the past. My coaches really helped bring out the best in me. I was able to improve a lot with this help. All the best-paid sports stars talk about the help they've gotten from their coaches to reach new levels of success." After a pause, Rick said quizzically with a smile on his face, "Are you some new kind of shrink?"

Learning How, Not Why, Promotes Growth and Change

Responding with a laugh, I replied, "You might say that. What's happening is that our knowledge about how people change is rapidly evolving. It's not enough to understand why we have a problem. We all need to develop a practical game plan to solve the problem. It starts with the warmth, caring, and consistency of the therapist. Being like a good parent helps the patient feel secure enough to take the risks involved in growing and changing. An understanding therapist is much more important than the specific theoretical understandings of the patient's problem. We all change from having new experiences, not just from intellectual insights. Like a good coach, my job is to help you to try new ways of doing things. The art of good coaching is to create the right balance. This involves helping to establish a safe environment from which experiments in living can be tried, and working with you in calculating risks in advance—so that if things don't work out, the result is still a positive learning experience, not a negative failure. Working with people in crisis offers a golden opportunity to promote rapid growth. People in crisis know that their old ways of doing things have broken down. Their increased vulnerability makes them eager to try new ways to ease their pain. They need a good coach, whom they can trust. All of us want to feel better and live healthier lives. We need help overcoming our fears and inertia. We need to practice, so our new skills become a part of our daily living."

"I can really relate to that," Rick said. "I remember in high school I was a terrible foul shooter. My coach helped a great deal. He showed me the error in my shooting motion and instructed me in the proper way to release the ball. I practiced a lot and became a good foul shooter. Late in the season, I was having trouble with my foul shots when the game was on the line. I guess the pressure was getting to me. My coach helped by having me rehearse it over and over in my mind. I'd practice in the gym, imagining I was taking the game-deciding foul shot. In our final game of the season, I really did win the game for us with two foul shots with only five seconds left."

"That's a good example of what I'm talking about," I said. "I'll bet your coach didn't 'analyze' you by trying to look for hidden meanings for your foul-shooting problem," I said.

"You're right. He didn't ask me if I had some mental block about standing still and putting the ball through the hole," Rick said, as we both laughed.

"Rick, I'm glad we have found some common ground in that the way I work reminds you of the positive work you did with your coach. I try to find the areas in which someone has had some successful experiences. This can serve as a positive model for you to see that you can make a difference in your life. It's easier to transfer skills from one area of success to another area of one's life than to have to start from scratch."

Healthy Self-Love Is Not Selfishness

"You talk about success," Rick said, with a sigh in his voice. "I don't think I've felt that for a long time. Money is tight, so I'm pushing to make more cold calls to drum up new business. Everyone seems to have an existing source for their software needs already. It's hard to break into established business relationships. I'm rejected so often, I guess I'm used to it by now."

"From a stress point of view, your body is not at all used to it," I replied. "A vicious cycle has developed. Both work and personal life are in escalating spirals of stress. At work, you are under great money pressures pushing you to cold-calling other people's clients. The constant rejection leaves you on a treadmill of real financial worries and constantly reinforced feelings of humiliation and failure. In your personal life, a similar stress cycle exists. You have the stress of not being able to make a baby and the emotional strain on your sex life with Laura. Now, on top of all that, the high blood pressure medication renders you impotent! Have you ever stopped to think about it? You must have enormous inner reserves of strength of character to still be standing under this combined onslaught."

Rick had a thoughtful look on his face as he responded, "You know, I've just never looked at it that way before. I've always just worked hard to do what I have to. I've always thought it would be selfish and self-indulgent to complain about things being rough. When I was a kid, I remember my dad worked hard and didn't say much. He taught me that a man has to take care of his responsibilities first. I just haven't had any time for myself to relax or have fun with things going on as they are."

"Rick, I am in agreement with your values," I began. "Hard work and a sense of responsibility to family are admirable qualities. I share those beliefs. I don't want you to change them. I'd like you to think about taking a little time for yourself to recharge your batteries so that you can be more effective in meeting your obligations."

From Couch Potato to Exercising

"What do you do after work?" I asked.

"I go home to be with Laura. She makes dinner. Then we watch TV for a couple of hours. I guess you might say that I've become a couch potato," Rick concluded.

"How about making a slight modification in that routine?" I offered. "For example, you might take an hour after work and do some jogging. Better still, you used to be a swimmer. Swimming is the single best exercise for the entire body."

"Doc, are you kidding?" Rick protested. "I'm exhausted at the end of the day. All I want to do is go home, kick off my shoes, have a drink and dinner. Where am I going to get the energy to jog or swim?"

"Here's how," I said. "Remember back in high school? After a full day of classes, you would be pretty exhausted. Then you would have a couple of hours of basketball or swim-team practice. Where did the energy come from? How did you feel before and after the team practices?" I asked.

Rick thought for a moment. Then a smile spread across his face. "Good point you're making. Sure, I was mentally tired after a day of classes. Most of the other kids went home to watch television. But I always looked forward to the practices. I was doing something for myself. I wanted to be on the team. Maybe burning up all that physical energy did actually recharge my batteries. Both my mood and my body would feel good. I'm sure it made it easier for me to concentrate on my homework later in the evening."

With a smile on my face I said, "I'm glad you remembered that. It illustrates my point perfectly. Your interest in sports was an example of healthy self-love, not selfishness. You felt good and you had more energy to do your school work. We now know that physiologically your body releases powerful mood-energizing substances called endorphins when you exercise. An hour a day spent doing something physical that you enjoy is like investing in yourself. It pays a dividend in renewed energy for the other parts of your life. It also helps you to lose weight, because you don't need to munch to lift your mood. It helps you to create a positive cycle of increasing self-esteem and self-confidence to aid you in tackling your problems."

"From my past experience of being physically fit, I know you're right. But I'm not a teenager anymore." Rick complained. "I've gotten so out of shape. I can't possibly look and feel sixteen again.

How to Get Back in Shape and Feel Good

"You don't need to look and feel sixteen again," I replied. "In just a couple of weeks, we can regain eighty percent of our fitness. We learned that—scientifically—when we started sending people into outer space. At first, the astronauts would come back after a month so weak that they needed stretchers to take them out of the capsule. At first, everyone was puzzled. The astronauts had hardly moved during the flight. They were seated or lying down most of the time. The lack of gravity in space, the weightlessness, magnified the problem. When subsequent astronauts performed some daily exercises during their trip, this problem didn't occur. The lack of gravity dramatized the fact that even physically fit astronauts need daily exercise. At first, maybe you won't like it. You'll feel the aches and pains the next day. But if you do things gradually, slowly increasing your effort, your stamina will build up. I'd suggest swimming twenty minutes every other day. That day of rest in between will help prevent muscle strains or other injuries. We now know, scientifically, that our muscles need a day off after a strenuous workout, to restore their energy. It's when you work out on an already fatigued muscle that you run a great risk of injury."

"What about the saying, 'No pain, no gain,' " Rick asked. "I remember my coach urging us to push through the pain."

"That may have worked for you when you were in rigorous, daily, supervised training as part of a sports team," I said. "However, now you're just like the rest of us. Trying to get back to a healthy way of living after a long time on the sidelines. Remember, that when you feel pain during exercise, your body is sending you a message that you're overdoing it. Listen to the message. If you ignore it, your body will have to scream out a louder pain message when you injure something. Pain doesn't necessarily mean *stop everything*. It's not an automatic red light. It's more like a yellow warning light, signaling caution. Pain certainly isn't a green light urging you to continue the painful exercise without pausing."

Lowering Your Own Blood Pressure

Rick nodded in agreement. "I guess I have to accept that my goal is different from when I was in competitive sports in school. Are there any risks for me in doing this, in terms of my blood pressure?"

"I'm glad you asked that question," I answered. "Not only is it not harmful—exercise will help you to keep your blood pressure normal. In a recent landmark study, patients with diagnosed heart disease lowered their blood pressure enough to be able to stop or decrease their medication. The treatment program consisted of learning how to deal with stress, exercise, and diet. We will be focusing on the same areas here. In addition, those heart patients in Dr. Dean Ornish's 'Optimal Lifestyle Program' lowered harmful cholesterol by sixty percent. Remember, they all started with diagnosed clogged vital arteries. You are in much better condition. At this early stage, you just have some elevated blood pressure."

"Great," Rick exclaimed, his face showing enthusiasm. "I was worried because I thought exercise caused blood pressure to rise."

"During exercise, there can be a brief increase in blood pressure," I explained. "That's why I'm recommending gradually increasing moderate exercise. You can handle that. Heart patients handle it. Remember, I'm not talking about your going back to the glory days of your youth in competitive team sports. This isn't to turn you back into a jock or even a weekend warrior. The moderate exercise helps to lower blood pressure in the long run by helping our overall conditioning."

Men and Feelings: Beyond John Wayne

"I'm beginning to feel some hope for the first time in a long while," Rick said with some animation. "I just haven't been feeling anything at all for so long."

"You've been going through a lot. What's your sense of why you haven't been feeling anything?" I asked.

Rick thought for a moment and said, "I guess for a number of reasons. I'm still able to work and we can make ends meet. Also, Laura needs me to be strong for her. A man who cries is weak and self-pitying and no use to anyone. You know the saying, "A man ain't supposed to cry."

"Yes, and we both know that other saying, 'When the going gets tough, the tough get going.' That's well and good for John Wayne cowboy movies. But in the real world, being in touch with our feelings is a sign of strength, not weakness. Our feelings are guides to help us stay in touch with ourselves. For example, if I touch a hot stove, the pain instantly informs me to pull back my hand. Our emotions serve the same function. If something upsets us or makes us sad, staying in touch with the feelings helps us to monitor if what we are doing is helpful. It's like our own form of biofeedback. Our feelings give us information about how we are doing. By blocking out negative feelings, we numb ourselves. If we couldn't feel the pain, we wouldn't take our hand off the hot stove. We would get severely burned. When we avoid painful feelings, we continue doing things that harm our body. Being in touch with feelings doesn't make you a sniveling wimp. Far from it. Feelings help us to monitor how we are coping. As we make changes in our life-style, our feelings get better."

"I hear what you're saying, and it makes sense," Rick replied. "But it's so different from the way I grew up. My father had to work hard to support us. He didn't like his job. Yet, he had no choice. He had to do it. What good would his being in touch with his hating his job have done for him?"

I answered, "Rick, times change. Today we have more choices. People change jobs frequently and many even change careers. Putting blinders on and plowing ahead unhappily takes its toll on our health and well-being. In addition to the pain and misery, you can't do well at something you don't like."

"I have to think about how this relates to me," Rick said in a slow, deliberate manner. "You've given me a lot of food for thought."

"Good," I replied. "We can discuss this more in our later meetings. Before we stop today, I want to get you started with your homework."

With a grin, Rick said, "I know what's coming. I've been watching Laura practice with her tape. She's told me what you said to her about using it."

"Great," I said. "I don't have to repeat myself, then. Do you have any questions? I know we have covered a lot of ground today."

"Not right now. You've answered the ones I've had as they came up," Rick replied.

"OK, if anything comes up between now and our next meeting, give me a call," I said.

Loving Feelings

I felt we had worked successfully together as we had begun the process of Rick getting back in touch with his loving feelings for himself. Over the years, he had gotten so out of contact with himself. He had turned himself into a nonfeeling machine to try to avoid the pain in his life. This could not work. We are endowed as living creatures with observation of our feelings to guide us. We cannot turn that recognition off and fly blind, and not run into trouble. Our feelings are essential to guide us in creating a happy and healthy life.

The good coach is like the good mother. Both help us to learn how to love ourselves in healthy ways. Our very nature, as human beings, requires that we get nurturance from others to grow and develop. The human bond of caring and consistency helps us to admit our pain and make the changes necessary to promote healing.

No matter how ill or despairing we may become, where there is life, there is hope. Rekindling the flame of hope is always the first priority. You can do this for yourself. As I did with Rick, let your memory take you back to better days in your past—to times when you felt good and healthy. Think of times when you solved a problem in your life and felt pride at your achievement.

Another way is to focus on someone in your current life who means a lot to you. This significant other that you love can be another living creature, or perhaps God. The important point is to take some of that love you feel and direct it to yourself. For example, let your love of God inspire you to treat yourself with more care and compassion. This is one way you can harness your faith and spiritual values to heal yourself. Remember, when we love, we care. We show respect. We give our time and energy. We are motivated to work through difficult times to get to better days. We become active participants in our life and our world in positive ways.

Winning by Letting Go

Rick arrived for his initial biofeedback training all geared up, as though he were about to compete in an important competition. "I'm ready to go at it," he declared. At the beginning, his hand temperature was about 85 degrees, indicating mild to moderate stress. After a few minutes, Rick was still hovering around the same level. "I can't believe that I'm not moving this thing," he said, as he stared at the digital reading on the biofeedback machine.

"Rick, where is your mental focus?" I asked.

"On getting that temperature scale up," he declared.

"That's probably the problem," I replied. "It seems that you have gotten caught up in competing with the machine. You need to shift your focus back to gently observing your belly breathing and letting go of any muscle tension you feel. The machine just registers your inner levels. You can't compete with the machine. You'll just wind up competing against yourself in terms of higher stress levels."

"OK," Rick concurred, "it sounds like some good advice my swim coach in high school gave me. There was a guy who I always swam neck-and-neck with. My coach kept telling me to forget that he was there and just concentrate on my own form and timing. I always performed better that way."

"That's a good example of what I'm talking about," I said. "You won by letting go of the competition with the other guy. You focused on doing the things that would let you do your best."

Rick was able to raise his hand temperature to nearly 90 degrees, as he kept his concentration on passively observing his breathing and relaxing any tension in his body.

Family Ties: Bonds or Knots?

Laura looked upset as she arrived for her fourth session. After we sat down, she didn't say anything for a while.

Finally, I broke the ice by observing, "You look upset. What's troubling you?"

"Rick and I just had another difficult weekend with my family. I just don't know how to relate to them anymore," Laura said with a look of exasperation. Then she fell silent again.

"Remember the other week when you were upset about Rick's problems?" I asked. "When we finally got to talking about it, you made a breakthrough in terms of your stress response. Perhaps we can achieve a similar result now."

"That's true, but this is different," Laura replied. "I've been talking about my family for years in therapy. Needless to say, they haven't changed at all. Rick is seeing you now, but *they* certainly won't get involved. So what's the use of talking about them here?" Laura asked.

"As I mentioned before, the way we work on problems here is different from traditional psychotherapy," I said. "Our focus is on quick and effective ways to change things in the here and now. It's a very functional approach. This complements the search for deeper meanings that occur in traditional therapy."

"OK, I'll give it a try," Laura responded. "I have a good understanding of why things are the way they are with my family, but it hasn't helped to make them any different. My father died of a heart attack a few years ago. Especially since then, my mother likes to have her children and grandchildren visit. Last weekend, she invited everyone over to her house by the lake. My sister has a new baby. My brother has a young child. My cousin and her two kids were there, too. All the adults were asking me, 'What's going on about a baby?' They were all full of advice and questions. 'What are you going to do, Laura?' one asked. 'Are you going to adopt?' asked another. 'What fertility drugs are you taking?' a third asked. My cousin was so intrusive, that she even suggested that Rick and I use condoms!" Laura exclaimed.

"What led to that suggestion?" I asked.

"Through the family grapevine, she had heard that our infertility specialist found that I produce antibodies to Rick's sperm. It seems she read somewhere that some doctors recommend using condoms during nonfertile times of the month. The idea is that less repeated contact would result in lower antibody levels. But that's not the point. I felt so humiliated. My cousin telling me how to conduct my sex life. If she only knew there isn't any," Laura said in anguish, tears streaming down her face.

"I understand what a sensitive spot your cousin touched," I said. "I had a good session with Rick and he did well in his initial biofeedback training. I'm hopeful that we can make progress in resolving the problem."

"I'm relieved to hear you say that," Laura replied. "Rick told me he felt positive about his start with you. He said he thinks of you as a coach, not a doctor. Coming from him, that's a compliment!" she added with a smile.

I smiled back, "Yes, I know. Getting back to your family, how did you feel amid this barrage of questions and advice?"

"I felt anxious and my body got tense," Laura replied. "Since I've been here, I focus on these things more. I said to myself, 'You've got to get some release.' So I went swimming. I began to feel a sharp pain in my lower abdominal-pelvic region. The pain felt like a knife cutting through me. I rested for a few minutes and the pain went away. Then I tried to swim again. The pain came back even worse. I had to stop swimming altogether and just sit. So, instead of getting relief, the swimming caused me pain. What am I supposed to do? I thought exercise was a way to work off tension."

"It sounds like an acute muscle spasm," I answered. "You were so tense, that the swimming led to spasm and pain. Rest brought relief. It's a good example of the fact that exercise isn't necessarily the answer to the relief of stress. Actually, focusing on the belly breathing you have learned by practicing with the tape will help break the spasm. Meditation can also help. By repeating one word or sound to yourself on each breath as you exhale, you can distract your attention away from the anxious thoughts that triggered the muscle spasms. Your body returns to a resting state, and the muscles relax giving relief from the pain."

"I'll try the belly breathing the next time I feel the pain," Laura said. "But I'm still too worried about everything to meditate at this point in time. Do I have to meditate to control my stress?"

"No single technique is absolutely essential," I advised. "Each person uses those that feel comfortable in the doing. While meditation can be useful, the same relaxation response can be triggered by belly breathing. The important point is to choose the techniques that work for you."

Laura looked pleased. "Good. I'm not sure if I could meditate for twenty minutes if my life depended on it. Too many thoughts are always rushing through my head."

"A lot of people have that difficulty in trying to use meditation to relax. In our fast-paced society, it's hard to turn off all our thoughts. Getting back to the weekend. What happened with your mother?" I asked.

"A lot," Laura sighed. "As soon as we got there, she pulls me to the side and says, 'Rick doesn't seem excited about being here. He's not interested in seeing your brother.' My mother is always putting Rick down. It's like she's always questioning my marriage. My brother is a dentist. My mother always wanted me to marry a professional, like my brother. To her, Rick is just a salesman. He's not good enough for a daughter of my mother. My mother is also always forcing my brother and sister on me. She thinks it will do me good. Well, it doesn't. Early Saturday evening my mother announces, 'Let's all eat dinner together.' Sounds nice, doesn't it? Well, to start with, Rick and I are the only ones around. Everyone else is on the lake with their kids. Rick and I are supposed to wait for all of them to return. In addition, I wind up cooking dinner for everyone. It was just like my childhood. It was expected of me. I was angry inside, but I didn't show it. My mother says to me, 'You're wonderful. You did a terrific job.' I don't want that. I want to be treated equal to my brother and sister. I was so upset, I told Rick we should leave and go home. He was very practical. He convinced me that at this point, we were hungry and should stay and eat the dinner that I cooked. He probably was right, but I got upset with him and didn't talk to him for a while." Laura paused and looked at me for my reaction.

"Were you upset with Rick for convincing you to stay?" I asked.

Laura thought for a moment and said, "It wasn't just that. I also told him that I can't stand my mother for forcing my siblings and their kids on me. Again, he was 'practical.' He said I should tell that to my mother. It sounds like a good suggestion, but my mother just doesn't understand. She thinks family is wonderful. The more family, the better."

"As you said before," I began, "you wind up feeling angry inside. This triggers the stress response in your body. You're not expressing your anger directly to the person you're angry with. Instead, you're deflecting your anger to Rick. Not only does this not help you to change your relationship with your mother, it also creates distance between you and Rick."

After a thoughtful pause, Laura replied, "You're right. I do take my frustration with my mother out on Rick. But my mother won't change. Telling her is like banging my head against a wall. It just hurts me more."

"The reason for telling your mother how you feel is to get it off your chest," I said. "I realize that your mother probably won't change. The anger you feel doesn't go away because it isn't directly expressed. It eats away at you in increased stress and you let it out at Rick because that relationship is safe."

"Let me tell you something else that upset me," Laura continued. "Some friends of my mother came over. Rick and I had wanted to take a boat ride on the lake. My brother said that he would take Mom's friends for a boat ride. Again, Laura can wait! I was so upset, I wanted to escape, to go home. I really felt the contrast between Rick's family and mine. The other week, some of his family came over to our home with a young son. Everyone chipped in to do things. I didn't feel like I had to serve everyone. His family isn't as well off financially as mine, but they seem more willing to share."

"Your experience points up that the attitude of the adults is what makes the difference, not the presence of kids. The problem is that you feel that your family takes you for granted," I said.

"Yes," Laura replied. "Also, they make me feel bad about not having a child. They make me feel guilty that I don't. The other week, I went to see my brother, the dentist. I told him I can't have any pain injections because I'm trying to get pregnant. He said, 'I'm glad my wife and I had an easy time getting pregnant.' I felt like I got a slap in the face."

"It seems clear that your family is unaware and ignorant of the effect of their comments on your feelings," I replied.

"That's very true," Laura said. "Yet I can't seem to separate myself from them. Even though they're always so negative. I always feel that I'll try one more time."

I said, "I certainly understand that you want the closeness of family. The issue for you is to feel comfortable expressing your feelings when they occur, whatever those feelings are, and directly to the appropriate person."

"They don't accept my expressing negative feelings," she replied. "They take it as a personal insult. Then I feel guilty about that."

"You are not responsible for their reactions," I began. "You have a legitimate right to express your feelings. The system that exists now doesn't work. You sit with the anger and frustration. You have rage eating away at your insides. Don't you think it's worth a chance to try an experiment to see if it's better to express your feelings?"

Laura responded, "When I said to my mother that Rick and I will eat when we want, she looked at me with puppy-dog eyes and said, 'You can always eat when you want. Please wait for the others. We're not often together as a family anymore.' My mother simply doesn't understand me. For my mother, family should be close and loving. She wanted us to wait for, and wait on, the others."

After a pause, Laura added the crucial part. "Even if I said that I was going to do what I wanted, her words would still be ringing in my brain. I'd feel guilty and not be able to enjoy myself."

"Why are you giving her such power?" I asked.

Laura thought for a moment and replied, "Part of me feels that she is right about being close with family, but it doesn't work. My brother doesn't really want a close relationship with me. He has his own family—a wife and child. They are his main concern. My mother feels that I should get more involved with all the children in the family. My mother will tell the kids, 'Go show your Aunt Laura this.' It just gets to be too much. I feel like running away."

"Well, how about just saying, "No, I don't want any more of this right now," I suggested.

"I can't do that. I feel guilty about offending them," Laura replied.

"I understand the conflict you experience between how you really feel and your fear of hurting other people's feelings," I began. "But you're entitled to your real feelings. Your obligation is to let others know what the ground rules are, what you can feel comfortable with. If you just remain silent and withdrawn, they may misread your message. Your mother may react to your quietness by feeling that you need more involvement with family. By making your true feelings clear, you let people know that you want them to respect your need for some privacy. You can't be responsible for pleasing others at the cost of your being upset. You have to let them be responsible for their own feelings about your legitimate needs."

"I know what you're saying is right," Laura replied. "But it's hard to put it in practice with my family, since I've spent a lifetime trying to please them and ignoring my own feelings."

I nodded in agreement. "I understand that. Try an experiment. See what happens by being more direct about what you can handle. The worst that can happen is that your mother gets upset. If you can accept that as her problem, and not your fault, then you will feel better and you won't take it out on your body or on Rick."

"I guess it's worth a try," Laura said. "Since it's not working now, I can see that I have a lot to gain and little to lose."

Laura continued to show evidence of progress in her physiological training session. Her hand temperature at the start was 81 degrees. She was able to relax and get to 86 degrees during the training. Slowly, but surely, she was readjusting her internal thermostat to a less stressed position. Still, something was holding her back from more fully relaxing.

Getting the Support You Need

Laura's experiences with her family are, unfortunately, very common. We tend to get stuck in old familiar roles dating back to childhood. These attitudes we have toward ourself and also our stress-related illness are crucial. Sadly, our culture and our family belief system encourage falsely 'blaming the victim.' These false prejudices leave many people feeling ashamed of their problems. If we feel that it is our fault that we have headaches or back pain or infertility, then we will relate to others from a position of embarrassment and hiding. Communication becomes artificial. How is it possible to ask for positive support from family and friends if we are hiding in shame?

The first step is to change our attitude. We need to accept that there is a real medical problem. Stress-related disorders are physiological processes. If we had a heart attack, we would feel OK about getting the support we need. We would not feel ashamed of having a heart attack.

It would be accepted as a medical problem requiring help from doctors, family, and friends.

We need to have the same attitude about stress-related problems. We have a legitimate right to express our wants and needs and limits. We have the right to ask for support in the ways that are most helpful. This differs with each individual. Laura, for example, needs her privacy respected by an intrusive family. The opposite problem may occur in another family. We may need more active involvement from loved ones who typically never ask questions and keep their distance.

The important point is to step back and allow ourselves to get in touch with our needs. Take a minute and a piece of paper and make a list of wants, needs, and limits. Remember, these will change over time. Just because we express a need for closeness now, doesn't mean that we can't ask for some privacy later.

Quitters Pay Double

Laura felt that her mother just didn't understand her. While this was true, Laura's withdrawal and unwillingness to say how she really felt compounded the problem. By maintaining a "stiff upper lip," we only fool ourselves. As long as we are going to continue to relate to someone, we can't quit trying to improve our communication with that person. The old saying, "quitters pay double" applies here. If we quit trying, we not only suffer the loss and feelings of failure, but also the gnawing doubt that just maybe, if we had tried, we might have been able to change things for the better.

By learning to share our real feelings, instead of hiding them, each of us opens up the possibility of getting honest support that is meaningful. We need to take control of the situation by expressing what is working for us and what is not. I have seen many examples of this with my infertility patients. Often, a woman will avoid a good friend with a young baby. Ashamed of their painful feelings, these women distance themselves and lose a needed friendship. Instead, by being honest, they can be accepted for their legitimate feelings and maintain the supportive friendship they need. Family and friends can be valuable assets when we are under stress. By being open and direct, we increase our opportunities to receive support from them.

Infertility: Rick's Experiences

Rick arrived for his third session looking like he had been through some trying experiences. "Between the infertility problem and Laura's family, I've had a difficult week," Rick began. "Where shall I start?"

"Laura told me about your weekend at her mother's," I replied. "While I want to hear how you experienced it, let's start with what you mentioned first, the infertility problem."

"We were just told that Laura has antibodies to my sperm," Rick explained. "So now, during Laura's fertile time, instead of having sex, we have to go to the infertility doctor for me to produce sperm. They are washed to decrease any antibody reaction, then used to inseminate her. Talk about being turned into a machine. Let me tell you, it was one of my worst experiences. Just thinking about going there makes me anxious. As you know, because of my blood pressure medication, I don't get a good erection to start with. I kept asking myself, 'How am I ever going to jerk off in this doctor's office?' When I got there with Laura, the nurse gave me a cup and, pointing to the bathroom said, 'Fill it up.' I looked at her in disbelief and said, 'You have got to be kidding. I don't think an elephant could fill that up!' She looked startled for a second and then laughingly said, 'That cup is for a urine sample. After you do that, then use one of the containers in the bathroom for a sperm sample.' The bathroom had a totally antiseptic, unsexy atmosphere. After producing the urine sample, I started to think about how I was going to switch gears and produce sperm. I looked around to see if there were any erotic magazines to help get me going and stimulate a fantasy. I couldn't find any. So I closed my eyes and tried thinking. I had to work so hard to get caught up in a fantasy that I forgot that I had to get the sperm in the little cup. Over half the sperm got ejaculated directly in the toilet, because I came with my eyes closed! I was really upset. I went out and told the nurse that I had an accident and only got a small amount of sperm in the cup. She told me 'Don't worry. Take a break for twenty minutes, then just go back in and produce more.' I was floored. I knew I didn't have it in me. I tried again, but nothing happened. Fortunately, the doctor finally said there was enough in the first sample to do an insemination. Boy, was I relieved."

"To tell the truth, Rick," I replied sympathetically, "I think you handled the situation really well. It's obviously an unusual situation. Many men have embarrassing episodes in producing sperm on demand in the doctor's office. One man was so overwhelmed, that he literally ran out of the doctor's office without producing a specimen. His wife was left sitting in the stirrups waiting for an insemination that wasn't to be. There is a whole repertoire of such stories among infertility patients. There is an element of black humor in them that only other infertility sufferers can really appreciate. By the way, did you ask the nurse why there weren't any magazines, so that you could keep your eyes open during the procedure?" I asked.

Rick nodded. "I did ask and she told me that I was probably so nervous that I didn't open the medicine cabinet in the bathroom. On the inner door, they have a couple of sexy magazines. I still think she should have told me where to look. The whole situation made me feel humiliated. The bathroom didn't even have any ventilation. I was really uncomfortable."

"Did you mention any of your feelings to anyone?" I asked.

"No, I just wanted to get it over with and get out. I felt so foolish."

"But if you don't ask, you will never know if you can get what you want. It would be nice if others could read our minds and anticipate our needs, but they can't. It's not foolish to ask. It may be foolish not to ask," I added.

"Well, maybe not foolish, but selfish," Rick said. "Laura has obviously been suffering for a long time about not getting pregnant. A part of me is tired of trying to have a baby. It's been a real long hassle. I want to have some fun with my wife. How can I say that, without looking foolish or selfish?" he asked.

"Well, I think a part of Laura feels the same way," I said. "Maybe if you talked about your feelings, that might help move things in a more enjoyable direction for both of you. That would be neither foolish nor selfish. It would be taking the initiative to help rekindle a more loving relationship."

"I would sure like that. But I'm afraid that we've been locked into our problems for so long, we don't know how to get things moving in the right direction. Got any ideas, coach?" Rick asked with a smile.

"Well, a good place to start is to bring some romance back into the marriage," I said. "Let's leave sex alone for now. You are making good progress with the relaxation techniques. Soon we'll be able to reduce your medications and you will get sufficient erections again. But before that, you can improve your communication and sharing of affection with Laura. Remember when you were courting, before you got married? Both of you were on your best behavior. Complimenting each other. Looking for ways to please each other. How about going out to a nice dinner and dancing for a starter?"

"We used to enjoy dancing. We could both let go a little and have some fun with that, I think. But what after that? And how are we going to improve our communication at this point?" Rick asked.

"Perhaps I can help with that," I replied. "I work with couples, as well as individuals. If the two of you want, I can see you together for some sessions."

"OK," Rick said, "that's good to know. Let's see how things go with a night out."

Regaining Normal Blood Pressure

After a pause, Rick asked, "Getting back to what you said just before about my blood pressure and sex—what time frame are we looking at for me to be able to function as a man again?"

"Very likely we're talking about just a few weeks' time," I replied. "You have mild hypertension. In your first training session, you warmed to ninety degrees from a good initial baseline of eighty-five. With ongoing home practice and building the body relaxation techniques into your daily life, your blood pressure will return to normal. You can then maintain the gain on your own, without the medication."

"That's great!" Rick exclaimed. "It seems amazing to me. Is this some new experiment that's getting you such good results?"

"No," I replied. "This is well established after years of study with thousands of blood pressure patients. Many large studies both here and in England have demonstrated the effectiveness of learning how to lower your own blood pressure."

"My doctor said that I have 'essential' hypertension. Does your approach work for this type of high blood pressure?" Rick asked.

As a smile crept over my face at his words, I said, "I have to tell you why I'm smiling. Over ninety percent of high blood pressure is called essential hypertension. It's a classic example of medical terminology hiding ignorance, rather than revealing useful information. Nobody knows what the cause is of essential hypertension. It's just a label. It would be more accurate to say, 'hypertension: cause unknown.' But the medical profession has difficulty admitting that it doesn't know something."

"That's a relief. When I read the word essential, I thought, damn it, *essential* in plain English means that something is necessary. Now I 'need' hypertension like a hole in the head. I'm glad to hear that there is nothing essential about it," Rick added with a wry smile.

Rick did well during the biofeedback-training part of the session. At the start, his blood pressure was lower than it was at the end of his prior training session. This showed that he was learning how to lower his own blood pressure. Today's initial reading of 135/85 was well within normal range. He was still taking his medication. However, before he had started the training program, his blood pressure had been 140/90— just on the borderline of being considered elevated. So medication alone had just gotten his blood pressure down to a borderline elevated level. Before he had started taking the drugs, his pressure had been 160/100— clearly high. Thus, medication alone had partially helped, but at the cost of his becoming impotent.

During the training session, Rick achieved deeper levels of physiological relaxation. His hand temperature rose to 93.2 degrees from an initial level of 91.1 degrees. His blood pressure fell to 130/80. Clearly, he was taking control of lowering his own blood pressure. The positive results were in line with the progress usually achieved at this stage of his training. He was on target for achieving his goal of being able to keep his blood pressure normal without drugs.

I wanted to see if he could maintain and possibly improve on these self-induced lower levels before suggesting a decrease in his drugs. We would have the answer by our next session. Rick was excited about the prospects.

The Rocky Road to Romance

After Rick left, I thought about him and Laura. Things were moving very fast for both of them. My initial goal had been achieved. They both were feeling hopeful again. They were also willing to try again to tackle the difficulties in their marriage. However, long years of experience had taught me that we were headed for some rough spots. Hope brings rapidly rising expectations for dramatic improvements. Yet, human interactions and feelings change gradually. Years of frustration and hurt don't just melt away instantly. The danger is in the inevitable disappointment when reality does not improve as fast as expectations.

Rick was ready to rush back to romance. Laura had her hopes pinned on Rick learning to lower his blood pressure and having his potency restored. I knew they would need to work on their relationship as well. That's why I told Rick they could see me together, if they ran into trouble as they tried to strengthen their bond.

I had told Rick to hold off from sex for now so he and Laura could get back in touch with warm and affectionate feelings for each other. The most erotic organ is the mind. He and Laura needed to move back into a more loving and communicating relationship to be able to enjoy each other physically again.

The Inevitable Crisis

The message on my answering machine didn't seem unusual. Just before his next appointment, Rick phoned my office to say he had to cancel. Last-minute time conflicts can arise. But since our work was at that delicate early stage of rising expectations, I called Rick back to see how he was doing and reschedule our appointment.

"Doc, since you called, I'm going to tell you straight out. I'm not making another appointment. You've done the best you could, but it's no use," Rick said with obvious sadness in his voice.

"What happened?" I exclaimed. "When I last saw you, things were going so well."

"Yeah, I really was excited. I thought I was well on the road to getting better. It's not your fault. You did everything you could."

"Rick, I hear how devastated you sound. I know it's difficult to talk about. But what happened that makes you so hopeless?"

"I know you would help if you could," he said. "But this is out of your line of work. The problem now is sexual, not stress."

"Hold on," I replied. "There's still cause for hope. Actually, sexual problems often have a relation to stress. I'd like to hear what's wrong. I'd prefer we talked in person, rather than on the phone."

"OK, if you really think you can help, I'll tell my boss I have a medical emergency and make our originally scheduled appointment."

Rick looked anxious when he arrived. "I was going to surprise you. I didn't expect it to have worked out the way it did. I thought I'd have good news to report," he began. "I left here feeling really optimistic, for the first time, that I was solving my blood pressure problem. You said you were going to be conservative and wait to see this week's results before cutting the dosage of the pills. I said to myself, 'Let me try cutting the dosage myself. What have I got to lose? Not much. My blood pressure is well within the normal range now. Maybe I can pleasantly surprise Laura and myself with the ability to do some good lovemaking again.' So, I figured I had a lot to gain and nothing to lose. So I stopped taking the pills. After a few days, I began to be my old self again. I'd wake up in the morning with a bit of a hard-on before going to the bathroom to pee. I began thinking about sex again. I took your advice and planned a romantic Saturday night with Laura. I took her out for a candle-lit dinner at one of our favorite restaurants. We usually only go there on special occasions. All through dinner she kept asking what was the big deal. I told her that when we get home she would find out. So when we got home, she said, 'OK, what's the surprise?' I said, 'Let's put on some music and do some slow dancing.' She seemed puzzled, because I haven't suggested dancing in ages. We were holding each other close and I asked her if she felt anything different. She didn't say anything for a moment and then started to giggle. She said, 'What's this pressing up against me?' I smiled too, and told her about going off the pills and being my old self again. She was thrilled and, needless to say, it took us no time at all to get into the bedroom and out of all our clothes. I didn't have any problem getting hard enough to enter her. The problem was that as soon as I did, I came. I felt awful. I literally had no control. This never happened to me before. I felt so humiliated. Laura was very understanding, but it didn't help. We waited a while and I tried to get stimulated again. I couldn't even get hard. I felt like a total failure. By the time I called you, I was really dejected. I just gave up. What's the use? I felt like I had gone from the frying pan into the fire. So, you said you thought you could help. Have you ever successfully treated anyone for what's happening to me now?" Rick asked.

From Impotence to Premature Ejaculation

"Yes," I answered. "Actually, your experience is quite common. It's just that men literally don't talk about it. They feel too ashamed. Potency problems, regardless of their cause, can lead to problems with coming too quickly. The man's focus is so preoccupied with trying to get and maintain an erection, that he loses his voluntary control over his ejaculatory reflex. As you said, you literally had no control. But with Laura's help, you can regain voluntary control again."

"But how can Laura help me? Isn't this my problem?" Rick said.

"No," I countered. "It's a shared problem between the two of you. Just as infertility is a problem of a couple—regardless of which spouse the medical profession diagnoses as having the problem."

Rick looked puzzled. "But it's *my* voluntary control that I have to regain. What is Laura's role in that?"

The Dance of Love

"Making love is like dancing," I began. "Each partner influences the other. Laura's attitude and how she moves are key factors in how stimulating sex is for you. She can significantly help you to refocus, both mentally and physically, on your own sensations, so that you can regain voluntary control over your orgasm."

"I understand the physical part, but what is the mental part? When I had good sex, I certainly wasn't thinking about it, I was just doing it," Rick said.

"That's right, Rick," I acknowledged. "When any mind-body function is going well, we are just doing it, not thinking about it. It's as true for sports as it is for sex. Let me use an analogy that relates to your own experience. You told me you were on your school's basketball team. All those practice sessions served an important purpose. You learned how to coordinate your mental awareness and physical sensations so that your moves on the court flowed smoothly. Your reactions became semiautomatic. Your mental focus was in the here and now of your active involvement in the game. Now, if you ran into difficulties in a part of your game, how would you learn to correct it? Let's say, for example, you were having trouble with your jump shot. Your coach noticed that your form was off when you were intimidated by a tall opponent. First, he'd have you work on your shot alone. Maybe you'd develop a higher arc so that the shot couldn't be blocked so easily. Then you would practice your shot with a teammate guarding you. You would make some adjustments to take into account the reactions of the other player. At all times you would need to stay in touch with the situation and be able to control your moves voluntarily. You would decide when to shoot the ball. You would develop a 'feel' for the game.

"Similarly, there are sensations in your genitals that precede orgasm. You can learn how to tune into them and use them as a guide to voluntary control when you come. It's just another form of biofeedback. The sensations in your genitals give you information. You can then voluntarily adjust your movements to delay reaching orgasm until you want to. So you regain voluntary control by using your mind and body together. You learn how to monitor your own sensations—similar to how you have been learning to monitor your own physiology to control your blood pressure voluntarily. Biologic feedback mechanisms are an integral part of all living systems."

"OK, I get the picture," Rick said. "What should I do?"

"Therapy for sexual problems is a form of couple therapy," I began. "I need to meet with you and Laura together. I'll be making suggestions for how you can learn together at home. Just as in our biofeedback work, the two of you will become active participants in healing yourselves."

"Fine, I'm ready," Rick said. "Let's make an appointment for us all to meet as soon as possible. I can't stand living with this problem any longer."

"First," I said, "I want to get Laura's views on us all working together. I meet with her next week."

"Doc, I know that Laura is just as eager as I am to get our sex life back on track. I'm going to talk to her about our session today. I know there won't be any problem."

"You may be right, Rick. However, Laura needs to decide for herself about us all working together. It's a good idea for you to talk with her about today's session. How about this suggestion? If Laura wants to, she can call me about us all meeting together this week. Otherwise, I'll just keep her individual appointment for next week. Remember, Laura needs to want to participate and not be pushed into it for the treatment to succeed."

"Fair enough," Rick replied. "I'm glad I kept today's appointment. I can see it would have been difficult to have this discussion over the phone."

"Yes, some things are so personal, that you need to sit and talk together about them," I replied. "Before we do some biofeedback training today, tell me where you are right now in terms of your blood pressure pills and your practicing the relaxation techniques."

"I'm still off all the pills," Rick advised. "I really can't stand them. I've been practicing religiously. I do the tape in the morning and evening. I focus on my breathing at various times during the day. I really want to be able to control my blood pressure myself and be able to function sexually."

"You certainly have a powerful motive for regaining control," I said. "I would have preferred that you had returned to your doctor for his consent before eliminating your medication. While we both were aware of the progress you made, I never recommend that a patient change his medication without his physician's approval. Changing or stopping medication can be risky. We need to respect the equilibrium our body is in, as well as the changes taking place."

"I guess I tend to rush things a bit," Rick acknowledged. "But that's because for the first time in years, I'm starting to think things will be OK."

"That's good," I replied. "Now let's see how things are doing."

Rick's initial blood pressure reading was 140/90. He had succeeded in getting his pressure to the level that the pills had previously achieved. During the session, he was able to lower it to 130/80. This equaled his prior session's low level. However, this time he was off all medication.

Rick's progress was fairly typical. This was his fourth session. The treatments were two weeks apart, so he was now at the end of six weeks of treatment. His daily practice was working. He was successfully controlling his stress response.

Many patients with mild hypertension succeed in just four or five sessions, as Rick did. Some stop treatment at this point and continue to do well. They are self-starters and continue to do these daily practices on their own. Others recognize that they still need to get a better handle on some stressful situations in their personal or work life. They continue for a few more sessions to get to a point where they feel better at coping with their chronic stressors.

My Reflections on the Crisis

After Rick left, I thought about the crisis he had experienced. One can never predict exactly where a problem will arise. My premonition that some crisis might occur is from long years of experience with people undergoing rapid change in their lives.

Rapid change, even positive desired change, is disruptive to our established patterns of living and functioning. Stress-related disorders don't just occur overnight. They are the result of gradual shifts over months and years to try to accommodate to chronic stress. By the time we feel the symptoms of aches and pains, or our doctor sees the signs of dysfunction, we have evolved to a new physiological equilibrium. Even though the new balance is one we recognize as illness, reversing the processes requires some time if the readjustment is to be smooth. However, in life, corrective processes can run a little too fast. Rekindled hope can outrun expectations. We can push a little too hard, too fast.

A good example is getting back into shape. If we are out of shape, we should get a physical exam from our local physician before plunging into a workout schedule. We also may tend to be too eager to make up for lost time. We may push until we get a message from sore muscles that we should slow down a little. If we ignore the message, we may suffer an injury. Our bodies need time to readjust, even to healthful exercise.

Rick's eagerness to get back to an enjoyable sex life was very understandable. It led him to advance the timetable for his being able to stop taking the drugs. As so often happens in life, an unintended effect occurred. It had been so long since he had had an erection, that he was out of touch with his feelings leading to orgasm.

My emphasis from the beginning was on an open, sharing, mutually trusting working relationship. This provides a supportive backup system, just as a good parent or good coach can be counted on to help if there is trouble.

Self-Fulfilling Prophecies and Informed Consent

You may be asking yourself, "Well, if you knew there might be trouble, why didn't you warn Rick about the possibility in advance?"

There are a couple of problems with such an approach. First, no one can foresee every possible negative consequence. Second, and more important, is the role of self-fulfilling prophecies. It is a well-established scientific and psychological fact that what we believe affects what we experience. A classic study showed this effect on teachers. Many students of equal ability were divided into two groups. The teacher was told that group A had exceptional ability, and group B was below average. The teacher's evaluation of the students' performance corresponded to the false beliefs about differences in their abilities.

In other words, I might have encouraged the dysfunctional behavior by predicting it.

"Well, why is this any different from telling a patient the possible side effects of a drug or medical procedure? Shouldn't Rick have been told about antihypertensive drugs causing impotence?" you may be wondering.

Yes, Rick should have been informed. The difference is that in taking a prescribed medication or undergoing a medical procedure, you have no voluntary influence on the course of events. You are merely a passive recipient of either a powerful drug or procedure. In addition, you have no choice but to live with possible outcomes that may have serious irreversible consequences. Thus, informed consent in these areas is an important way of safeguarding your freedom to choose how to regain your health.

Maximizing Your Choices

Laura and Rick's experience is a good example of how stress can affect us on many levels. Not only had the stress of infertility affected Laura mentally and physically, it also had affected her relationships with husband, family, and friends. Similarly, Rick's high blood pressure was both an effect of stress in his work and personal life and a cause of sexual problems that strained an already pressured marriage.

Resolving these problems required a flexible and multilevel approach. Both Laura and Rick had gotten off to good starts working individually. Now Rick was at a point where short-term couple therapy with Laura was needed to make progress sexually. On the surface, it looked like Rick's problem. Yet, sex and intimacy always involve the couple. Whatever problems Laura may have been having in this area would be hidden by Rick's overt difficulties. In a way, it was the mirror image of their infertility problem. Overtly, Laura was suffering most in not getting pregnant. Rick's difficulties with not being able to be a father tended to be hidden under Laura's more overt complaints.

Long-term infertility struggles typically interfere with a woman's enjoyment of sex. The causes are many and can include combinations of factors: resentment toward her own body for not functioning as it should; feelings of unworthiness from not conceiving; anxiety and tension with every monthly cycle; despair, depression, and sadness about ever getting pregnant; feelings of guilt and self-punishment; anger at one's husband for not appearing to be concerned; and grief and a sense of loss in not producing a baby.

At this point in our treatment, Laura hadn't explored any of these possibilities. The focus had been on learning new mind-and-body skills, coping with her family, and supporting Rick in his treatment.

Laura needed to decide if it was time to work jointly with Rick. She might have felt that she needed more work alone. She might have wanted to pursue both approaches—working more individually and working with Rick. By encouraging Rick to talk to Laura, but not changing prior plans with Laura, helped to maximize Laura's choices as to how she wanted to proceed.

Laura's Decision

A couple of days later, Laura called. "Rick will be joining me at my appointment time," she announced. "He told me about his session with you. We talked about the various options and I thought about things myself for a few days. I feel that right now, working on our marriage is my first priority. Rick was really devastated the other day. I hate to see him like that."

"I certainly understand your concern," I said. "In your last session, we began exploring some of the stressful aspects of your relations with your family. Do you also want to work some more on these areas not directly related to Rick?"

After a pause, Laura replied, "I'm sure there are a lot of things I could work on for myself. But I just can't justify taking the time for that right now. Rick is my first priority."

"All right," I said. "Let's see how this approach works. I'd like us to stay open to the possibility of using some of the time for individual work, if it seems appropriate."

"Fine," Laura replied.

Getting in Touch with Yourself

My conversation with Laura gave me a clue as to what was holding her back in the training sessions from getting to deeper levels of relaxation. Laura found it difficult to focus on just herself. She was constantly preoccupied with how others were feeling—Rick, her mother, other family members. Laura was literally brought up to focus on pleasing others rather than tuning in to her own feelings.

As children, we are all dependent on our parents for our survival and well-being. Unfortunately, many parents give their children the powerful unspoken message that the child will get love and protection only by pleasing the parent. This leads to the type of guilt Laura felt whenever she tried to stand up for herself. She felt as though she were doing something bad and would be punished.

In addition, it was very difficult for her to focus on her own feelings and needs. She mislabeled it as selfishness and felt guilty about being self-indulgent. Laura's initial difficulty in finding time to practice the tape was related to the guilt she felt that time spent on herself was not productive. Also, Laura's motivation for treatment was to resolve her infertility. She needed encouragement to see that getting help for her self could help her achieve her goal of getting pregnant. This ongoing self-neglect was an important factor in Laura's inability to relax further physiologically.

This powerful pattern of self-neglect is so ingrained that it occurs out of our conscious awareness. For many of us, it literally came with mother's milk. I have found that the mind-body training enables us to see the physiological reality of mentally neglecting ourself. For example, biofeedback training helps the person to focus on tangible effects such as muscle tension that the pattern of self-neglect is causing. Concretely seeing the link between mind and body aids in motivating the individual to take the risks involved in changing such causative factors of stress as their way of relating to their loved ones.

Strategy and Tactics

It is easier to change these old patterns when those we love encourage us to do so. The couple work provided me with an opportunity to have Rick directly see his gain in Laura's focusing more on her own feelings.

The immediate problem was to help Rick get back in touch with his own sensations, to regain voluntary control over his orgasm. Premature ejaculation is best defined as the man coming too quickly, thus not enabling the woman to reach orgasm. Significantly, the definition focuses on the couple's experience, not on the absolute amount of time it takes before the man has an orgasm. The goal is mutual satisfaction, not setting a time record.

Masters and Johnson proved that a short-term behavioral treatment provided an effective cure. The treatment strategy involves the man clearly identifying his intense preorgastic sensations, and avoiding being distracted by his wife's needs. This approach obviously requires a cooperative wife, willing to encourage her husband to focus on himself, not her, during the treatment. Laura's desire to please was a plus for this part of the work.

Good sex, however, is more than just mechanics. Love, romance, and open communication all are necessary ingredients. Good sex involves our feelings, heart, and mind, as much as our body. As Rick gained confidence that he could control his orgasm, our focus could shift to Laura and her enjoyment. The more Laura could focus on her own pleasure, the more Rick could focus on his, and the more they could mutually enhance their relationship.

Improving their sex life could generate positive energy for other parts of their lives. Laura could learn that it really was better to be in touch with her own feelings, that she could both feel good and have a better marriage with Rick. Both of them could regain a better perspective on their infertility as a part of their life, not all-consuming. Rick could feel better about himself and his marriage, and have more positive energy for both his work life and for making life-style changes that would enhance his health and well-being.

Having a sense of my overall strategy, I could now focus on my initial approach to get Laura and Rick moving. When I met with them, I would first provide each with time to talk with me alone. This would enable me to get a clearer picture of each of their sexual histories. Often, members of a couple find it easier to talk about an aspect of their sex life without the partner present.

A person may have preferences or dislikes, but may never have communicated them to a partner. Patients may have some sexual secrets that they want to unburden, but are afraid to tell their partners. The initial individual time enables the person to discuss these things with me. Knowing that confidentiality is assured, we can discuss how to make use of the information shared.

Having had four individual sessions each with Laura and Rick prior to this meeting had given me some useful information already. I didn't expect any revelations that might jeopardize our work together. I hoped to get a clearer sense of each one's personal preferences and dislikes.

Chapter 3

Intimacy—
Working Together
as a Couple

Sharing Yourself

Laura and Rick seemed nervous as they sat down together for our meeting. After a brief initial silence, I spoke.

"I see you're both a little nervous. I certainly understand that. Let me help us get started. I've met with each of you a number of times. Our work together is part of that same process of healing that I have been pursuing with each of you individually. I know that the overt problem that you are here for is a sexual one, and we will use a tried-and-proven approach to enable Rick to regain voluntary control over his orgasm. But that is a small part of what we are here for. The bigger picture involves restoring the positive feelings of warmth and closeness that come with the joy of shared intimacy. The regeneration of that positive energy of love can help each of you to feel better about yourself and to create positive motivation to make changes you want in your life."

I could see the anxiety start to lift from both of them as they connected to my message. "I would like to start by talking alone with each of you for a few minutes. This will enable me to get a clear picture of your individual experiences with each other. Then we will meet together and mutually decide on what the two of you can do to begin. As in all therapy, the basic principles of respect for each other's wishes and needs applies. There is no healing in trying to do anything you are uncomfortable with. All physical intimacy exercises will, of course, be done by you in the privacy of your home. Here, we will talk about your experiences and work toward further growth and intimate sharing. If you have any questions at this point, let me know. Then I'd like to start talking with one of you."

Laura and Rick looked at each other and shrugged their shoulders indicating they had no questions at the moment. Rick then said, "Laura, why don't you start. I've been talking a lot to the doctor about my sexual experiences." Laura agreed and Rick stepped outside into the waiting room."

"Well, what do you want to know?" Laura asked.

The Best of the Past

"Let's start at the beginning," I replied. "I recall your mentioning your being a virgin when you met Rick." Laura blushed as I said this. "What was sex like with Rick at the beginning?"

Laura, blushing even more, replied, "We never went all the way, until we became engaged. I grew up in a home of traditional values. I was not a child of the sixties. I wanted to save myself for my husband. Once we were engaged, I felt it was like being married. We had a commitment to each other."

"That sounds very romantic," I interjected. "I noticed you were blushing before. Do you have a sense of what that's about?"

"I guess talking about sex has always been a little embarrassing for me. We never talked about sex at home when I was growing up. I was brought up to be a 'good' girl."

"Yes, and you are 'good' in the best sense of the word. I understand that it seems a little awkward for you, but could you tell me what you enjoyed with Rick?"

Blushing again, Laura said, "Well, to start with, I met him at a party. I was immediately attracted to his outgoing personality and sense of humor. I'm more reserved, as you can tell," Laura said with a little smile. "He made me laugh. I thought he was fun. But that's probably not what you're asking about."

"Actually, it is," I answered. "I want to get a clear picture of what you find attractive about Rick, what you enjoy in the widest sense. I'm not only interested in your sexual experiences."

Laura replied with a smile, "That's a relief. I thought that sex was what shrinks thought was the basis of everything."

I laughed and said, "You don't have to be a shrink to realize there is more to life than sex. The real basis of everything is the quality of the relationship of which sex is a part. Making love is an expression of a good relationship. I think the sixties taught us very clearly that sex without love can lead to emptiness rather than fulfillment."

"I'm glad to hear you say that. Some friends of mine thought I was 'square' to wait for the right man and the right relationship."

"You acted in a way consistent with your personal values. That's a healthy approach to life," I replied. "When you were most able to enjoy Rick, including making love, what helped to make everything go right?" I asked.

After thinking for a moment, Laura replied, "Well, I guess the best times were right after we were married. I wasn't completely comfortable with us fooling around even when we were engaged. But when we got married, I really knew he was mine. After a year, when we started focusing on having a baby, sex became less enjoyable."

"During your first year of marriage, when everything was at its best, what contributed to setting the right tone and mood for making love?" I asked.

Alcohol and Sex

"I was really happy being married," Laura began. "I wanted to make Rick happy. Mostly, he would take the initiative. Thinking back, I guess knowing that we had a romantic evening planned would get me in the mood. I would look forward to a nice dinner out and dancing afterward." Laura started to giggle and continued, "I was thinking of our first New Year's Eve as a married couple. The champagne was great! Even a little goes right to my head." With a laugh, she added, "I guess if I weren't so careful, I could be a cheap drunk!"

"Did you find that wine would help you to relax and enjoy making love more?" I asked.

"Definitely," Laura responded emphatically. "I think that being a little tipsy always has helped me to let go more completely," she added with a smile. "Now that I'm thinking about it, I recall that when I started to focus seriously on getting pregnant, I stopped drinking, because I had heard that alcohol might cause problems."

"It sounds as though—like many people—you used alcohol as a way to relax," I responded. "You may find that focusing on your breathing and the other relaxation exercises helps you to let go without the harmful potential that drinking has."

"I've been so preoccupied these last few years with getting pregnant, that I think I'd have to get totally drunk to relax," Laura said.

"That's an unfortunate misperception that millions of people have," I continued. "Actually, increasing amounts of alcohol just anesthetize us so that we don't feel anything. You may remember seeing old TV westerns where the local doctor had his patient drink whiskey to dull the pain during surgery. They became anesthetized and obviously couldn't function. As Shakespeare said about drinking, 'It giveth the desire, but taketh away the performance.' In small amounts, alcohol has an initial positive effect by functioning as a disinhibitor. If we are feeling uptight or inhibited, a small dose of alcohol turns off that part of the brain that has the distracting thoughts and inhibitions. Larger doses of alcohol turn off more areas and result in diminished sensitivity and decreasing ability to perform. Excessive drinking is actually a major cause of impotency."

"What you're saying is really what I've experienced," Laura said. "When I would have just a drink or two, it would turn off my thoughts and I could enjoy things more. But when I really got smashed, I either got numb or just passed out."

I replied, "In effect, the benefit you get from alcohol in small amounts is that it turns off whatever negative thoughts or inhibitions you may have. You can learn to distract yourself from such negative thoughts, with what you're learning here, without the effect alcohol has of dulling your responses."

Getting in Touch with Yourself

"But how can just belly breathing and muscle relaxation accomplish that?" Laura asked.

"It's more than just physical," I countered. "By focusing your mind on your breathing, you are distracting yourself from any negative thoughts you may have. In effect, you are freeing your mind. This allows you to tune in more sensitively to what you are feeling and experiencing in the moment. This heightened sensual awareness enables you to take more pleasure in lovemaking. In essence, you can shift your focus to your immediate sensations and away from any intrusive thoughts."

"Listening to what you're saying, it does make sense to me," Laura began. "Yet I don't see how I can do that. When I'm with Rick, my thoughts are on pleasing *him*. I can't focus on me until he has had his pleasure. But when that happens, he stops making love."

"How do you feel about that?" I asked.

Laura first looked puzzled and then upset at my question. "What am I supposed to feel?" she began. "I really haven't thought about how I feel. I feel good when I'm physically close with Rick and he's happy. I like when he holds me, and sometimes I'll ask him to after we make love. He always does if I ask him."

"What about your physical pleasure—about having an orgasm?" I asked.

"As far as that is concerned, I guess I've never focused on it," Laura said. "Don't get me wrong. I'm not a prude. If it happens, fine. If it doesn't, I'm not going to make a big deal out of it. I'm not going to complain to Rick and make him feel inadequate if one doesn't occur when he makes love to me."

As I listened to Laura, I was thinking to myself that indeed she was certainly not a child of the sixties. Clearly, asking for something for herself she perceived as being selfish. In addition, she felt that her pleasure was Rick's responsibility and didn't want to hurt his feelings. I also felt that Laura's avoidance of the word *orgasm* indicated how uncomfortable she was. Her traditional value system did have positive aspects, such as her not being obsessed with an orgasm as being the acid test of good sex. Knowing the necessity of always working with a person's value system, I decided to begin my response as follows:

"I agree with your emphasis on closeness, rather than just focusing on orgasms. As I said earlier, when Rick was here with you—I'm interested in the bigger picture of restoring the positive feelings of warmth and closeness. What is your sense of what has happened to those feelings over the years of your infertility grind?" I asked.

"I guess I've felt ground down over the years," Laura began. "I gradually started to resent my body for not functioning the way it's supposed to. I began to feel empty. I felt incomplete. I even started to feel less attractive. Instead of making love, sex became a chore to perform during my fertile time. I wanted to get it over with as quickly as possible. Instead of being held, I would lie still with a pillow under me after sex, because the doctor said it would help the sperm travel up my uterus. As the years of frustration have gone on, I think I've become more and more alienated from my body. It's been a source of pain and humiliation for me, not pleasure. I've sensed Rick withdrawing, too, over the years. Even before his present potency problems. I don't know—maybe he sensed my negative feelings about myself."

"I can appreciate what you've been going through," I said. "Unfortunately, your alienation from yourself, your body, and enjoyment is common with infertility problems. However, you can help both Rick and yourself to get back the closeness you have had."

"How can I do that?" Laura asked.

"When the three of us meet together, I'll talk about how you can help Rick. Now I'd like to discuss some ways you can help yourself get back to a more positive feeling about yourself and your body."

"I'd like to do that," Laura replied. "In my psychotherapy, I've gotten to the point of intellectually accepting that I deserve to feel good, but I'm having trouble doing it."

"The suggestions I'm going to talk to you about offer you the opportunity to get some experience in a positive way for yourself. Let me ask you, do you like bubble baths?"

Laura smiled and said, "Yes, but it's been such a long time since I took one. I remember even liking them as a kid. I could sit and play in the water endlessly. Now I guess I could just soak in the tub and get away from the world."

"Yes—literally good, clean fun. I'm glad you have had positive experiences with it before. Have you ever tried creating your own environment of sound, textures, and aromas?"

"No. I'm not sure what you mean—in the bathtub?" Laura asked.

"Yes, listening to soothing music, using your favorite fragrance bath oil. Pampering yourself, in other words."

"Sounds decadent," Laura said with an approving smile. "I might never want to get out of the tub. Wouldn't I get spoiled?" she asked, half jokingly, half seriously.

"Not a chance," I responded, in a similar way. "But we can set limits. I'd like you to try this for a half hour three times during the next week. Note what you feel, what you like, and if anything makes you feel uncomfortable. We'll talk about your experiences and make adjustments accordingly. How does that sound to you?"

"All right. I'm willing to give it a try."

"Good. Let's stop here," I suggested. "I want to talk to Rick alone, before we all meet together."

As Laura left, I thought to myself that we had gotten off to a good start. By finding common ground with her prior good feelings about bubble baths, we could build a bridge for her to get back in touch with positive feelings. By regaining her own sense of her sensual self, Laura could improve her self-esteem while she worked with Rick on his problem.

As Rick sat down, I thought to myself that I wanted to find out more of his individual reactions to the infertility struggle to gain a better understanding of how to start building bridges with him, as I had done with Laura.

Men Hurt, Too (Even If They Don't Show It)

"As with Laura, I'd like to start by getting a clearer picture of your reactions and experiences of how your love life with her has been affected over the years. Let's begin with when you met Laura," I said.

"We met at a party. I had a good feeling about her right away, since she laughed at my jokes." Rick smiled in remembrance. "She seemed different in a way I liked. She was quieter and paid more attention to me than anyone else I had ever known. I got the feeling she was genuinely interested in me. Laura grew up in a proper, conservative way. Everything developed really slowly. It may sound old-fashioned, but I respected her for it. I felt that what we shared together was special. For a while, it was like being a teenager again. Necking, petting, having limits. After we got engaged, we finally had sex. I like the fact that Laura wasn't demanding. I could just be myself and she felt good. You know, with some women, you feel you have to work so hard to please them, that you can't enjoy yourself. I never had that problem with Laura."

Rick paused, then continued, "I guess everything was great until Laura got serious about having a baby. Don't misunderstand me, I wanted a baby, too. Laura would just get so upset every month when she got her period. I felt I had to be the strong one, for her to be able to lean on. Gradually, our sex life started to fall apart. Laura seemed to lose interest in sex and even in being affectionate. I could see that it was because she was upset with herself, so I never complained to her. After a while, it seemed that we only got together during her fertile days. It became like a job. She would tell me in the morning, 'Tonight's the night.' I began to feel like a machine. She seemed to just want to get it over with as quickly as possible. Then she'd lie there with a pillow under her to increase the odds of conception. I used to enjoy holding her after making love. I got displaced by a pillow! Now that I'm recalling it, I remember starting to come quickly just to get it over with. In a way, I guess I did have my current problem, that you call premature ejaculation, except I didn't feel out of control. I just felt I was getting the job done quickly and efficiently. Also, Laura wanted me to, so I wasn't depriving her of any pleasure."

"It sounds like you were hurting pretty badly, as a result of the infertility problem," I said.

"As I'm talking about it now, I guess that's right," Rick replied. "I hadn't looked at it that way before. I always saw it as mainly Laura's problem and her suffering with it. Also, family and friends who know have always consoled *her,* never me. I was always told that I needed to be strong and understanding for her, which I have really tried to do."

"Yes, you have," I acknowledged. "Unfortunately, our culture tends to push men into the 'Rock of Gibraltar' role. It's frowned upon for men to admit their hurt. Yet, men suffer, too. Getting in touch with the hurt helps to relieve the pain. Sadly, women often mistake their husbands' 'strong, silent' role as meaning an indifference to their suffering. Not seeing the hurt, a woman mistakenly feels there isn't any pain being shared by her husband. The stereotyped 'macho' role often leads to alienation between the couple. The solution lies in the direction of getting in touch with your feelings, not blocking them out to be 'strong.' "

Rick's voice was choked up; as he spoke he seemed to be fighting back tears. "I've felt so alone for so long now. I've felt pushed away. I've felt that Laura just didn't want or need my comfort," Rick mumbled as he began to cry.

After a moment, I tried to encourage him by saying, "It takes a real human being to cry. Only inert rocks don't express feelings. You have been so focused on the role of being strong and performing that you have lost touch with your inner self. The road to self-healing is the road of being in touch with your feelings and needs."

The End of Macho Man

"But doesn't Laura need me to be strong for her? Won't she feel a loss of security if I'm crying?" Rick asked.

"Tears express a feeling," I began. "They are a way of communicating where we are. Being in touch with and sharing feeling gives us strength to carry on as part of a team that has a bond of *shared* feeling. This is what Laura wants and needs, as you do. The 'macho' approach is a hollow, bankrupt, cardboard image. It's not real. It's all surface, no real depth. Maybe it had survival value, when unfeeling brute strength was necessary. We live in a world where accommodation and change insures survival. Macho may be useful for killers. Sensitivity is necessary for lovers."

"I hope you're right," Rick said. "It sure would be a relief to feel it's OK to be myself."

"Don't take my word for it. Check it out with Laura," I said.

"How am I going to be able to do that? What if you're wrong?" Rick asked.

"Do a little experiment," I suggested. "Take a calculated risk. For example, you might say that you miss holding her. If you put it that way, you can share your feeling of loss in a way that appeals to her to get closer to you. Everything depends on how you do it. If you are going to accuse her of pushing you away, you will get a defensive response," I said. "The idea is to phrase things in a way that she can respond positively, not have to defend herself against an attack."

"I see what you're saying. I never realized how the way you say something is so important. I don't know that I can watch every word I say."

"You don't have to," I assured him. "If you just focus on your caring and loving feelings for Laura, and think about how you would like to be approached—you will do just fine."

"OK, I can focus on that—all right," Rick said.

"Well, that's your individual assignment for this week," I said with a smile. "Think about your feelings and how you share them with Laura. Also, keep track of how she responds. We can look at your experiences next week, and learn from whatever happens."

"OK, coach," Rick said with a smile.

"Good, let's have Laura come back and join us after we all take a five-minute break," I suggested.

Changing Stereotyped Roles

As Rick left, I thought about the enormous toll in pain and stress that our lingering "macho" cultural stereotype has taken on men and women. Fortunately, as a society, we seem to be moving in a direction that encourages men to acknowledge their feelings.

Being stuck in stereotyped roles had created distance between Rick and Laura. The rigidity of their patterns had alienated both of their own selves. By becoming more flexible and being able to respond more freely to his feelings of vulnerability, Rick could grow and share more intimately with Laura. Laura, by getting more in touch with enjoyable sensations, could be more open and responsive to Rick, as well as improve her own self-esteem.

Both of them had individual assignments to practice at home. I wanted to reinforce, as a couple together, what they would be working on individually. To do this, I would suggest a return to romance and enjoyment of each other. Any activities to encourage them to grow in friendship and communication would be supported. At this point, I would strongly recommend that they not engage in foreplay or intercourse, so as to remove any performance demands from them temporarily. In addition, this would help them to experience their sensations more fully—which was the immediate goal.

Mind-Body Treatment of Intimacy Problems

Laura and Rick's intimacy problems involved many levels of sharing: communication, feelings, trust, as well as sex. By its very nature, intimacy involves a delicate balance between maintaining our own sense of self and sharing with the one we love.

I have found that this new mind-body approach offers a uniquely valuable way of enabling rapid progress to be made. The reason is that the focus is on here-and-now experiences that are simultaneously worked on by each partner, both as an individual self, and as part of a couple.

This overcomes the problem that often occurs in traditional treatment approaches to intimacy problems. Typically, one or both partners will be seeing different therapists individually, as well as possibly a third therapist for couple work. It is virtually impossible to coordinate so many different therapists into a smooth, coherent treatment. The unfortunate tendency is to reinforce the artificial division between a person's experience as an individual and as one of a couple.

Sexuality is a classic example of an activity requiring that sharing and communication, as well as individual experiences, be balanced and coordinated simultaneously. The major advances in the last twenty-five years in effective short-term couple therapy, sex therapy, and biofeedback have paved the way for this new integrated mind-body approach to intimacy problems.

Responding to Concerns

There are two major concerns that classical Freudian analysts have had about the new integrated mind-body approach. Both concerns have been successfully addressed in actual treatment experience, and both arose from the classical model that the key to change was only in the unconscious of the individual. Thus, the first concern was that if a person's symptom, such as premature ejaculation, was cured by here-and-now behavioral techniques, another symptom would arise as a substitute expression of a hypothetical unconscious conflict, such as castration anxiety. Masters and Johnson and the last twenty years of sex therapy have conclusively proven that there is no symptom substitution.

The second concern also arose from the theory that the key to resolving a person's problems was only working alone with that person's mind. Twenty-five years of successful couple and family-therapy treatment approaches have conclusively proven that many problems are best resolved by a combination of individual work and working together with the couple or family. Typically, a couple or family therapist may do some work with individual members as well as the couple or family as a unit. If there are any potential conflicts of interest between serving the best needs of the individual, as opposed to the larger unit of the couple, then a separate therapist can work with the individual.

Working Together as a Couple

After the five-minute break, Laura sat next to Rick, and they both looked at me to get things going.

I opened with, "I can see you're wondering where do we go from here. Well, meeting alone with each of you has deepened my knowledge of your experiences. Each of you now has some individual assignments to do. You certainly can talk with each other about what you shared with me, if you want to. It isn't essential though, and if either of you thinks it's better not to discuss it, that's OK, too. As a couple, I want you to work together in a way that both enhances your intimacy and is consistent with what you are each working on individually. Therefore, the initial homework—remember this isn't like school work—will be to have some fun together."

Laura and Rick looked at each other and smiled.

Also smiling I said, "I'm not sure that it's the kind of fun you may be thinking of, right now. I'm suggesting a return to romance, candle-lit dinners, and dancing. You both have talked of having fun together that way. But—and this is a big one—I am urging you both not to engage in any sexual activity at this time. This means not only no intercourse, but no foreplay."

"Hey, Doc, I thought you said this was going to be fun," Rick protested.

"Yes, I did. And at this stage, to keep it fun, we need to put off limits any activity that might interfere with the two of you beginning to get closer and to share. I don't want any pressures to perform and please the other sexually to interfere with your getting back in touch with mutual feelings of warmth and closeness. Don't worry, sex will come later, when it's a natural outgrowth of your renewed intimacy."

Laura turned to Rick and said, "Well, Hon, it kind of reminds me of our courtship. Waiting a while did make us both more eager to enjoy each other."

"That's true," Rick replied, sheepishly. "OK, I'll behave."

"Good," I said. "I know you're eager to run with the ball, Rick. I understand your motivation, but I'm glad to hear that you can live with this restriction for now."

"I'm with you, coach. I can restrain myself for the good of the team," Rick said with a smile. We all laughed. Rick's good spirits carried through to his biofeedback training. He began at 130/80 and lowered his blood pressure to 125/75 by the end of the session.

Using Your Imagination: Visualization and Imagery

During her physiological training, Laura continued to show steady progress. She started at 84 degrees hand temperature and eventually reached 89 degrees during the training. I had the sense that intellectually, she now saw that she needed to focus on herself more, but that she still was trying to find out how to do that experientially. I felt that the "homework" would help her to do this. Then I could encourage her to use visualization and imagery techniques to help her relax more thoroughly.

Our imagination is as much an ongoing part of us as breathing. We all daydream, recall memories, do inner talk in our mind. These are all examples of our imagination in action. We can voluntarily direct our imagination. Thus, we can harness powers of mind that we typically assume are out of our conscious control. This is similar to using our breathing to shift our physiology.

You can visualize a scene. It's like making your own movie in your mind. You can create the atmosphere, mood, and action you want. As you focus on pleasant images, they will help you to relax.

Visualization is currently being used by Olympic champions and professional athletes to improve their performance. By picturing in detail all the steps of a successful event, you program the right reactions into your mind and body. At the Olympics and professional level, physical skills are all outstanding. It's the mental edge that makes the difference between winning and losing.

By visualizing a calm scene, such as a perfect day at the beach with loved ones, we can alter our physiology toward body and mind relaxation. It's a great way to take a stress break.

We can also monitor our inner talk, and remembrances. If they are focusing on the negative, we can consciously choose to redirect our inner dialogue and memories to more positive, self-affirming directions.

Mid-Course Assessment

I felt we had gotten off to a good start in our first couple meeting. Both Laura and Rick appeared ready to work together, as well as progressing individually on their intimacy issues.

For each of them, this was their fifth session, a mid-course milestone in the usual ten-session treatment program. As is typical, both had established their capacity to perform the basic skills correctly, such as belly breathing and muscle relaxation. At this point, the focus shifted more to the mind side of the stress equation. Dealing with some ongoing stressful situations in personal life and at work became the center of attention. In Rick and Laura's experience, the problem of intimacy had led to the combined individual and couple approach.

The individual parts of their session confirmed my sense that each of them had his or her own intimacy and sexual issues to work on, as well as working on their problems as a couple. Their evident goodwill and cooperative spirit with each other and the treatment were important factors in my being able to work rapidly with them in this way. If there is overt hostility between the couple or deep-seated resentments, progress will be stymied until the anger is resolved. This makes the process more lengthy, and may require separate individual work to resolve longstanding rage.

Fortunately, neither Laura nor Rick was out to sabotage the process. Their understandable hurts and disappointments could be dealt with by rebuilding positive bridges of good experiences together, as well as individually.

My plan would involve individual and couple "homework" assignments that dovetailed with each other. Each would reinforce the other. This way, they could each progress simultaneously. If Laura and Rick had gone through standard sex therapy, they would probably have had each of their problems dealt with sequentially. Typically, Laura's problems would wait, while she helped Rick with his first.

Approaching their problems from a stress point of view, it made more sense to have them work simultaneously in helping themselves and each other. It is both quicker and builds self-confidence and self-esteem in a mutually reinforcing way. This was particularly important because their sexual difficulties were part of the larger picture of themselves and their marriage being stressed by their struggles with infertility.

Desire Returns

When Laura and Rick arrived for our next meeting, we agreed to continue with the same format as the prior session. Laura went out and sat in the waiting room, while I began with Rick. He seemed eager to talk.

"A lot has happened since our last session, both in terms of myself and my assignment with Laura," he began.

"Let's start with how you presently feel," I suggested.

"OK. But, first of all, I have to tell you, this time I did follow doctor's orders. I didn't 'fool around' with Laura," he said smiling. "Physically, I'm getting back to my old self, now that I'm off the blood pressure drugs. Not only am I waking up with an erection more often, I'm having wet dreams during the night. As a matter of fact, my desire's gotten so strong that I tested it the other day," Rick said with a puckish grin.

"What do you mean?" I asked. "I thought you just said you had followed 'doctor's orders.'"

"I did. I did," Rick continued. "When I say 'I tested it,' I mean the equipment," he said with a smile. "I figured it could use a trial run, and I'm happy to announce that I found the equipment totally in working order," he concluded, with a grin.

"I'm glad to hear that. I'm not surprised that you would go ahead on your own," I replied. "In terms of your regaining control over your orgasm, which is our goal, what was your experience like with masturbating?"

"Great!" Rick exclaimed. "Seriously, I had a good hard-on. I guess you would call it a full erection," he said with his puckish look. "I was able to stay in touch with and enjoy my sensations. I finally came, when I wanted to. It was a relief in more ways than one," he continued with a smile. "It's good to know I can be in control of myself again. I guess I tried it, without talking about it here first, because I always had good control when I was in charge. I felt this would be a safe place to start from. Anyway, who wants to ask his doctor's permission to play with himself!" he said with a laugh.

With a smile I replied, "You're certainly in a good mood today. Actually, your intuition was correct. One standard treatment approach to your problem involves the 'stop-start' technique, in which the man reestablishes his ejaculatory control in progressive stages—initially alone, then eventually with his partner."

After a moment, Rick continued in a more sober tone. "I'm not sure that this so-called 'stop-start' technique will work for Laura and me. I have no idea how it will work when I'm inside her." Rick said.

"The same way as when you are masturbating," I replied. "You vary your movements, stopping and starting again according to the sensations you feel. After a couple of times of stopping just before orgasm, you then continue until you climax. Your focus is on your sensations, not distracted by trying to please Laura."

After a thoughtful pause, Rick said, "That sounds good in theory, but I see a real problem in our situation. Quite frankly, part of my problem is that it's difficult for me to monitor my sensations when I'm inside Laura. I just feel like I'm gliding in an open space. It's very different from when we just got married. Then, she felt very tight around me. She had a good grip on me, that gave me a consistent pressure. What are we going to do about that?"

A Quick Way to Better Sex

"Actually, your experience is a common one and there is a quick and easy solution to the problem. All Laura needs to do is voluntarily contract her vaginal muscles to re-create a consistent, tight fit. They are called the pubococcygeus (PC) muscles. It is known as a Kegel exercise, after the gynecologist who did the initial work. This is common element in many sex therapy programs."

"Laura told me you're encouraging her to do things *she* enjoys, not just to please me. Is this going to mix her up about that?" Rick asked.

"No," I replied. "As a matter of fact, Kegel's exercise is specifically designed for women to experience more pleasure for themselves. Its main use is to help women who are having difficulty reaching orgasm themselves. It's a win-win situation. Both you and Laura will benefit individually and as a couple."

"I'm glad to hear that, coach," Rick said with a look of relief.

"Both of you will get more pleasure. This will encourage more intimacy. A positive cycle will replace the current negative cycle of guilt and resentment that has built up over years of frustration," I concluded.

"Let's switch gears to how your main homework assignment went," I said. "What has happened in terms of rebuilding the romance?"

"I think we're doing good," Rick said. "I've enjoyed myself. I took Laura out to a neighborhood street fair last Saturday night. There was a band and everyone was dancing in the street and the whole evening only cost me ten dollars. We both had a great time. In addition, I'm complimenting her on little things that I like. It's amazing to me, she really glows when I tell her something simple, such as that I like the outfit she's wearing. She really looked great Saturday night and loved me telling her."

"Yes, the little things add up," I said. "We're usually unaware that we can create a positive atmosphere with just a little thoughtfulness. It sounds like the fair was a really creative idea of yours."

"Also, I'm taking your advice and trying to watch how I say something that I'm upset about," Rick continued. "Before, I'd say something like, 'This is terrible.' Now I'll say, 'I'd appreciate it if we could please change this in such-and-such a way.' I guess it's easier for her to respond positively if I make a specific suggestion that she can do something about. I know she really does want to please me. I'm finding myself falling in love with her all over again."

"That's beautiful," I encouraged. "Let's continue keeping the good times rolling. You're seeing that sensitivity and praise pays off, whereas the strong, silent approach creates alienation. Let's stop here so I can talk with Laura."

Relaxing in the Bath

Laura had a pleased expression on her face when she walked in for her individual part of the couple session. She got right to the point by saying, "I really enjoyed my homework. It's so soothing and relaxing to soak in a bubble bath. I am trying to find the time to fit it in every night. I get so relaxed, I'm ready to go to sleep afterward. Usually, I would need to read in bed for a while to get sleepy."

"I'm glad that you're enjoying it," I said. "The tension reduction for both mind and body certainly promotes the shift to getting a good night's sleep. Some people find that by relaxing in the tub when they get home from work they are able to make a nice transition to enjoying the evening. For many it replaces having a couple of drinks to unwind from a hard day's work."

"Won't I just want to go to sleep afterward?" Laura asked.

"Not really," I answered. "Taking a relaxing bath between five and seven P.M. is different from taking one before your regular bedtime. You're more awake, so the transition is just to a more relaxed state."

"I think what really worked was creating a private little world for myself. I was able to shut out all the daily pressures and demands. Your idea of my appealing to many different senses really helped. I put on some soft mood music I like. I got a bath oil that gives me a silky feeling and smells like lavender. I sat back with an ice-cold Coke—not a diet one, either—the regular kind. After settling in, I closed my eyes and imagined myself floating in a pool on a nice sunny day with a comfortable breeze in the air. Just talking about it makes me feel good," Laura said with a smile.

"Yes, you appear more relaxed as you talk about it," I observed. "You may find it helpful during your biofeedback training to close your eyes and let yourself visualize this. Such a positive inner focus will help you break through to deeper levels of physiological relaxation. Up to now, I suspect your focus has been distracted by thinking about what you need to do. This has created a resistance to deeper relaxation."

"I like that suggestion," Laura replied. "I have been having difficulty letting go of worrying. When I try to stop the thoughts, it's been hard to do. I start to think I'm failing and then I just get more anxious. Maybe I can focus on this instead."

"Yes, and the more relaxation you experience, the more energy you will have later," I added. "When Rick rejoins us, I'll ask you about how things have been going for the two of you together. Before we stop now, I'd like to propose some additional ideas for you."

"As long as it's as fun as the bubble baths," Laura said with a laugh.

"I expect it will be," I replied. "I want you to continue your self-exploration of sensual pleasure. Does that sound like fun?"

"I'm not so sure," Laura stated slowly. "I haven't been in the mood to enjoy sex with Rick. I guess I'm not exactly sure what you're suggesting."

Sex and Morality

"Sexual pleasure is a combination of fantasy and friction. It's a classic mind-body interaction. Since the ultimate sexual organ is the mind, let's start there. You have shown that you have both a good imagination in creating a wonderful bubble bath environment, and the capacity for visualization as exemplified by the pool scene you created in your mind's eye. How are you at fantasizing erotic situations?" I asked.

After a pause, Laura said with a frown, "Not so good. I guess I'm too uptight. The way I was brought up, the whole idea was wrong. Good girls just didn't think about sex. They certainly didn't play with themselves," Laura said somewhat self-righteously.

"There certainly is a lot that is positive in the traditional values in which you were raised," I replied. "We certainly have seen the excesses of too much permissiveness on the part of parents and society in terms of the explosion of teen pregnancies and drug addition. Yet, there does seem to be a happy medium between the extremes of abstinence and excess permissiveness. As a society we're searching for it. I believe it involves a combination of instilling healthy values, sharing accurate information about sex and drugs, and fostering a sense of individual responsibility. However, that's a big separate subject. Let's focus on you. We are dealing with you as an adult, married woman, who is trying to help make her marriage work. It seems to me that to enjoy sex with your husband more, greater knowledge of your own sexuality can only help. What do you think about that?"

Laura thought for a moment and said, "I see your point. I need to deal with what's right for me at this stage of my life. I really want my marriage to work. But I guess I want to both be a moral person and enjoy life. Is that possible?"

I shook my head in agreement. "I believe it's not only possible, but that the two go together. The essence of being a moral person is being a good person, in the sense of not only not harming others, but also encouraging their healthy growth and development. Enjoying life in a positive way involves both being a moral person and experiencing our senses and feelings in natural, healthy ways. We have the capacity for pleasure, including sensual and sexual pleasure, so that we can live a full life and re-create ourselves in our children."

God and Guilt

Laura began to cry. "What you're saying sounds right to me. But I feel like I must be guilty for something, and God is punishing me through my infertility."

"Why would God be punishing you?" I asked.

Laura thought for a moment and replied, "I broke one of the Ten Commandments: Honor thy father and mother. I didn't obey my mother. She didn't want me to marry Rick. Therefore, I'm to blame and am childless."

Now it was my turn to think for a moment. Finally I said, "It seems to me that there is a very real misperception in what you said. It sounds as if you believe that God works through your mother. Not obeying her wishes is falsely equated with disobeying God."

"Well," Laura replied, "my life is more unsettling now. When I was younger and doing what my mother told me, I felt protected."

"It seems to me that you're being very hard on yourself," I said. "You're assuming that if you married someone your mother approved of, you'd be a mother by now yourself."

As I paused and studied Laura, I could see that this is exactly what she thought. "Was your mother right about everything, Laura?" I asked.

"Well, she sure thought she was," Laura replied. "And when you disagreed with her, she let you know it. All it took was a look and I felt like I was in the doghouse."

"And now, do you feel that way about God as well?" I asked. "Has He turned into the Great Gestapo in the sky? Is He just waiting and watching, and out to 'get you' if you mess up in any way?" I asked.

"It sounds really ridiculous when you put it that way," Laura said, starting to smile. "But I do feel really angry at God. He has the power to give me a child but he doesn't. Sometimes I feel like Job. Why is God punishing me?"

"I think you're still focusing on blaming yourself and feeling guilty," I began. "I have lots of questions as to why things are the way they are in life, and I certainly don't have all the answers. But as awful as feelings of blame and guilt are, they aren't so bad as feeling lost and out of control. So we jump on the bandwagon of guilt—and I say *jump* because I mean it—somewhere along the line we choose to feel guilty, since it makes us feel better than feeling out of control. If you believe God is punishing you and you feel the blame and guilt—well, then at least you're on the same side as God. There is a very strong reality of letting ourselves feel self-righteous when we feel guilty. We are accepting the punishment we feel we deserve, so even in our misery, we can find a place to feel good about ourselves, not truly good, but self-righteously good. But I don't believe God is punishing you. I think this bandwagon was taught to you by your mom and it's time to jump off and deal with the issue at hand. We can re-create ourselves in loving an adopted child or a biological one. Many exceptional people don't have any children, but re-create themselves in their love of God and the entire human family."

"I'm not that exceptional. I want a baby," Laura said.

"Well, that's human. The important point is that one way or another, biologically or through adoption, you will have a baby to love and nurture. I think if you just focus on the reality that you will be a mother, it will help you to find peace within yourself, with Rick, and with God," I replied.

"What you're saying feels right to me," Laura replied. "I've always known we could consider adoption at some point. I'll just have to sit with it for a while to get more comfortable with the idea that I will get my main wish, which is to be a mother, and that I don't have to feel guilty about being a failure if I don't get pregnant."

"Before we meet together with Rick, I'd like to tie up some loose ends from before, if that's all right with you," I said. "We have traveled quite a distance from the sensual to the spiritual side of life. Can we switch gears for a moment back to the sensual?"

"Sure," Laura said, a smile brightening her face. "I think our discussion about God and babies has begun to free me up to feel more deserving about enjoying pleasure."

"I'm glad to hear you're feeling less guilty," I said. "You mentioned before that given your upbringing, it's difficult for you to fantasize erotically. There are some books that can help you if you are interested. They are written by women for women. They are sensitive and sensual."

"That sounds like a good idea to help me get started," Laura replied.

"OK. Two classics are *For Yourself,* by Lonnie Garfield Barbach, and *My Secret Garden,* by Nancy Friday. Flip through the books to find a fantasy that appeals to you. As you get more comfortable with the process, let your own mind create your own enjoyable fantasies."

"What do I do then?" Laura asked.

"I'll leave that to you," I replied. "See how you feel. You may want to just fantasize and not do anything with yourself. Only do what feels comfortable. Don't try to push anything that doesn't feel right. We're not here to prove a point, but to aid your self-relaxation and enjoyment."

"OK, I'll keep it light and fun. I'll try not to tie myself up in knots over this," Laura said.

"Yes, I agree with you. The process of becoming more comfortable with yourself is important," I said. "Let's take a five-minute break before meeting together with Rick."

Forgiving Yourself

My time with Laura underscored the importance of focusing on the client's concerns as they arise. On her own, Laura got in touch with long-term troubling issues ranging from morality and God, to her mother, and guilt over sensuality and infertility. Long-buried conflicts in all these areas can be hidden sources of chronic stress. By providing an open, nonjudgmental environment, one creates the atmosphere of trust necessary to enable the patient to find the courage to talk about these things. There are no easy answers or pat formulas to these dilemmas.

However, by helping patients to see that they can travel a path that meets their needs as they define them, great relief from stress can be achieved. As patients begin to see themselves back in control of directing their destiny, their energy is freed up for self-healing and growth. In her case, Laura will be able to try some experiments in living to find out what feels right to her. This can replace the pain and confusion of inherited values that don't quite fit Laura as well as her mother intended. As with the fantasy exercise, the goal is the process of getting in touch with what feels right, not achieving a specific end-point. Life is a process, an ongoing adventure. End-points have no future.

We all need practice in forgiving ourselves. The only value in looking at past mistakes is to learn something from them. It just adds stress to beat ourselves up today for real or imagined sins in our past. If we seriously believe we're in error, it can be helpful to make amends. But even in doing so, it's important to focus on the positive. Learning to identify the difference between misplaced guilt and real guilt can be difficult.

If you need help, get it from someone who is open and nonjudgmental—someone who cares enough to help you help yourself.

Express Appreciation

In the couple part of the session, I began by stating, "We have covered a lot of ground individually. I'd like to discuss how the two of you can work together to help Rick regain voluntary control of his orgasm. Before doing that, I'd like to hear about how last week's assignment 'rebuilding romance' went."

Laura and Rick looked at each other smilingly. "You go first," Rick said to Laura. "I want to hear how you felt about it." "OK," Laura replied, laughing, "but you talk, too, Rick." As Rick nodded, Laura began, "I really like what's changed between us. While going out is wonderful, the best part for me has been all the little things. Like Rick complimenting me on a dress I'm wearing, or making an appreciative acknowledgment about something I've done for him. I can really see how much I've missed those little things. I guess that before, I was feeling taken for granted and unappreciated. I feel like giving more to him now that I know he cares."

Rick added, "I'm happy to hear that. I was a little nervous that being so complimentary now might sound sappy. I guess through the years I overdid the old 'strong, silent, macho type.'"

Laura laughed and looked at Rick while she said, "I'm thrilled that you're saying nice things to me. When you don't say anything, I think you either don't notice or don't like what I'm doing. Either way, that's discouraging to me. I need to hear from you. It shows me you appreciate my efforts."

I added, "Laura, I'm glad to hear what you are saying. One of the biggest problems couples have is expressing their appreciation to each other. Yet, a few words of praise or gratitude are so important in showing that we value what is being given. So many couples wind up with each member feeling unappreciated because of a lack of positive feedback. Sincere compliments are a proven way to rekindle warm feelings and the desire to give to your partner."

Laura replied, "I feel more like helping Rick with his problems now. I would have tried before, but now I realize it would have been more out of a sense of obligation. Now I'm more eager because I feel appreciated."

I agreed. "That's very important. Your attitude is crucial to making things work. If you begrudgingly do something out of obligation, that takes away any joy or spontaneity. A positive attitude helps to inspire reciprocal feelings of warmth and love."

The Squeeze Technique

Now that Rick and Laura were more comfortable with each other, the stage was set for them to work together. I was able to explain the next step of treatment.

Masters and Johnson developed a treatment approach that is currently used to enable men to regain voluntary control of their orgasm. Although their work was exclusively in sex therapy, their treatment essentially involves principles of biofeedback. The focus is on getting the man back in touch with his genital sensations before orgasm. By experiencing these sensations, he can learn to control his orgasm voluntarily.

The reason this works is that orgasm is a reflex response. Sensations build up to a point where involuntary muscle contraction or climax is triggered. By staying in touch with the sensations, a man can put off climax as long as he wants to. The basic principle of learning voluntary control over a reflex response is similar to using biofeedback to adjust muscle-tension levels voluntarily in other parts of the body.

Rick would be responsible for learning to listen to his body to understand the sensations that were telling him that the reflex response of ejaculation would occur. Laura would help him by gently, but firmly, squeezing the penis just below the rim of the glans at the time when Rick told her to. When this pressure is applied right before ejaculation, it would allow Rick to delay his reflex. Learning to sense when it is right before the reflex is triggered is done by trial-and-error training, as in other forms of biofeedback.

Again, the principle is used of building upon successful experiences. At first, a woman uses her hand only. When the man masters voluntary control that way, the next stage is intercourse with the woman on top and the man guiding her movements. Finally, voluntary control with the male on top, or missionary position, is achieved.

Masters and Johnson reported a 98-percent success rate with the squeeze technique. Premature ejaculation is the most common sexual problem of men, including those who are psychologically healthy. Before this quick and effective approach was developed, nothing really helped. "Common sense" approaches ranging from counting sheep to using alcohol, sedatives, and tranquilizers all had failed. Likewise, psychoanalytic, marital, and classical behavioral desensitization approaches also failed because they did not address the immediate cause of the problem. Only when the man's focus is on monitoring his sensations does treatment succeed. Men continued to try treatment approaches that failed before Masters and Johnson found the solution. When a man has an emotionally painful and humiliating problem like coming too quickly, he is going to try almost anything to solve the problem. Each failed treatment approach was based on a wrong assumption of the cause of the problem.

The error in "common sense" approaches was to assume that the problem was excessive stimulation and that the cure would be in diminishing the sensations. Even medical doctors got caught up in this error. Physicians would prescribe drugs, anesthetic ointments, condoms—all to no avail.

Psychoanalytic treatment made the error of assuming that the man had unconscious conflicts about women. Sadly, many years have been wasted by men searching for presumed unconscious hostility toward women. Marital therapy failed because it erroneously assumed a conflict within the couple as the problem. Classic behavioral desensitization failed because it wrongly assumed that anxiety was the cause of the problem.

After sharing this information with Rick and Laura, I asked if they had any questions.

"Could you be more specific about exactly what I'm supposed to do?" Laura asked as a blush widened across her face.

"Yes. I'd be glad to," I replied. "You place your thumb on the cord-like frenulum on the underside of the penis. Your first and second fingers are on the topside of the penis, one on either side of the coronal ridge. This ridge separates the head from the shaft of the penis. You squeeze the thumb and first two fingers together firmly for three to four seconds. Rick will immediately lose his urge to ejaculate. He may also lose some of the fullness of his erection. About one quarter to one half minute after releasing the pressure, you can return to actively stimulating the penis. Repeat this procedure two or three times. Then you can stimulate him to orgasmic release."

"The procedure seems simple enough," Laura said, still blushing. "Isn't it going to hurt to squeeze like that?"

"No, this is a painless procedure," I assured Laura. "The erect penis can tolerate this pressure without any discomfort. A flaccid penis might experience some pain if it were squeezed this way."

Turning to Rick, I continued, "Your main focus is to continue experiencing your premonitory sensations before the orgasm reflex is triggered. That way you can signal Laura when to squeeze. As you gain more confidence in identifying that point, you will find the procedure a pleasurable experience. You will be learning how to extend the time you feel pleasurable sensations before coming."

"You mean I can even enjoy this work?" Rick asked with a surprised look.

"Yes. Good lovers have fun and enjoy what they're doing. You can get to 'play' with your pleasurable sensations. You can prolong lovemaking in a way that is both enjoyable to you and to Laura. Most important, the shared pleasure and intimacy can reenergize both of you and your marriage."

"I like that idea," Laura said. "It reminds me of the fun and closeness we had at the beginning of our marriage. I really felt free to enjoy making love with Rick then. I've missed that since we've gotten bogged down in our fertility ordeal."

Sex, Intimacy, and Fertility

For the next few minutes, I gave Laura and Rick an overview of clinical findings about mind-body theories.

"In addition to a renewed marriage and better feelings about yourselves, an enjoyable sex life can help improve fertility. Recent research is showing that positive emotions such as pleasure, happiness, and a sense of closeness with the one you love all contribute to reestablishing normal physiological balances. Conception and pregnancy are finely tuned orchestrations requiring just the right balances of hormones and biochemical reactions.

"We know that positive emotions can enhance our immune system, while chronic negative feelings can depress our resistance. Similarly, our nerves are calmed by enjoyable experiences and frazzled by chronic stress. Many women are aware that an increase in stress can result in a late or missed period. Stress has the power to disrupt the normal sequence of hormonal and biochemical changes in the monthly menstrual cycle.

"I find it interesting that we are endowed with powerfully pleasurable emotions relating to sex to insure reproduction. We know know scientifically that many pleasurable experiences are associated with an increase in a powerful substance called endorphins. Recent studies have shown that endorphins can beneficially affect important hormonal balances necessary for pregnancy to occur. I believe that the key to currently unexplained infertility is in these delicate biochemical orchestrations. I also believe that the unexpectedly high rate of pregnancies I see in this group who learn to control their stress is probably due to the re-creation of internal biochemical harmony."

"If that's true, why are so many obviously tense and stressed-out women able to get pregnant easily?" Laura asked.

"We know that stress affects people differently," I continued. "It's likely that some women are more vulnerable than others to disruptions of the delicate sequencing necessary for successful pregnancy. Remember, unexplained infertility only accounts for a small amount of infertility problems. My clinical experience with these women has been that they are suffering considerable physiological stress. Their ability to get pregnant appears to correlate with their learning how to control stress in their daily lives—not just in the treatment session. Coping with stress is a balance between how we handle situations and the severity of the stress. Anything that tips the balance in our favor is helpful. For example, unhappiness results in decreasing amounts of endorphins. Enjoyable sex increases our endorphins. This can help to shift the scale toward successful pregnancy."

Laura exclaimed, "What you're saying is very helpful to me. It clears up a lot of confusion. I had felt that in some way being unhappy might be a form of penance that would make me more deserving to get what I wanted. It makes sense to me that God created pleasure in sex to promote reproduction. It helps me to resolve a conflict I have had about sexual pleasure taking away energy from my drive to become pregnant. So, as you're saying, instead of a conflict, enjoying sex actually improves my chances."

Rick added, "It's a lot like my experiences with sports. I played my best when I was enjoying the game. My team did their best when we were all having fun playing together."

Standing Up for Yourself

The room got quiet suddenly as Laura and Rick were obviously absorbing all of this. After a few minutes, with a big smile on her face, Laura stated emphatically, "I'm looking forward to enjoying life more now. I'm now able to see that feeling good is healthy, and not selfish as I was brought up to think. You know, my mother really poisoned my mind about sex. She was always warning me that men just wanted one thing and when they got it, they had no respect for you. Honestly," she paused, "thinking about it now gets me mad at her. Really, it's a wonder I could enjoy sex at all, even after marrying Rick. But I feel more ready to stand up to her now when she becomes overbearing, rather than just complaining to Rick about it. I can see now how my not standing up to her just spreads her unhappiness between Rick and me."

"I'm glad to see that you're making a priority of not allowing anyone to make you unhappy," I began. "It's given you new courage to stand up for yourself, even in the face of such a powerful authority figure for you as your mother. I think you will be pleasantly surprised if you behave in such a way that you expect your mother to respect you. When you make it clear that you'll settle for no less, you'll find that she will respond. I think you'll find that she will accept you on your terms. Remember, you are not a little girl anymore, relatively helpless in relation to your mother. If anything, now she needs you more than you need her. She may act in the same old way of assuming that she knows what's best for you because you have not made it clear that you expect to be treated with the respect she offers others."

Laura thought for a moment and said, "Now that I can clearly see the importance of not sacrificing my happiness to please others, it frees me to stand up for myself. I was brought up to believe that if I pleased others, they would take care of me. I can see now that just isn't true."

"Even if others were to honestly have your best interests at heart," I said, "they don't know you as well as you know yourself. Only you know best how experiences feel to you, whether you're comfortable or not. You need to make that clear to others. You mentioned respect before in relationship to your mother. Well, respect for each other's feelings is the basis for any healthy relationship."

Making a Breakthrough

Laura made a breakthrough by using her own imagery in her biofeedback training session. She started at an 89.5-degree hand temperature, which was higher than her prior level even after training. Her continuing practice was paying off. In addition, she went into the session on a positive note from her realization that it was healthy to be happy.

Her new-found resolve to stand up for herself was also evident in her initial level of relaxation. It was as though she had lifted a great burden off her shoulders that had been holding her back. She eagerly let herself visualize relaxing in the bubble bath. Within two minutes, her hand temperature rapidly rose to just over 95 degrees! Laura's stress was melting away. She maintained the gain through the rest of the session. The next step for her was to maintain this level of calm in her daily life. Laura had reached an important turning point. She now knew that she could get to a level that she hadn't thought possible before. Her hard-won achievements needed time to consolidate. This was a particularly vulnerable period. To reinforce her gains, Laura had to continue to do the positive things that got her to this point. Her new understanding of how positive emotions promote healthy functioning would help her to stay on track.

Perhaps Laura would face an early test of her new resolve to be respected by her mother and family. They might sense that she was trying to change the rules of her interaction with them. This would frighten them into redoubling their efforts to maintain the old system.

Maintaining the Gain

Rick maintained the blood pressure of 125/75 that he had achieved at the end of his previous training session. During today's training, he briefly lowered it to 120/70, then maintained it in the range between 125/75 and 120/70.

Rick was doing his daily practice and stated he was enjoying the discipline. It reminded him of his daily training when he was in high school sports. Although Rick had been suffering with the more visible problems—impotence, and then premature ejaculation—he had an easier adjustment to make than Laura had. His experience with the disciplined training required in competitive sports, while enjoying playing the game, gave him a good framework for doing this work. Laura actually had the tougher task. She had to change ingrained attitudes that were instilled in her from childhood.

Chapter 4

Family Ties— Loving Bonds

Coping with the Inevitable Crisis

"I'm finally trying to stand up for myself with my mother," Laura announced at the beginning of the individual part of our seventh session. "It isn't easy and it makes me anxious just talking about it, but I know I have to," she continued, trying to disguise the hesitancy in her voice.

"I want to help," I said. "Tell me, what's happened?"

"My brother decided that he and his wife need a weekend together away from their baby. My mother called me and told me that she thought it would be a good experience for Rick and me to take care of their baby during their holiday. It's this coming weekend. We don't have any special plans for that time."

"What did you tell your mother?" I asked.

"I said I wasn't sure. I said I needed time to think about it and that I'd get back to her today. I didn't tell her this, but obviously I chose today so I could talk with you about it. I feel good that I did not tell her I needed to talk with Rick about it. After our last session, I'm determined not to use Rick as an excuse with my mother. Of course, I will discuss it with Rick, but that's none of my mother's business."

How to Do Things Right for Yourself

"I'm glad to hear how you have been dealing with the situation so far," I began. "You bought yourself some time to figure out what you want to do. This is probably the single most valuable thing we can do to avoid the stress of making poor decisions when we are being pressured. When you really think about it, it's very rare that we face a life-and-death emergency that requires a decision on the spot. For most things, we can take some time to resolve conflicting feelings that we may have about what is being asked of us. The old saying, 'Let me sleep on it, and I'll let you know in the morning,' is a wise rule of thumb. Taking the time to feel comfortable with a decision can save a lot of heartache later. Not only does it give you time to think, it also gives you the opportunity to talk with a trusted friend about the situation, as you are now doing with me. That's always a positive approach when dealing with a tricky problem."

I continued, "Another positive aspect of your response is in what you did not do. You did not use Rick as an excuse with your mother. You cannot avoid dealing with your mother. Putting Rick in the middle just sends the wrong message to her. It says that you are intimidated by her and cannot deal directly as an adult with her. It reinforces her belief that you are still a little girl. It makes her feel that it's a battle between Rick and her to determine what you do. This causes further strain in their relationship and you feel torn being in the middle.

"By speaking up for yourself," I emphasized, "you are showing your mother that you have a mind of your own and she needs to respect that she has to deal with you directly. This will decrease the sense of manipulation you feel. Your mother has been appealing to your guilt by saying, 'Do this for your brother, or for the family.' Now you are showing her that *you* have specific wants and needs that must be respected. By standing up for yourself, you are changing the interaction from mother-daughter to two adults.

"It's OK that you're consulting with Rick," I added, "without feeling the need to tell your mother. You need to get his feelings and reach a common ground with him about requests like these. I'm very encouraged by the way you are approaching this. It's clear that you really have a new determination. Indeed, courage *is* standing up in the face of fear and uncertainty. Now, tell me, how do you feel about taking your brother's baby for the weekend?"

Feelings Are Not Thoughts

"I've had ambivalent feelings," Laura responded. "My initial reaction as my mother was talking was, 'Oh, no, here we go again.' I could feel my stomach tense as she spoke. Later, I got caught up in the old guilt stuff. I was thinking that they need a break—and family members ought to help one other. Fortunately, I realized pretty quickly what was happening in my mind and I realized that it was just the old programming from my childhood coming back to haunt me. But then I started to feel that I'll probably want my brother and sister-in-law to take *our* baby for a weekend. If I don't take theirs now, they won't take ours later. So, I'm confused about what to do."

"It's interesting to hear you describe what's been going on in your mind," I began. "Part of your confusion is due to a misperception that is very common. At first, you did talk about your feelings. The 'Here we go again' and tense stomach. Then you spoke about what if you didn't take the baby this weekend. Wouldn't that mean they wouldn't reciprocate later. That's a thought, an hypothesis. It's not a feeling. We often get confused by mixing feelings and thoughts together as though they were both feelings. So far, the feelings are negative about taking the baby. Your later thoughts indicate your guilt and anxiety about saying no."

The Usefulness of Dreams

"OK," Laura replied. But she looked distracted. I could tell her thoughts were elsewhere. Before I could inquire as to what she was thinking, she blurted out, "I had a nightmare last night. It was so vivid and upsetting, I can't get it out of my mind."

"Dreams can be a useful tool to help get a clearer picture of how we really feel about something," I encouraged. "Typically, wishes and fears are played out in dreams that may be too disturbing for us to be aware of more directly in our waking life. I've often used dreams to help people get in touch with the unconscious sources of their emotions."

"I don't think I usually dream," Laura replied. "Anyway, I always thought that what I dreamed was pretty worthless."

"Actually, we all dream every night," I replied. "The problem is that dreams are very fleeting experiences. Within a few seconds of waking, they slip out of consciousness. However, there is a good way to capture more of them before they disappear. It might be helpful to explore your dreams. Before going to sleep, put a pen and pad by your bedside. As soon as you awake, write down your dream. Don't wait. You need to capture the dream immediately. Even if it's just fragments that you remember, write them down."

Laura had a wry smile, "It reminds me of taking my basal temperature as soon as waking to find out if I was ovulating. I had to do that immediately on waking, too!"

"I can understand your association with that anxiety-provoking ordeal," I said. "But this can be more fun and a lot more interesting for you. After you write down your dream and any immediate association to it, put the paper away until our next session. I'll ask you what you remember before you look at the paper again."

"What's the point in that?" Laura asked.

"I've found that it's useful to see what we *forget* about our dreams," I replied. That tells me more about what's emotionally important. The reason we forget most dreams so quickly after we have them, is that they contain things that are disturbing to our conscious mind. My approach serves as another screen to see what gets forgotten after we write down the dream. Often the forgotten part contains the most useful information. That's the way our conscious mind works to forget—or more accurately, to repress—material from our unconscious that is too painful for us to deal with at the time."

"The dream I remember is pretty painful," Laura said. "Why do you think I'm able to recall it? It sounds like you're saying we forget painful dreams."

I explained, "It's not the painfulness of the dream, but our readiness to deal with the underlying conflicts. Remembering an upsetting dream usually indicates that we are prepared on an unconscious level to work on the problem that the dream symbolizes. Do you want to make a go at the nightmare you recall?"

"It still seems so real to me," Laura began. "In my dream, I was visiting my mother. My sister came over with the baby. She was slicing a tomato, and cut her finger. My mother rushed her to the doctor's office. My mother told me to stay at home with the baby. The baby screamed and cried continuously for her mother. I couldn't soothe her no matter what I did."

"Let me guess how you felt while you were with her screaming baby," I smiled.

"Exactly," Laura responded and grinned. "I felt trapped. I felt like I was in a hopeless situation. The baby wanted her mother. I was not an acceptable alternative. There wasn't anything I could do to calm her."

"So what thoughts do you have now about the dream?" I asked.

"Well, that's exactly how their baby really is. Whenever Mommy is away, the baby cries until she returns. That's why I don't want to babysit for a weekend despite my mother's telling me it would be a good experience in mothering."

"I can see how stressful it would be," I replied. "I certainly understand your not wanting to put yourself through that. In addition to that main point, there is another interesting part in your dream: Your sister cuts her finger slicing a tomato. Have any thoughts about that?"

Laura looked down for a moment and then replied, "She is such a princess. Everyone caters to her. If she has to do a simple thing for herself, she will botch it."

"I can see that," I said. "When I heard you relating that part of the dream, my mental association went back to the weekend visit to your mother's—that you told me about a while ago. You were responsible for preparing dinner. When we talked about it, you expressed your anger at cooking for everyone. I think your dream reflects your resentment at her being catered to. She cuts herself doing a simple thing like slicing a tomato. But then comes your conflict. Your mother rushes to help her and puts the responsibility to looking after her baby onto you. It's an emergency situation, so how can you say no without feeling guilty?"

"That's right," Laura said. "I wind up being asked by our mother to carry my sister's responsibilities. I'm beginning to realize how unfair this is. I don't want to be a part of this anymore. I can see from our last session this is working against me."

"It sounds to me that you have a new-found determination to stand up for yourself," I said. "Learning that your emotions can affect your well-being has helped to motivate you in a positive way. Fortunately, your real-life situation with your mother and sister does not involve an emergency as your dream did."

Creating Positive Change in Family Relationships

I continued, "By changing how you act, you can alter existing family interactions in a way that is healthy both for you and for them. You have been in the 'good daughter' role to please your mother. That is how you have gotten your mother's approval. From early childhood, you were the responsible one, the giver. Your sister has been the taker. Your mother is well-meaning in that she wants harmony in the family. She has been reinforcing your good behavior because it has been helpful to the functioning of the family. She probably knows that your sister gets indulged, but she doesn't see that there is any harm in it for your well-being. What's more, you have not been objecting, but have been going along with her requests. So your sister demands and gets catered to," I said.

"How can I change this pattern?" Laura asked. "I really want to, but it's been going on for so long."

"You can change the pattern by acting differently yourself," I replied. "This will force both your mother and sister to have to take your wishes into account. All change comes about when someone takes the energy to start doing things differently. The problem is that many of us just hope for change, but don't make the effort necessary to create change. Unfortunately, just crossing our fingers and hoping that others will do what we need is not the way life works."

Refocusing on Laura's case specifically I said, "I believe in you and your right to be treated with respect for your feelings. You say you wanted to be treated with more respect by your family. You can be, but you have to be willing to take the first steps to start the change. This can be done in lots of ways."

I could see that Laura didn't look convinced, so I continued. "For example, when you were at your mother's and she suggested that everyone eat dinner together, you could have told her that everyone should pitch in to make it."

"As I told you," Laura replied, "only Rick and I were around. Everyone else was at the lake."

"Well then, don't be so available." I added, "Go on and do something somewhere else until the others come back to do their share. No one has a gun at your head forcing you to work in the kitchen by yourself. You don't have to feel guilty about not serving them."

"You're right about the guilt," Laura said. "It doesn't take much to make me feel guilty."

"That's right," I continued. "I'm glad that you see that clearly now. Let's look at the anger you felt at the time, which you hid from your mother, but expressed to Rick. When you start to feel anger, ask yourself why. What specifically made you feel put out?"

"I felt angry because no one cared that I wasn't having any fun, but was doing all the work," Laura answered.

"OK," I said. "Then you need to stop what you're doing. When you feel angry and have discovered why, then you need to decide what you want to do about the situation. Anger is a feeling. It alerts us to think. Anger by itself is not the answer to a problem. You need to act in a way that helps to resolve the situation causing your anger. You need a plan of action that helps to influence the situation in a way that is consistent with your taking good care of yourself."

"I know that what you're saying makes sense," Laura said. "I'm going to try to act more assertively with my family. But they sure are going to be upset."

"You might be right about their resisting," I replied. "However, you may be positively surprised, if you express yourself before your anger turns to resentment. By stating your wishes in a positive manner, you appeal to their sense of fairness. I've seen many family members change when they were approached in a direct and positive manner. Remember, they want and need a relationship with you as well as you want one with them. It certainly sounds like your mother would probably make some adjustments if you stood up for yourself. After all, as you point out, she accommodates your sister, who is demanding. Your mother doesn't want to lose any of her children. I'm sure each of you is very important to her."

"This sounds so new to me. You make me think that it just might all work out for the better," Laura said with a bright look of hope.

"Yes, it can," I replied. "Your mother loves you, but only in the way she knows how. She needs to hear from you how to relate better to you. As a therapist, it's easier for me to be a 'good mother' to you because, unlike your real mother, you don't have to meet any of my needs. So I can be one hundred percent for your self-development and growth. I can help to encourage you to be more for yourself than you are. I can teach you how to care for yourself better. More important, I can believe in you in a way that perhaps no one ever has before. You were brought up to do for others to get the love you needed to survive. As an adult, you can meet your own basic survival needs. You can achieve a greater happiness. You can create loving relationships based on a mutual respect for one another's wishes and needs. I believe you want that happiness, too, or you wouldn't be here in my office today."

A few tears welled up in Laura's eyes. "I want to feel good about being me. It's more than having a baby—as much as I want that. I want to feel secure that my mother and Rick really love me. I'm tired of feeling that others have things that I'm not allowed to have."

"You can make it happen," I said. "I'll bet that you feel a little better about who you are right now."

"I do," Laura replied with a laugh. "How come?"

"You took a chance. You took the risk of hearing and feeling that you are worth being happy. You are beginning to believe in yourself. Why don't you focus on that good feeling when you do your biofeedback later. It will help you to relax more, just as your visualization of taking your bubble bath helped you to relax physiologically."

"I like that idea," Laura said. "It's a new experience for me to feel more positive about myself. It would be great if I could feel this way more often. Maybe this will help me relax more."

Healthy Values You Can Live with

"Good," I said. "I'm really pleased that you're feeling better about yourself. Now, let's look at how you did with your homework. What happened with the fantasy exercise?"

"I surprised myself," Laura exclaimed. "I must be on a roll with my new positive attitude. I bought the books you suggested and was able to use them to construct my own romantic, sensual fantasy. I even combined it with a bubble bath. It felt so good that I even let myself go and began touching myself." Laura started to blush as she spoke. "I gave myself an orgasm." She smiled and said, "I guess I haven't yet learned how to stop blushing."

"You will as you become more comfortable with your new self," I said. "It sounds like you have really been letting yourself explore pleasurable sensations. I know what a big step this is for you. I want to congratulate you on your courage and success. Tell me, how do you feel now about opening up these new areas for yourself?"

"It's a bit scary," Laura replied, slowly. "Thinking about myself and my pleasure is really new to me, but I'm convinced that I need to acknowledge my feelings in order to be healthy."

"How does this new attitude fit in with your value system?" I asked.

Laura thought for a moment and replied, "My basic beliefs and value system are the same. I still believe in God and in being a good person. I still believe in marriage and commitment. The only thing that's changed is I'm not ashamed of myself for enjoying pleasure in my body."

"I'm glad to hear that you have been able to integrate your new attitude toward yourself and your body with your existing traditional value system," I concluded.

Before ending with Laura, I gave her some more "homework." On the mind side, Laura was going to think more about our discussion of family, and respond to her mother's request of her to baby-sit. On the body side, I spoke with Laura about what Kegel exercises are. She agreed that she would try to experiment with it.

How to Enhance Your Sexual Pleasure and Orgasm

Kegel's exercises are easy to learn and practice. The following discussion and instructions are adapted from the excellent chapter by the Grabers in the *Handbook of Sex Therapy* edited by Joseph and Leslie LoPiccolo.

The pubococcygeus muscle attaches to the woman's pubic bone in front, under the pubic hair, and the tailbone in back. Both these bones remain stationery, so the PC muscle doesn't get used during one's daily life, in contrast to most other muscles in the body. Yet, this muscle is the one that contracts involuntarily during orgasm. Kegel's exercises enable you to learn how to contract these muscles voluntarily. This results in better control and strengthens the muscle—and both enhance sexual pleasure and orgasm.

Kegel's exercises can initially be practiced while urinating. Keep your belly muscles relaxed by resting your forearms on your thighs to support your weight. As you sit on the toilet with your legs separated, let a little urine out and then completely stop the flow by contracting the PC muscle. Then let another teaspoon out and again stop the flow. Continue this until your bladder is emptied. Once good control is achieved, you should stop doing the exercise while urinating so as to avoid the possibility of a bladder infection. You can then practice anywhere—for example, in your car while waiting at a stoplight—you can alternately contract and relax your PC muscles.

In essence, this is another form of biofeedback training to bring under voluntary control a previously automatic response. As with all such training, there is a cumulative benefit from practicing. If you find the exercises boring, you can entertain yourself with music or TV while doing them. Alternatively, you can make good use of your time by practicing while waiting in line for something. No one will be able to see that you are contracting your PC muscle.

Once you have mastered the basic exercise, you can use it during lovemaking. Just do the same voluntary contraction of the PC muscle to create a tight grip. To maximize the tightness, you can do a visualization in your mind as you contract the muscle. Imagine that you are bringing together the two sides of your vagina, as though you were clapping your hands. This helps to get the entire muscle moving and gets the smaller upper part of and sides maximally involved. With practice, you fine-tune the amount of contraction of the muscle during lovemaking. Thus, you can voluntarily vary the amount of tightness. This results in enhanced pleasure and more enjoyable orgasms for both you and your lover.

Maintaining Motivation

Every crisis can be perceived as a threat or an opportunity to grow and change. Laura's mother's idea that she baby-sit is a good example. Laura was just beginning to develop a more positive sense of self. Yet, her mother still had expectations of Laura based on the past. Thus, the inevitable test of her new resolve had been made.

Our talk had helped reinforce Laura's new attitude. It had enabled her to see that there were positive outcomes possible from her standing up for herself. Over many years, Laura had been locked into the false assumption that being assertive would only lead to more pain for her. It was crucial for her to see that it would be less painful for her to express her true feelings than to submit again, as in the past. Laura had been trained from early childhood to please others, regardless of her own wishes. Fear of losing their love had blinded Laura. She could not see that now as an adult, she was able to take care of herself and confidently share her life with Rick. She needed help to see that now, her mother needed her. It was an eye-opener for Laura that her mother might change to preserve a relationship with her.

Maintaining motivation is essential to changing lifelong patterns. The ability to see the possibility of a positive outcome is crucial to maintaining motivation. Too often we lose our determination in the face of obstacles, because we lose faith that things can really get better. As in Laura's case, this misperception is the result of unconsciously accepting that we are still in the role of a powerless child, rather than in the reality of being an independently functioning adult.

Particularly in relation to parents and other authority figures, we need to see that we have the power to stand up to others and assert ourselves successfully. This is true in our relationships with doctors, therapists, and supervisors at work. As clients, consumers, and workers, we have rights as individuals to be treated with respect for ourselves and for our feelings. We are not helpless children without alternatives. If necessary, there are always other doctors, therapists, and other jobs. We are not at anyone's mercy. We deserve respect for our individuality.

Integrating Ourselves and Our Values

Establishing life-affirming values and beliefs is crucial to regaining and maintaining our health. Again, Laura's experience is a good example of how to reintegrate ourself and our values in a positive way. Laura grew up with solid traditional values, including concern for others and faith in God. Unfortunately, she learned to be suspect about enjoying pleasure. She was able to make a successful change in this area because she could integrate the new information about positive emotions into her existing belief system.

Too often we accept something logically, but it doesn't fit into our belief system. When this happens, we ignore doing what we know intellectually is best, because it doesn't feel right in terms of our values. Laura's situation is a good example. As long as Laura believed that enjoying herself was selfish and against God's will, she would not be able to change, regardless of the amount of scientific evidence she learned. Only when she could see that pleasure was part of God's plan could she be free to act on the new information.

As human beings, we are governed by our values and belief systems, even though we may not be consciously aware of them. They are built into us at an early age and guide us semiautomatically. By and large, this is healthy for us. Traditional values have helped us to lead productive lives by instilling in us expectations for appropriate behavior. Unfortunately, we also grow up with some prejudices and misinformation instilled in us. For instance, many of us need to struggle to see that being for oneself in a healthy way is not selfish. Sadly, many good people, like Laura, feel guilty about normally asserting their wishes. Correcting this misperception can free us of much needlessly self-inflicted pain and anguish.

Now that Laura was acting in a way consistent with her beliefs and values, she was free to more fully experience herself and her emotions. The process of positive change could now be increasingly reinforced by the positive feelings she had as she experimented with her new self-awareness.

Staying on Track by Staying in Touch

Rick had a smile on his face and a relaxed air about him as he sat down for his individual part of the session.

"You look like things are going well," I said.

"Yes, they are," Rick replied. "I'm feeling increasingly optimistic about our situation."

"Good. Tell me what your experience was with Laura and the squeeze technique," I asked.

"We had some trouble at first," Rick began. "Laura was very tentative at first in applying the squeeze. She was afraid of hurting me. I told her she could be firmer and she gradually increased the amount of pressure. So, on the first try, she didn't succeed in stopping me. However, a few days later, on our third attempt of the week, she succeeded in applying the right amount of pressure."

"I remembered Laura expressing some concern about squeezing too hard," I said. "I'm glad to hear that she was able to overcome her fear rather quickly. Tell me, were you able to stay in touch with your sensations?" I asked.

"That got better as we went along," Rick said. "At first, we were both a little nervous. I felt a bit distracted. When Laura didn't squeeze hard enough the first time, I was beyond the point of no return."

"How did you react to that?" I asked.

Using Humor Instead of Blame

Rick replied, "My immediate reaction was one of upset. Then I mentally stepped back from the situation. I remembered my coach telling me not to beat myself up over a busted play, but to get on with the game. It may sound corny, but I actually tried to make a joke of it to break the tension. I said to Laura with a smile, 'Let's not cry over spilled milk.' It helped relieve her guilt about not getting it right the first time. I think it let her get on with the game the next time we tried a few days later."

"Great idea," I said. "Using humor—instead of blame—is a great way to defuse tension when an error is made. You knew that Laura would be feeling bad. If you had criticized Laura, you would have made her more tense and defensive. By using humor, you let her know that everything was all right. Your vote of confidence in her helped her to be comfortable enough with herself to get it right the next time. You avoided the vicious cycle of a mistake causing increasing pressure that leads to other mistakes."

"I'm feeling good about how things are going," Rick said.

"I am, too," I replied. "Since you're doing well and your homework involves Laura, how about us all meeting together, now?" I asked.

"Fine with me," Rick replied.

Regaining Prior Levels of Functioning

During the break, before seeing Laura and Rick together, I thought about the homework I would suggest for them. They were making rapid progress individually and as a couple. This is common in situations where there are no deep-seated couple conflicts and a previously existing level of functioning is being restored.

Laura had been doing a lot of work to resolve her own attitudes. Her ability to integrate new information into her existing value system was permitting her to move rapidly. Laura had stated that she was occasionally able to reach orgasm in the past. Thus, our task was to restore that former capability and enable her to achieve pleasure voluntarily by relaxing and going with her feelings. Obviously, if she could not integrate having pleasure into her value system, her progress would be much slower.

Success breeds success. Both Laura and Rick were in a positive cycle of increasing mastery leading to growing self-confidence and self-esteem, which permitted rapid progress to occur. I would continue to raise their levels of mastery gradually, according to well-established treatment protocols.

For Rick, the next level involved maintaining voluntary control of his orgasm during intercourse with Laura on top. For Laura, the next step involved her achieving orgasm through self-stimulation while Rick was inside her and stroking her. Each step involved achieving further mastery and self-control. Each success would build self-confidence in their ability to enjoy and actively participate in lovemaking. The ultimate goal was the natural mutual enjoyment of intercourse.

Love Is the Key to Great Sex

To reduce stress and promote healing, it is more important to focus on the growth of warmth and sharing rather than just on techniques of performance. Rick's use of humor to defuse the tension when Laura didn't squeeze correctly was helpful.

While specific techniques can improve sex, love brings our heart and soul into the experience and is necessary to create the environment for great sex. This is why my main focus with Laura and Rick was to rekindle the spark of love between them that had been temporarily buried under the stress of their infertility and sexual problems. Improving their sex life is not just a goal in itself, but a means to regenerate the healing powers of shared, loving intimacy.

Personally, I believe that there has been an overemphasis on sexual techniques and an underemphasis on the primary importance of warmth, love, and caring in our society during the last twenty years. Fortunately, we are beginning to shift back to emphasizing the primary importance of the quality of the relationship rather than the intensity of the orgasm.

As we met together, it was evident that Laura and Rick felt comfortable working with each other. Most important, I could see the warmth and love they had for each other. For the first time, they sat close together with their legs touching. They spoke more to each other than to me. Laura expressed her gratitude to Rick for not getting upset but instead, reassuring her when she didn't squeeze correctly. They both agreed that maintaining that atmosphere of warmth and acceptance made it possible for them to experiment in a more relaxed and secure manner.

Laura's breakthroughs in our sessions continued to be reflected during her biofeedback training. Her increasing self-esteem and growing self-confidence was facilitating a more relaxed physiology. The rekindling of her loving relationship with Rick was fostering a positive cycle. For the first time, Laura's initial hand temperature reading was 90 degrees. From a baseline of 92 degrees, Laura relaxed further by using a combination of visualizing her bubble bath scene and letting herself reexperience the good feelings of self that she felt during our individual talk. She reached 96.1 degrees, indicating a truly relaxed physiology.

Rick continued his steady progress. In this session his blood pressure went from an initial reading of 120/70 to a low of 115/70 during the biofeedback training. He was maintaining his daily work with the relaxation tape and focusing on his breathing. He, too, was benefiting from the shift from stress to renewed loving and sharing in the marriage.

Learning How to See New Solutions to Old Problems

Laura and Rick had made excellent progress so far, both individually and as a couple. He was controlling his blood pressure and regaining control of his sex life. She was emerging in her own right, from a vicious cycle of stress. Together, they were rebuilding a close, intimate, loving marriage.

Yet, the chief problem that had been plaguing them for years still had not been directly resolved. They were still struggling with infertility. They were dutifully following their infertility specialist's orders every month. He was diligently prescribing the latest regimens of medications and high technology and continuing to inseminate Laura with Rick's sperm. Unfortunately, each month brought another emotional roller coaster going from hope to despair. Moreover, from a stress point of view, there was no end in sight to their ordeal. Chronic stress without prospect of resolution is very damaging to our physiology. Our systems get increasingly exhausted and distorted away from normal functioning.

Now that Laura and Rick had experienced some much-needed success in our work, the time had come to deal directly with their thoughts and feelings about the infertility grind they were going through. Now that hope and self-esteem and love were all being restored, they needed to explore different possibilities for resolving their infertility problem.

Earlier, because of their demoralized state, it would have been too overwhelming for them to deal with this issue directly. To see new solutions to old problems, you first need to regain some self-confidence and optimism. Old problems seem insoluble when we are in depression and despair. Exploring alternatives and seeing that a mutually acceptable resolution could be achieved would remove an enormous amount of stress. Knowing that they could get on with their lives, that indeed there could be life after infertility, was the final crucial step Laura and Rick had to take both as a couple and as individuals. Then our work would be done.

Our focus continued to be on the resolution of stress. The goal was peace of mind and body. There was no right or wrong path to choose. They could consider setting a time limit to their current infertility treatment. They could explore adoption. They might choose to try other recently developed technological approaches. They might choose to live childfree.

Rick and Laura needed to develop a mutually acceptable plan of action that would enable them to reestablish control over their lives. They needed to restore their sense of active determination of their destiny, instead of feeling like hopeless victims month after month.

Playing the Percentages

In order for Laura and Rick to make a responsible decision, first they needed information. While every case has individual variations, it would still be helpful to examine current statistics to learn what percentage of infertility patients do conceive. There was and is a great need for more scientifically controlled studies of large numbers of infertile women to develop statistically significant results. Unfortunately, women have long been neglected when it comes to finding funding for these investigative studies. The present understanding of conception rates are as follows:

Currently accepted fertility treatments for women with antibody problems, as Laura had, result in varied low rates of pregnancy, according to the treatment employed. Only approximately 10 percent of these women get pregnant naturally.

About 20 percent get pregnant during ovulation if the husband had used a condom for intercourse during nonfertile times of the month. It is believed that using condoms decreases the amount and intensity of the woman's antibody production to her husband's sperm by decreasing the frequency of her contact with the sperm.

About 25 percent get pregnant with in vitro fertilization. IVF involves surgical removal of eggs from a woman's ovaries. They are washed to decrease the possibility of an antibody reaction occurring, before the husband's sperm is combined with the eggs in a culture dish. If fertilization occurs in the following twenty-four hours, then the resulting conception is returned to the woman's uterus.

About 30 percent of women get pregnant using a combination of an immune-system repressor such as prednisone, which diminishes antibody reaction, and artificial insemination using the husband's sperm. This is the procedure that Laura and Rick had been following every month for a long time now. The infertility specialist might vary some of the elements if pregnancy did not result. The dosage of immune-system repressor and length of time the woman takes it might be varied, as well as the specific drug used. The timing and frequency of the inseminations around the fertile time of the month might be varied slightly, too. The infertility specialist might also prescribe a drug that stimulates egg production to increase their number in the hope of increasing the chances of successful fertilization.

It Is Control of Stress, Not Adoption, That Increases Pregnancy Rate

In my experience, there appears to be a commonly held belief that after adopting a baby, a woman is more likely to become pregnant. Actually, infertile women who adopt have only the same subsequent pregnancy rate as those who don't adopt. This "spontaneous cure rate" is very low—about 5 percent in either case. It has also been hypothesized that when a woman adopts, her stress is reduced and therefore, she should be able to become pregnant.

In reality, just because a woman adopts doesn't mean she no longer has physiological stress. Infertility is only one contributor to stress. As we can see with Laura, many factors added up to triggering her chronic-stress response. Adoption doesn't turn off the chronic stress response. If Laura only adopted a baby but did not alter the chronic-stress response caused by other factors, she would indeed be no more likely to get pregnant than other infertile women.

In my work, I have observed a similar transformation among all the women who have gotten pregnant. Before the training, these women, like Laura, would react with anxiety and worry to daily life events. This would trigger their physiological stress response. However, these women used the mind-body techniques to make a crucial positive change in their coping style. Instead of reacting with anxiety, they learned how to stay calm and take a problem-solving approach to situations. This decrease in anxiety led to a resolution of the chronic-stress response enabling the body to shift back to normal physiological balances. I believe that this accounts for the very high rates of pregnancy in the women with whom I have worked.

Stress and Feelings

Chronically experienced emotion, such as anxiety or hostility, can trigger the stress response which can cause dysfunctional, physiological changes. This sequence of mind-body events explains how chronic anxiety can lead to unexplained infertility in some women, just as chronic hostility has been shown to lead to heart attacks in some men.

There are many anxious women who do get pregnant and many hostile men who don't get heart attacks. However, some people are more sensitive and their bodies are more reactive to their emotions. These people are referred to as sensitive "mind-body" reactors and are more likely to suffer physiological dysfunction caused by their emotions.

Each of us is born with our own unique emotional temperament and our own degree of mind-body sensitivity. Just as some children are born with a low frustration tolerance and are quick to express anger, other children demonstrate emotional distress with upset stomachs or other physical symptoms. This is part of our inheritance—it is not our "fault." As a matter of fact, some of the most admired people in our society— gifted actors and artists—are often extremely sensitive mind-body reactors.

It makes no sense to "blame the victim" for being biologically prone to being anxious or quick to anger or being born with a high degree of sensitivity. What does make sense is to use our current knowledge that mind-body training can turn off the stress response to help these individuals get back to normal physiological functioning. By learning to trigger the relaxation response, a chronically anxious woman suffering with unexplained infertility can have her fertility restored. Similarly, as we shall see later in this book, men who are quick to anger and prone to hostility can prevent heart attacks by using the mind-body methods to turn off their stress response.

Being a sensitive mind-body reactor does have health benefits. Positive emotions such as joy and happiness can trigger the relaxation response and help keep our physiology functioning well. Just as sensitive reactors are more prone to chronic negative emotions leading to physiological dysfunction, they are also more likely to have positive emotions lead to renewal of healthy functioning. Sensitive reactors also are particularly effective at using the mind-body techniques to restore a sense of inner calm and get back in control of their life.

Another Crisis Creates a New Opportunity

Laura began the individual part of our eighth session by bursting into tears. "I almost called you yesterday, when I found out," she sobbed. "I couldn't sleep at all last night, I was so upset. I felt I was doing so well until this happened. I don't know how to deal with it," Laura cried.

"Obviously, something that feels overwhelming has hit you," I replied, encouraging Laura to continue.

"My sister-in-law is pregnant," Laura blurted out between uncontrollable sobs. "It's so easy for her. I feel like such a failure! I'm jealous of her having what I want so much and can't have."

After giving Laura the time she needed to dry her eyes and compose herself, I said, "I've been thinking it's time to discuss this issue directly with you. You can have a baby, too."

Laura looked up at me with puzzlement. "What do you mean? How?"

"Have you and Rick ever discussed adoption?" I asked.

Laura was silent for a moment. Then she replied, "Not really. I've always felt that Rick would be disappointed if I couldn't give him a baby."

"That sounds like some of your old thinking about what it takes to please others," I said. "I haven't spoken to Rick about this, but most men in similar situations feel different from what you imagine. Typically, they want to start a family and end the pain of unsolved infertility. Whatever Rick's feelings are, you can only benefit by talking to him about this. Continuing this way, you are constantly being stressed by the lack of an end in sight, and being plagued with this issue that you are a failure."

Laura thought for a moment and then said, "I guess you're right about talking to Rick. He has been supportive and he does want to start a family, too. But as we're talking now, I'm getting in touch with my own thoughts. Maybe I feel that not having my own kid is second-best. If my sister-in-law can have them so easily, why can't I have one of my own?"

"I don't think her ability to conceive is relevant to what you have been experiencing," I replied. "It's common for us to compare lives and set up scenarios of how unjust the world is. While this may make us feel a bit better for the moment—as there is usually someone around to give some sympathy to a victim—it really gets us nowhere. To use energy to justify a position we don't want to be in is pointless, but it's up to you."

Laura thought for a while about what I said. "You're right. It is a blessing from God to be a mother. It's not that important if it's a biological or adopted child. I want the opportunity to become a family." After a pause, she continued, "I'm glad we talked about this. I know I don't have to feel so unworthy and jealous anymore. I know I have a lot of love to give to a child. I know Rick does, too. I'll talk with him. This is a big decision. How does one decide when to stop trying and to start the adoption process?" Laura asked.

"There's no set formula," I replied. "The process of transition can take many forms. For example, some couples who have been trying for years, as you have, may set a date a few months ahead. If they aren't pregnant by then, they go forward with adoption planning. The important thing is to talk it over with Rick and get to a mutually agreeable decision."

"OK," Laura said. "I know Rick has some things to talk to you about before we meet together. I'm beginning to feel better. My homework went great. I was able to identify the muscle contraction to practice the Kegel exercise. I started experimenting with contracting when Rick was inside me. It was a little strange to stimulate myself this time, but I found that by enjoying the sensations, I was able to relax and have an orgasm. I'm sure glad that we did all our homework before I got that call from my sister-in-law. Last night would have been a disaster to try to enjoy lovemaking."

"Yes," I agreed, "obviously if something disturbing like that occurs, don't even try to push yourself. It's normal not to be in the mood when you're so upset. It sounds like things are going well. Let's stop here so I can see Rick."

Harnessing Frustration

"I'm getting very frustrated," Rick began. "I need your advice on how to deal with our infertility doctor. What he is suggesting is continuing to interfere with our sex life. This week really highlighted the problem for me. We were having sex with Laura on top, as you recommended. I could feel her muscles contracting around me. Finally, when it was time for me to let myself come, Laura asked me to put on a condom as the infertility doctor had ordered. I guess I'm my old self again. I functioned well with it on, but it's not as much fun as without it. I want to know if I really need to use them?"

I replied, "I assume your infertility doctor prescribed condom therapy for the antibody problem Laura mentioned?"

Rick nodded affirmatively.

"Do you know how serious the problem is? What were your test results?" I asked.

"Recently, we were tested again," Rick answered. "The infertility doctor said the results were the worst possible. It seems Laura had a maximum antibody response to every part of my sperm. She had a one hundred percent reaction to the head, body, and tail of my sperm. The doctor has prohibited us from having sex without condoms. He said that unprotected sex would just rekindle the antibody reaction that he is trying to suppress with immune-suppressor drugs. The problem is he has had us using condoms for a long time, yet this test was even worse than the one before. The condoms don't seem to help the antibody problem. What do you know about this?" Rick asked.

I responded, "The experts disagree as to the effectiveness of using condoms to help treat a sperm antibody problem. Some feel that it marginally shifts the odds of conception a couple of percent in the right direction. Others believe that condoms are useless as an antibody suppressor and may actually be counterproductive if they interfere with enjoying sex and contribute to stress. Nobody knows for sure. In your case, it appears that the antibody results have gotten worse during condom therapy. How upsetting is it for you?"

"Very upsetting," Rick retorted. "You know I always thought that one of the benefits of being married was that I wouldn't have to worry about needing condoms for safe sex. So since I don't need them to prevent venereal disease, and they aren't helping the antibody problem, why do I need to use them?"

"How does Laura feel about this?" I asked.

"That's part of the problem," Rick said. "Laura wants to do everything according to doctors' orders. She won't listen to me about this. She might listen to you, though."

"I'll tell Laura what I just told you," I began. "Remember, this is a delicate situation. Laura needs to feel comfortable about not using condoms. It won't help your enjoyment if she feels pushed. She won't be an active partner if her concerns aren't respected."

"I know what you're saying is right, but I wish there was an end to this. Did Laura tell you how upset she got from her sister-in-law being pregnant?" Rick asked.

"Yes, she did," I replied. "Laura wants an end to the ordeal, too. How would you like to see things resolved?"

"I want to start a family," Rick said. "I'll do anything that can make that happen."

"Have you thought about an alternative to your present approach?" I asked.

"I want the experience of being a father. I'm for anything that Laura can go with. A friend of mine has an adopted kid and they have a great family," Rick replied.

"I'm glad to hear that," I said. "I know Laura will be talking to you at home about planning some resolution. I'm sure she will be pleased to hear that you are open to considering alternative ways of starting a family."

Mind over Body

Before seeing Laura and Rick together, I reviewed in my mind where we were in the treatment process. Things were going well. Each of them had shown ability to trigger the relaxation response and turn off the stress response throughout biofeedback training. What remained was to resolve the psychological contributors to stress that I had talked about with each of them individually. In my experience, this is often the key to shifting the balance of forces in the person's daily functioning toward normal relaxed physiology.

We were at a similar point in their sex therapy. Together and individually, they were well on their way to mastery of the necessary behavioral techniques. Significantly, the remaining areas for resolution were on the mind side. Laura needed to continue the development of her sense of self-worth. Rick and Laura needed to feel comfortable about how to balance their needs and desires in relation to their antibody problem. They needed time to talk this through. Also, in terms of their infertility problem, they needed time to work out a mutual plan for resolution.

The mind and the brain are the ultimate determinants of the balance between stress and normal physiology. Mental phenomena such as low self-esteem, chronic conflict, and negative emotions interact with brain chemistry to produce stress responses in our nervous, immune, and hormone systems. Resolving conflicts, improving self-worth, and fostering positive emotions help shift the balance away from stress and back to normal, healthy physiology. Just as in sex, where the mind is the ultimate erotic organ, so too, in stress, the mind ultimately determines the balance. The good news is that we can change our minds for the better.

Planning a Vacation Wisely

Laura and Rick were each relieved to discover that the other wanted to find a resolution to their infertility problem, and both were open to alternatives, such as adoption. They agreed that they needed to talk more on their own about the timing of such a transition.

Laura listened to Rick's feelings about using condoms. She asked my opinion and I told her what I had told Rick. I suggested they talk with their infertility doctor about their difficulty with condoms, and their plan to pursue alternatives to childbirth, such as adoption. They agreed that it was a good idea to do that. I told them I would be happy to talk with the infertility doctor if they felt it would be helpful. They decided that they wanted to approach him first and see what he had to say. I agreed that it was a good first step for them to talk directly with him.

I told them my thoughts about their nearing completion of our work, and that the main concerns to be dealt with were on the mind side. They agreed and mentioned that they would be taking a two-week break for vacation. We all felt that might provide an opportunity for them to communicate in a relaxed setting and discuss their options for resolution.

We spoke about their vacation plans. They had used the problem-solving approach that they had learned in our work together. Initially, they had different ideas about what would be fun and relaxing. Rick wanted to go to Atlantic City to see the shows and have some fun at the gaming tables. Laura wanted to go to New England, which she felt would be more romantic. They reached a good compromise. They planned a trip to the Jersey Shore at Cape May. They could take a day trip to Atlantic City and have romantic evenings by the ocean.

The Art of Successful Negotiating

They created a win-win situation. Both got important things they wanted. They could now look forward to a vacation that each would enjoy. This style of negotiating builds trust and closeness. Instead of denying her wishes in order to please Rick, Laura had asserted herself in a positive way. Rick could relax, as he did not bear the responsibility of having made the decision alone; Laura found herself more enthusiastic because she was doing what she wanted rather than sacrificing her wishes. This was so much better for both of them than if Laura had passively and resentfully gone along with a plan that she would have felt to be self-sacrificing.

Many people confuse negotiating in intimate relationships with business dealing. Actually, the bottom line is very different. In ongoing personal relationships, the payoff is in feeling good about yourself and the other person. The process of how you reach a decision is as important as the decision is itself. At its best, the process involves mutual respect and working in a problem-solving manner instead of placing blame on each other. It's important that both participants feel that they got something important that they had wanted. This approach fosters trust, which is the foundation of a good intimate relationship.

Unfortunately, in our materialistic world, this style of personal negotiation often resembles the worst aspects of business dealing. Personal attacks, grandstanding, and winning at the other's expense are destructive in conducting personal affairs. Sadly, many popular advice books on how to get what you want focus on getting your way regardless of the human cost. Even in business, where the bottom line is money, such tactics often backfire, especially if you expect to do business with the same people again.

Making the Most of Your Vacation

Laura and Rick had already experienced the process of change in our work, and their vacation planning enabled them to extend those gains. They could more fully explore their return to romance and complete the last stage of their sexual "homework."

A vacation can be an opportunity to rest, to take a break from your daily routine. It gives you time to have fun and renew yourself. Vacations are necessary to help you cope with life stress. Getting away from problems for a while will not in itself solve those problems. However, you can get the most benefit from vacation time by using it to help the process of making adjustments in your daily life when they are needed.

In planning a vacation, consider those facilities that have programs to help one cope with tension. A growing number of resorts now include classes in stress management, where you can learn belly breathing, muscle relaxation, and other self-help techniques offered in a relaxing and fun-filled atmosphere.

A vacation can also be an opportunity to explore a new adventure. This can range from developing or expanding a new hobby, to honing skills in a sport that can be continued in daily life back home. For example, you can improve skills in tennis or skiing, which are not only sports but are also stress-relieving aerobic exercises. The possibilities are as wide as the imagination. A vacation can be both fun and part of the process of learning how to take control of your health.

What Feels Better

In talking with Laura and Rick about the next stage of their sexual homework, they each expressed a desire to learn more about what the other liked sensually. I suggested an enjoyable game I call "What feels better?" Have your partner pick a spot on his or her body and indicate how that spot feels best being touched. In some areas, gentle stroking feels better. In other areas, firmer pressure is more pleasurable. Everyone is different. There is no "right" technique. The fun is in asking, "What feels better?" and discovering what each of you enjoys. There can be wonderful sharing in the giving and receiving. This game helps you to reach your prime objective—generating warmth, closeness, and increasing physical intimacy. To reach these goals, it's more important to learn your partner's individual preferences than to slavishly follow every detail of a textbook treatment regimen.

Since Rick and Laura had two weeks of vacation planned, I was able to give them Laura's final sexual homework assignment, too. If they succeeded in the first week with Rick completing his mastery of voluntarily controlling his orgasm, they could proceed to Laura's assignment. Specifically, Rick could then engage in intercourse with Laura while she achieved orgasm with or without finger stimulation of her clitoris.

The New Macho Myth

The silver screen has substituted new myths to replace the old John Wayne stereotypes. In the new version, the male hero has been transformed from the strong, silent, bashful-around-women type to the suave, sophisticated, sexual athlete who unfailingly brings his female prey to repeated orgasms with his machinelike phallus. Needless to say, everyday reality is far different from the movies. Some basic knowledge of anatomy and physiology will help to explode this latest macho myth.

Orgasm is a reflex response. All reflex responses involve two parts: the first is the sensory input received by stimulation of appropriate nerve endings; the second is the muscular contraction that is the motor or movement final part of the reflex. We are all familiar with the knee-jerk reflex, which is tested in the standard physical exam. The sensory input is provided by tapping on nerve endings just under the kneecap. The motor response is provided by muscle contraction causing the leg to kick forward.

In the male, the sensory input is provided by the network of nerve receptors in the head of the penis. Rick was now learning how to monitor the degree and intensity of these sensations to regain voluntary control over his orgasm reflex. When climax is reached, the muscles at the base of the penis contract. This release of muscular tension is accompanied by the pleasurable sensation associated with orgasm.

In the female, the clitoris is the nub underneath the folds at the top of the entrance of the vagina. It is a network of sensitive sensory nerve receptors. Stimulation of the clitoris, either directly or indirectly, provides the necessary input leading to orgasm. The muscles that surround the vagina provide the contraction that completes the female orgasm reflex response.

Two out of three normal, healthy women require some direct clitoral stimulation to activate the orgasm reflex. Statistically, fewer than one out of three women get sufficient indirect stimulation of the clitoris during intercourse to achieve orgasm.

Orgasm and Relaxation

A man cannot "give" a woman an orgasm. A man can help to create an atmosphere of love and trust that enables honest communication about sensual likes and dislikes. A woman needs to feel confident that she will get the kind of touching she wants, so that she can relax and enjoy the experience. She can then focus on the positive sensations which will naturally build toward climax.

Laura was now learning how to stay in touch with and maintain these pleasurable sensations. She needed to feel free to get the stimulation she needed either from Rick or by lending a helping hand herself to the process of lovemaking. She needed to be an active participant. In so doing, she would both enjoy herself and be a more sensual partner for Rick.

At its best, such sexual sharing provides a unique bond of love that enhances our sense of self and well-being. Our attitude, our openness, our mutual love and respect is much more vital to good sex than mere technique, devoid of human connectedness. As in treating stress-related disorders, mastery of the physical techniques is the easy part. Opening our hearts and minds requires the real effort.

Outgrowing the Need for the Biofeedback Equipment

The emphasis on resolving problems on the mind side of the mind-body equation was reflected in the amount of time spent talking with Laura and Rick. This part of the treatment sessions gradually increased as the couple's mastery of physical techniques was achieved. The biofeedback part of the training continued in order to integrate the mental advances into deeper levels of bodily, physiological relaxation. For the mind and body are two integrated aspects of the same whole—the individual as a fully functioning human being. Advances in one aspect need to be integrated immediately into the totality of the larger self. (Biofeedback is described in detail beginning on page 190.)

The final stage of treatment involved integrating the new skills more and more into daily life. At this point, the biofeedback training also served as helpful practice in this transformation toward healthy coping responses.

Both Laura and Rick maintained their prior levels of gain in their biofeedback training. This was a positive sign indicating that they were beginning the process of consolidation at these relaxed and healthy levels of physiological functioning. Even though each of them had had some upset in the past week—Laura with her sister-in-law's news, and Rick with his dissatisfaction with "condom therapy"—they both were consolidating their achievement of nonstressed physiological functioning. Obviously, there would be temporary setbacks when something stressful occurred. The important point was to develop the resiliency to bounce back by using the coping techniques to restore physiological equilibrium.

The biofeedback part of the session is a laboratory to measure progress. By now Laura and Rick had a feel for the difference between stressful and relaxed physiology. They would continue to carry this into their daily lives. When they experienced stress they could focus on the techniques that trigger the relaxation response. They were in the process of outgrowing the need for the biofeedback monitoring equipment. They were internalizing the cues that the instruments put them in touch with.

This is similar to our experience with monitoring our body temperature. After a while, we sense the correlation between different levels of body warmth and the readings the thermometer gives us. We can recognize on our own if we have a fever. The thermometer merely fine-tunes our knowledge more precisely. We can learn how to monitor ourselves in good health and maintain our well-being without the biofeedback measuring devices.

Resolving the Remaining Conflicts

Laura looked tanned and relaxed as she arrived for our individual part of session number nine. "The vacation was a really good experience," she began. "We both had fun and made progress in resolving how to go about becoming parents. I feel a great deal of relief knowing that Rick and I are together on this and that one way or another we will be parents. You were right about how stressful it is to be in limbo about the outcome. I didn't realize it until we resolved the issue and I felt so much more at peace with myself."

"I'm glad to hear that," I responded. "What's the game plan that the two of you have agreed on?"

"We started out by using the problem-solving approach you talked about with us. We quickly realized that both of us want to start a family as soon as possible. We talked about our feeling worn out by the years of this ordeal. So we immediately felt better that we agreed that we needed a solution. Then we started talking about possible strategies to achieve our goal. At first, this led to some difference of opinion. At this point, I want a baby now. I don't want to wait any longer. I'd adopt today. Rick feels that he'd like to find out if the work we're doing here to reduce our stress can help us conceive. So we thought about how you might direct us in resolving these differences. We thought about what you said in relation to our vacation planning—that we should try to satisfy both of our wishes. We then decided to continue for a couple of months with the inseminations while beginning the adoption process. This way, we will have two tracks, each moving in the same direction—starting a family."

I smiled and said, "It sounds like the two of you have really been applying to your daily life what we have been talking about here. That's great. It's wonderful to see you working together so well. In terms of the specifics of your plans, I have a question. We both know it can take quite a while to adopt. Have you thought about dealing with the waiting time involved?"

"Yes," Laura answered, "we're planning a private placement rather than an agency adoption, because of the time difference. Someone I know at work has a girlfriend who adopted privately and got a baby in less than a year. She's very happy with her baby and will give me the name of the attorney who helped her."

I noted, "I understand that can be very expensive—between fifteen and twenty thousand dollars. Will the two of you be able to afford it?"

"Do you want to hear the good news?" Laura asked.

I nodded affirmatively.

"My mother is lending us the money. She is really coming through for me for the first time that I can remember. You were right about her. I believe she does love me. I finally asked her straight out for something I really needed and why I needed it. She understood and said the money was there for important things like family." As Laura spoke, tears of joy welled up in her eyes. After pausing a moment to collect herself, she added, "Actually, I was the one who insisted on it being a loan. I guess I still have some guilt about deserving to take it."

"I can understand that," I replied. "But the important point is that you were assertive. You asked your mother for what you wanted and needed. You found out that she really means what she says about family being number one. She put her money where her mouth is. I'm thrilled for you. I'm not surprised, though. As I said, your mother loves you all and wants the security of family around her. I'm sure she wants to be grandmother to your child, too."

Renewed Self-Confidence

With a warm glow on her face, Laura said, "Asking for and getting the support of both Rick and my mother has really given a great boost to my ego. I feel so good, I have to pinch myself to make sure it's really happening. Realizing that by being assertive I can make a difference in the response I get gives me a whole new sense of self-confidence. I can't even put into words how good it feels."

"You've worked hard to make the changes you needed to get back in control of your life," I said. "I give you a lot of credit for working so persistently. As we can see, you're reaping the rewards of your efforts.

The best part is that this is only the beginning. I think you will be even more pleasantly surprised, as you see how being confident and assertive can open many doors for you. There are a lot more good things ahead."

"I appreciate what you're saying," Laura replied. "However, I know that I couldn't have done this alone. Right from the start I could sense your faith in me, even when I didn't have faith in myself. You made me feel there was hope that things could get better."

"That's what a good mother or good teacher or good coach does," I replied. "I saw the potential in you and have tried to help you to realize your own capacities to get back in control of your life."

Love, the Ultimate Aphrodisiac

Laura continued, "Rick and I are having such a good time that I just always want to be with him. Our resolving how we can definitely have a baby has brought us closer together than ever before. I feel so good whenever I'm with him. Like you said, this wasn't an assignment at all. I *want* to make love with him for the joy of it—instead of for his sake or to try to get pregnant."

"It sounds like you have discovered the secret of great sex," I said with a smile. "Love enables us to trust and be vulnerable. We can let our guard down and let go."

"It's still difficult for me to say this without blushing," Laura began. "I felt such a bond of closeness with Rick, that I lost my inhibitions. I was able to both tell him and show him what I wanted. I thought I knew what an orgasm was before, but this was a whole new experience."

I looked at Laura with a warm smile and after a moment said, "I'm really proud of you. I think you're doing a great job. Let me talk to Rick and see how he is doing."

When Opportunity Knocks, Open the Door

Rick also looked tanned and relaxed. "Things are going great," he began. "Laura and I are enjoying each other in ways we never did before. I'm sure she told you about how we worked out our plans to have a baby. It amazes me how assertive and flexible she was. That's not even half of the good news. Laura was a different woman in bed. She was really there, actively involved in getting as well as giving. I've always loved Laura. It makes me feel great now that I'm confident that she knows it."

"You make my job easy," I said with a chuckle. "I never have to ask a lot of questions to find out how you're doing. It sounds like you're doing fantastically well. It almost seems silly to ask how your homework went."

"Since you asked, I'll tell you," Rick replied with a big grin. "In a word, great. It's difficult even to think of it in terms of an assignment. With Laura being an active partner, I could focus on going with the flow of my own sensations. I didn't have to worry about how to please her. She made very clear what she wanted, when she wanted it. It made things so easy. I didn't have to wrack my brain trying to think of what might feel good for her. We developed a natural rhythm together. We got high off each other. I found it easy to just let things proceed. Even having to use a condom didn't bother me. You know, it's funny. It reminds me of when there's great team work and you're on a roll in sports. Everything just comes together," he said with a laugh.

Then Rick's expression became serious. "However, there is something I need to talk to you about. The timing looks like we're due for an insemination this weekend. Our infertility doctor doesn't work weekends. Once in the past this happened and he sent us to the clinic at the hospital. I couldn't stand that place and neither could Laura. It's such an inhuman, humiliating atmosphere. No privacy, no private bathrooms, just the stalls in the men's room. I think you get the picture. I couldn't produce a semen specimen in that environment if my life depended on it. Laura had been disappointed and I just couldn't deal with it. We also told the doctor that we were going ahead with adoption if this didn't work soon. He was cool about it and said he understood. I also told him how I couldn't stand 'condom therapy' anymore, but that Laura insisted on following his orders. Then he really surprised me. He was very sympathetic. He suggested that under the circumstances, we could try unprotected intercourse over the weekend. He said that now that we had made plans to adopt and felt good about that, we should focus more on enjoying the marriage. Personally, I think that he feels we won't get pregnant with these high antibody levels, but that it doesn't matter now."

"Is that what he said?" I asked.

"No," Rick replied. "He said that it was better to have intercourse than to have another upsetting experience at the clinic. That is a sure loser. He said having unprotected intercourse one time wouldn't really make the antibody problem worse. I don't know. Now that I'm talking about it, maybe he does feel we have a shot."

Stress, Antibodies, and Infertility

"Yes. I think you do, too," I replied. "Not only is he right in what he said about one intercourse not worsening the antibody problem, but the work the two of you have done here may have diminished the antibody response. It's been a while since your last antibody test. Both of you have made marked progress, particularly in the last few weeks. Also, no one knows for sure if it's a high antibody level that's causing your infertility problem. Our existing knowledge only shows a correlation—no cause-and-effect relationship between antibodies and infertility has been established. It may just be a coincidental finding. For example, it's possible that chronic stress is altering some necessary hormonal sequence, or the speed at which the egg travels down the tube—or stress could have a detrimental effect on implantation of the fertilized egg in the uterus. We do know that chronic stress can do all of the above. We just don't know for sure which mechanism is causing your infertility. The bottom line is that there is reason to maintain hope. Remember, hopelessness tends to create a negative self-fulfilling prophesy. If your doctor says, or you believe he thinks, that it can't work, then you are affecting your chemical balances in a way that creates a self-fulfilling prophesy."

"That's an eye opener for me," Rick said. "I guess it's like my high blood pressure. The first thing I had to do was to believe that I *could* learn how to control my pressure. If I thought it was impossible, I would never have succeeded."

"You got it," I said with a smile. "You're taking charge of your life now. How about we meet with Laura?"

"That's fine," Rick replied.

Reunited in Love

Laura entered the room and slipped in beside Rick, nudging him over with her hip. As Rick moved, he lifted his arm around Laura and draped it over her shoulder. As she rested her head against him, I responded, "Well, you two certainly look comfortable together."

Laura started to smile shyly and glanced up at Rick before she looked at me. "I guess it's kind of natural," she said, hesitantly.

I laughed. "Don't apologize. I'm feeling good about the successful treatment you've experienced. The positive results are before my eyes. Individually and together you're doing the right things in a natural and healthy manner. It seems that your talk with your infertility doctor has gotten a response that makes it possible for you to enjoy intercourse without using a condom. I'd like to know if you both feel comfortable with this."

Laura piped up immediately, "Let *me* start because I've been the most concerned about this. I'm feeling better that it's the right thing to do now. I was never crazy about condoms to begin with. Now that our fertility doctor thinks we have nothing to lose, I'm glad to throw them away. Now that I know that I'll be a mother one way or another, I'm more interested in having fun with Rick. We had such a great time together on vacation. It will be a relief not to have to mess with them."

Rick chimed in, while beaming at Laura, "What you're saying is music to my ears. You know me, honey, I'm always ready to make love to you."

"OK, big boy, cool it," Laura said, nudging him in the ribs, laughing. It was obvious she was enjoying every minute of this.

"Another issue resolved," I said dryly, as we all laughed.

Completing Treatment

In my role as therapist, I summed up all we had been working on. "Both of you, together, have successfully accomplished the goals you set out to reach, including resolving your infertility and sexual problems. Individually—Laura, you have learned to strengthen your relationship with your mother and family. Rick, you have taken control of your blood pressure. Underlying all these accomplishments, each of you has learned new ways of coping so as to take charge of your own lives. You both understand how stress has hurt you. More important, you have shown that you can successfully manage the stresses in your lives. From here on, you can continue to maintain your gains on your own. All you need to do is to continue what you've been doing here—namely, take good care of yourselves. Make yourself—each of you—the first priority in a healthy, life-affirming way. You have seen that loving and sharing with another requires that you first love and respect yourself."

"But there is another thing bothering me," Laura said. "While I agree that Rick and I have been responsible for making the changes in our lives, we have done it knowing that you are there. A part of me still feels a little scared about doing it on my own without you there at all."

"I'm glad you're able to be honest with me about that,". I said. "It's great to see that you're using your feelings as a guide to talk about what you need. Your concerns are natural and quite typical. It often takes a number of months before we fully integrate in our mind the new ways we are living. You're on that road and more time will enable you to have memories of your recent success to help support your self-confidence. There are two things that I can offer to help you bridge that time span until you feel more secure about your standing on your own two feet. First, a good parent lets his child know that he is available if the need arises. This is often the only reassurance required and the child can continue growing on his own, knowing that loving support is available and that he isn't being 'punished' with abandonment for healthy growth and independent functioning. If the need arises, I hope either of you would feel welcome to call me. Sometimes, just a phone call may be all that's necessary. Even as fully functioning adults, it's comforting to know there is someone who cares who is available. Second, I have found that at times a gradual weaning process is helpful. For example, your vacation created a natural increase in the time until this session. Perhaps we could have a 'Let's see how we've been doing on our own' session in, say, a month from now."

"I like that idea," Laura said. "It's long enough away for me to get a good feeling that I'm on my own, but soon enough that I can sense it's not too far in the future." Laura laughed. "You know that this infertility struggle has conditioned me to keep time in monthly cycles."

"Rick, how do you feel about this?" I asked.

"I'm feeling OK, now. But I can see how I will benefit if another meeting helps Laura to make this transition smoother in her own mind. I've certainly learned that the more relaxed and self-confident she feels, the better life is for me. Who knows? I might need some more coaching down the line myself. Anyway, if I do, I'll call. I know I have a tendency to jump the gun," he concluded with a laugh.

"I'm pleased to see that you're in touch with that tendency of yours, Rick. Being aware of it is more than half the battle in keeping it under control," I concluded.

Maintaining the Gains

The ultimate challenge, of course, is for individuals to maintain the gains on their own. Both Laura and Rick were off to a good start in doing this. Their training focused on this from day one. In the initial phone call inquiring about the program, I emphasized the active role patients play in regaining and maintaining their health and well-being. This was reinforced in the first session with the initial homework assignment of practicing the relaxation tape twenty minutes, twice a day.

In my program, each session involves review of how the homework is going, plus new mind-body assignments. The emphasis is continually on the necessity to build these changes into daily life. Progress in daily life is monitored in every session. Each session involves work on further mastery and independent functioning with different mind-and-body techniques. The approach is tailored to the specific needs of each individual. Throughout the training, I emphasize that my role is to help patients learn how to help themselves. Like a good parent or good coach, I'm there to help motivate, teach skills, and keep progress on track.

So by the end of the typical ten-session program, the individual has had a number of months of making changes and incorporating them into daily life. Interestingly, it often takes from three to six months for people to feel confident about new ways of doing things. It's as though the mind needs a period of time to experience the new "me"—to gain the confidence that the changes can be lasting. Perhaps the mind needs to have some time to build a library of recent "positive coping" memories to reflect on and inspire the self-confidence that the new ways will last.

In Laura and Rick's case, their sessions were weekly. As I noted earlier, Rick actually had the easier road. He didn't have to change his fundamental attitudes as much as Laura did. His experience in team sports had trained him to be more comfortable "running with the ball" on his own. Laura's anxiety about having fully integrated the changes so as to be self-confident was understandable given her history of being trained to be dependent on others.

As in all good care, medical or psychological, individual differences must be appreciated and respected. Therapists must always work with clients personally and not put them through an assembly line as though they were interchangeable parts indistinguishable from one another.

As expected, both Laura and Rick maintained their prior levels of relaxed responsiveness during the biofeedback training part of the session. At this stage, near the end of treatment, I always look for this type of consistency. It's an indicator that the techniques are being integrated into daily life. "Laboratory" results, however, must also be viewed in the broader context of how the patient is actually doing in daily life. As in all good medical care, the whole person, not just his or her lab results, must be considered and treated.

"I'm Pregnant"

Laura exclaimed with joy when she arrived a month later for our scheduled appointment. "I'm pregnant! I still can't fully believe it," she beamed. "It feels like a dream come true. We succeeded with our unprotected intercourse during my fertile time."

Smiling delightedly, I said, "You look radiant. You've got joy written all over your face."

"I'm keeping my fingers crossed that everything goes right," Laura continued more soberly. "I want to do what I can and I'm not sure what that is."

"Just keep doing the same things that got you to this point," I replied.

"But everyone is giving me such unwanted advice," Laura rushed on. "Every time I speak with my mother or sister, they warn me about something that could endanger my pregnancy. It's putting me under a lot of pressure. I wish they would stop it."

"So what are you doing about that?" I asked.

Laura looked surprised that I had turned the question back to her. She had obviously thought that I was going to give her an answer. "I hear you," Laura replied. "I need to tell them that I don't want to hear their scare stories. I need to talk to them. I can do that," she stated emphatically.

"Why do you think you haven't spoken up already?" I asked.

Laura thought for a moment and said, "I guess partly because they've been voicing some of my own fears. I don't want anything to go wrong."

"I can certainly understand your concerns," I replied. "But what have you learned here about that?"

Laura sheepishly replied, "That worry and anxiety are useful as signals of how we feel, but since they are only emotions, I don't have to choose to let them control me. I need to stop and take some time to think about what's going on around me. I need to figure out how to use my family as a support system instead of letting them get to me."

"Yes," I replied. "Taking a problem-solving approach is a more effective means of coping."

Laura nodded in agreement and said, "I'm following my doctor's orders and I'm continuing to practice what I learned here. The breathing exercise really helps when I start to feel panicky."

"Do you remember when I told you about all the new research showing that positive attitudes and emotions promote physiological health? I remember that as an important turning point for you in being able to stand up for yourself when dealing with your family."

"I'm glad you're reminding me of that," Laura replied. "I really thought about what you said. But it's not just *your* word anymore. I've experienced how I function better when I'm relaxed and positive, instead of being anxious and worried."

"That's right," I agreed. "Also remember that you are not alone. You have a team working with you. You are the captain. You need to get the best out of your team—including Rick, your family, friends, and doctors. By continuing with a problem-solving approach, you can best get the help you need, the way you want it. People want to be helpful and the more specific you can be in telling what you need and how they can help, the better your chances are of receiving from them."

"You're right," Laura replied. "I really do know these things. As long as I keep believing I'm worth it, I can ask for the care I need. I *am* in charge." Laura paused. "It's funny hearing myself say it, but I *am* in charge of myself. I *am* the captain of this team I have put together. It feels good saying it!" she exclaimed.

I smiled broadly. "It's good to hear you say it. Repeat it to yourself as often as necessary. All any of us can do is try to do our best. You have and you can see that your best is good enough. You can get the most that's possible out of life. There are times in life when things can get difficult, but on balance, we can have fun and stay healthier if we see life as an adventure to enjoy."

Laura nodded her agreement. "I'm finally feeling that I really can continue to do what I've been doing without these sessions. I know I'll miss you. I feel like I'm leaving home to go to college. I like knowing that I may call if I need to," Laura said with a nervous laugh.

"That's an appropriate analogy. You have grown up and are ready to leave," I said. "As all good parents know, that is part of normal growth and development. However, leaving home doesn't have to mean saying good-bye forever. As I told you, you are always welcome to call. It doesn't have to be an emergency. You might just want to touch base with a brief message about yourself. On the other hand, you may not want or need to call. There's no right or wrong in this situation. The important point is for you to know that there is that special bond of trust and shared experience that one has with a good parent, good teacher, or good coach. That special connection never dies, as long as you keep its memory alive in your spirit."

"I love you," Laura said. "I don't know how to thank you for all you've done."

It was my turn to blush. "Your appreciation is all the thanks I could possibly want," I replied. "Gratitude is a rarely expressed feeling. I feel honored to be the recipient of it."

A Successful Pregnancy

Laura's pregnancy was uneventful. I didn't hear from her until she called to tell me she gave birth. When I saw her with Rick and the baby, she told me that she had continued to use what she had learned in our sessions throughout the pregnancy. Laura and Rick took Lamaze training and found that the work we had done had already taught them many of the basics.

Laura's situation was typical in my experience, in that I don't usually see the woman after she has become pregnant. This is due to the short-term nature of the treatment and the feeling of most of these women that especially if they have become pregnant, they have succeeded as much as they possibly could. I mention this because I've learned through follow-ups by telephone that some women do have complications during their pregnancy that might also be stress related. I feel it would be valuable for others working in this field to explore this area, to develop a meaningful body of clinical experience in this uncharted territory.

In addition to my work with cases such as the one just reviewed, my clinical experience includes treating infertility patients with diagnosed anatomical problems, such as blocked tubes, which obviously cannot be unblocked by mind-body techniques. All the infertility patients do, however, benefit from the training in achieving greater peace of mind. All infertility struggles are stressful in the sense that they take an emotional toll and often physical toll in aches and pains. All of these women have reported that the mind-body techniques helped them to get back in control of their lives, cope better, and move toward resolution of their infertility. The resolutions may take different forms, including adoption and deciding to live childfree.

Harvard Study Confirms Treatment Effectiveness

As often occurs in medical science, different doctors simultaneously study the same issue. While I have been successfully treating infertility patients with the approach I have described, a team of Harvard researchers has been conducting a study to determine the effectiveness of mind-body methods in curing infertility. Their recently published report shows the success of this approach with a larger number of women than I, as an individual physician, have had the opportunity to treat. This is how medical progress often occurs. Individual doctors observe on a case-by-case basis how a new method they are refining benefits certain patients. But anecdotal evidence needs to be confirmed by a study of a larger number of subjects. As in this case, this usually occurs with the support of grants from foundations and the National Institutes of Health at a major research center such as Harvard.

How and Why the Treatment Works

As in my experience, the Harvard researchers found that the key factor in treatment involved training infertile women to turn off their stress response and shift their physiology back to the relaxation response.

As I emphasized to Laura in her initial phone call, and as the Harvard group also discussed, "emotional stress can cause tubal spasm, anovulation, abnormal gamete transport, progestational deficiencies, hyperprolactinemia, and can potentially lead to the luteinized unruptured follicle syndrome." Thus, as the Harvard study reports: "There is a tenable physiological explanation for a connection between anxiety and infertility."

Most significantly, the Harvard group confirms my main finding when they state in their report that "all subjects who became pregnant showed decreases in situational anxiety before pregnancy." The study concludes: "Our data clearly demonstrate that in women with unexplained infertility, elicitation of the relaxation response is capable of reducing anxiety, depression, anger and fatigue, while increasing a sense of well-being."

Individual Versus Group Treatment

The Harvard study involved a group-treatment approach. This enabled researchers to obtain the type of broad-based results that a scientific study requires, not only premised on a larger number of subjects, but on a more uniform and more easily reproducible treatment design. But there are some disadvantages to using a group approach for mind-body treatment. In a group setting, it's difficult to resolve the deep-seated conflicts that often underly an individual's chronic mental stress. For example, problems with self-esteem often require an individual treatment approach to help the patient find new solutions to specific habitual stresses with family, friends, and work-life.

My experience is that using well-established techniques of short-term, focused, issue-oriented individual and couple therapy—as shown in Laura and Rick's case—can be very effective in resolving mental stress. Laura and Rick could not have solved their multiple problems of impaired self-esteem, intimacy, sexuality, and infertility just by being in ten group sessions. The Harvard program followed a predefined schedule involving a lecture on techniques of mental-stress management. In such a group format, there isn't the opportunity to individualize treatment.

The fact that one third of the women in the Harvard study did become pregnant using their group-treatment approach is a statement of the effectiveness of mind-body methods. As I noted earlier, in untreated infertility, there is about a 5-percent pregnancy rate.

I encourage you to read the entire Harvard study for yourself. The title is "The Mind/Body Program for Infertility: a new behavioral treatment approach for women with infertility." Alice D. Domar, Ph.D., Machelle M. Seibel, M.D., and Herbert Benson, M.D., are the authors. It can be found in the journal *Fertility and Sterility,* 1990, Volume 53, Number 2, pages 246–249.

Part II

Health:
Taking Charge of
Your Life

Since this book focuses mainly on detailed case studies of how people can work together with a doctor to help themselves, I have led off with such an example—Laura and Rick's story.

In this section, I am going to discuss in more depth how you can help yourself by gaining a deeper understanding of the ways stress affects you and what you can do to make positive changes in your life.

Lists of signs and symptoms and stress-related disorders (beginning on page 163) will help you determine how you are doing and if you need to work with a specialist.

The descriptions of mind-and-body techniques can serve both as self-help tools and as a guide to gaining an understanding of the approach a doctor will take in working with you.

Chapter 5

Stress and Our Health

Stress: The Number-One Killer

You can make the difference in your own health and well-being. Life-style has been shown to be the key factor in the leading causes of death before age seventy-five. The reason for early death in over half of these cases relates to life-style factors. Thus, life-style is more important than all other factors combined—which include biology and environment! The source of this astounding estimate is the United States Centers for Disease Control.

Let's just think for a moment about the enormous significance of this finding. Such leading causes of death as heart disease, cancer, motor vehicle and other accidents, stroke, homicide, suicide, and cirrhosis of the liver, all are mostly due to life-style—which we can change for ourselves!

Life-style is simply the way in which we lead our life. How and what we eat, our hobbies, our work, exercise, are all parts of our style of life. The two most powerful forces affecting our life-style are our mind and our body. How we view the world and how we react to it are the key ingredients of our health and happiness. How we deal with stress is the most important part of our life-style.

It's the Little Things That Count

"A vacation would solve all my problems." How often we think that. Yet, a month after we're back from a holiday, we feel we need another vacation! I'm all for vacations. They do help us to renew ourselves. But it's what we do in our daily lives that really counts. Recent research suggests that everyday minor hassles play a bigger role in stress-related illness than major life crises. My clinical experience leads me to the same conclusion: How we handle normal everyday hassles is very important to maintaining health and happiness.

For many of us, our daily routine continually triggers our stress response. Bob gulps down two cups of coffee, on an empty stomach, as he runs out of the house in the morning to drive to work in the city. Bumper-to-bumper traffic and honking horns during his forty-five minute commute both enrage and frustrate him.

Upset that he is a few minutes late for a scheduled meeting in his office, he rushes in as his phone is ringing. His secretary is late so he has to take the call, while everyone else is still waiting in his office. Bob's secretary arrives in a few minutes. She takes ten calls for Bob, while he is in his hour-and-a-half meeting. At 10:30, he emerges tense, with a knot in the pit of his stomach. In a hurry, as usual, he gulps down more coffee and inhales a donut for quick energy. This being his third cup of coffee, the caffeine still is triggering the stress response. The donut gives him a temporary "sugar high" from which he will rebound down to a "sugar low" later.

The rest of the morning he tries to wade through piles of papers on his desk. He is interrupted constantly by calls from people demanding his immediate attention to their problems. Bob rushes out, after noon, for a scheduled business lunch. Arriving late, as usual, he apologizes by blaming the traffic, and orders a strong drink to try to calm his frazzled nerves. A high-cholesterol meal is washed down with two more drinks. To finish off the two-hour business lunch, he orders coffee (to rouse himself from the sedating effects of three drinks) and a rich dessert (to give him another sugar boost). Criticizing himself for being out of control, Bob says to himself, *I really don't need these extra calories.* Yet his sugar craving determines his behavior.

Afternoon back at the office is much like his morning. Not until after 5:00 P.M., when the phone calls decrease, can he do the work that "must" be done today. At 6:00 P.M., he remembers to call his wife, Carol, to tell her that he will be late for dinner—as usual.

Carol is upset because she has rushed home from her job to make a nice family dinner for Bob and their two kids. With the kids in the background screaming, "Where's daddy? We're hungry!" Carol begins to cry over the phone to Bob that she can't go on like this. Feeling guilty about neglecting his family, Bob can't concentrate on his work.

To help drown out his sorrows, he goes to the local bar for a few drinks to fortify himself for the trip home. Exhausted as he opens the door at 9:00 P.M., he is pounced on by his two kids eager for their daddy's attention. He grabs a beer and slumps in a chair in front of the TV. It's Monday night in autumn. You guessed it. It's time for *Monday Night Football!*

Carol is torn between rage and tears. She pops another Valium to try to calm herself. She grabs a piece of chocolate. Angry at Bob, she forgets about her "diet." She says to herself, *Who cares? Why should I lose these ten pounds?* Bob wants to tune out from the hassles of his daily life and escape into the football game. The kids are beginning to fight with each other over who gets control over the other television set in the den. The whole family is in distress.

Turning Your Life Around

Bob's daily life was unfortunately a mess. He was reacting to his day, not acting on his own behalf. Could he really do anything to make it better? In our work together he began to see for the first time the links between how he lived and how he felt—and the links between how he treated himself and the quality of his health and relationships with family and friends.

Bob gradually started to take himself seriously in a way that he never had before. He began to assume responsibility for his state of being; to make as his first priority doing what he needed to do to stay in healthy balance and equilibrium. For the first time, he consciously chose to do things that were right for himself. He began to anticipate and plan how to deal constructively with the daily pressures in his life. Instead of automatically reacting by going for the self-destructive quick fix, he started to show mature concern for his health and happiness.

Step by step, he gradually but consistently acted more and more in his own true self-interest. He made changes in his life-style, his eating and drinking habits, and in his relationship with his family. He did it because he began to believe that his life was worth his caring, loving concern and effort. As he made some changes, he could directly experience the benefits of increased energy, peace of mind, and better times with his wife and children. The process of self-renewal began to take on a life of its own. Feeling healthier and happier became the most powerful reward for his efforts. Free people are motivated best by experiencing their wants and needs being truly met by their own efforts.

Feel Better and Be More Productive

To Bob's surprise, he was also more productive at work. Like most of us, he had the false belief that if he took time and energy for himself, he would have even less for his work. He was suffering from a common misperception. He saw life as a zero-sum game. He thought he had only a fixed amount of time and energy. After all, he reasoned, there are only twenty-four hours in a day and that wasn't enough for him to keep up with his commitments. How could he possibly take time for himself and not fall further behind with everything else?

The answer to this riddle is found within ourselves. When we are in balance, healthy and happy, we are more effective and efficient. We are more productive. We think better, more creatively. We solve problems quicker. We get to the heart of things instead of wasting time. Just the difference in eliminating wasted time more than repays our investment of time spent renewing ourselves. When we feel good and have positive energy, we experience control over life.

Who and What Are You Living for?

If you think seriously about the following questions, you are taking the first steps in your recovery: What is it all about? What really gives me peace of mind? What is just tranquilizing my mind? What really makes me happy? What is just a quick fix?

I've posed these questions and described Bob's typical day to point up basic life-style issues. Is your life in balance and harmony? Are you eating right and getting some exercise? Are you involving yourself with family, friends, and community to meet your basic human needs for love, affection, caring, and sharing? Are you happy with your job? Are you in touch with your feelings? Are you nourishing the spiritual side of your life, including your values and beliefs?

If the answer to some or all of these questions is *no*, then you need to ask yourself: Who and what am I living for? Without being consciously aware of it, we often make ourselves, our health, and our well-being the last priorities in our daily life. We often act as though we can push our minds and bodies endlessly, without giving it a second's thought. We live under stress because we are in a constant state of reacting to pressure.

Stress has become the buzz word of our time. Stress has almost become a cliché in daily conversation. This is due in part to the pervasive effects stress has in our lives. In a recent cover story, *Newsweek* magazine put the overall cost of stress to the economy at $150 billion a year. The article noted that the Surgeon General of the United States indicated that two thirds of all illnesses before age sixty-five are preventable. In the same article, *Newsweek* asked me to explain what stress is. As I responded, our bodies are in a state of stress because we are repeatedly triggering their emergency response systems. We are still carrying the same physiology our ancestors had in prehistoric times. The problem is that today our stress is not subject to quick resolution by the "fight or flight" response.

Stress, in terms of our body, is like having one foot on the accelerator of a car, with the other foot on the brake. We wind up stripping our gears. This is because our civilized life-style does not allow us to discharge the stress response as our caveman ancestors did. We can't reach through the telephone to throttle someone who is getting our blood boiling, nor can we ignore our responsibilities and just go off to the South Seas. This chronic buildup of stress takes an enormous toll on our body in terms of wear and tear. Over half of all visits to the local doctor are for stress-related ills. Headaches, backaches, upset stomachs, trouble sleeping—these are just a few of the problems caused by stress. But we can use new scientific understanding to help restore our natural internal body harmony and avoid the harmful effects of such stress.

Over fifty years ago, physician Hans Selye, the father of modern stress research, observed that stress affects our systems' coping abilities. His concept of stress in humans is analogous to the phenomenon of how a strain or extra load distorts a physical system. For example, a support structure may sag under excess weight. If nothing is done to relieve the overload, the system may break down.

We have complex and intricately balanced systems. Fortunately, we are endowed with great natural restorative powers. However, like all systems, we require proper care to function well. Simple changes that are easily in our power to make can spell the difference between health and illness.

How You React Is the Key

Human beings have been blessed with the most advanced brain power on the planet. This has enabled us to make great achievements. Our capacity to perceive, interpret, and give meaning to events is a great gift.

However, as with most gifts, how we use our mental powers can cause us either happiness or despair.

Let's look at Jim and Barbara and how they each react very differently to the same situation. Both of them work in the same office and are supervised by Tom. He gives each of them a new assignment. Barbara reacts positively. She sees an opportunity to demonstrate her skills and be rewarded. She accepts the assignment as a challenge and performs at her best. She gains in self-confidence and self-esteem. Jim, however, interprets the assignment negatively. He experiences it as yet another demand from a boss whom he feels always wants more. He sees the situation as another burden on his day. He has to swallow his rage, because he needs the job. He feels defeated and demoralized. His energy is habitually sidetracked into triggering his stress response without any resolution. Jim's example demonstrates that it is how we react that determines whether an event is a positive challenge that promotes growth, or results in stress and strain that triggers the harmful emergency response on a chronic basis.

Barbara's response is an example of successful coping. She felt energized and motivated. She had the self-confidence and the skills to do the job. She could anticipate being rewarded with perhaps a promotion or pay-raise for doing well.

Jim's response is an example of being overwhelmed. His feelings of failure and demoralization sap his energy. His reaction is clearly one of distress. If this pattern continues on a chronic basis, it will take a toll in wear and tear on his body. He may develop symptoms such as fatigue, poor sleep, headaches, or upset stomach. He may further the vicious cycle of stress and demoralization by trying to cope with anxiety and depression through alcohol or drugs. Eventually, he will exhaust his mental, emotional, and physical resources. This end stage of the stress response is commonly known as burnout.

I chose this typical example to illustrate the single most important factor in stress: How we perceive and interpret what is going on is the key to whether we cope successfully, or instead, trigger the harmful stress response. The higher centers of our mind are involved in this process, which is called cognitive interpretation. Later, we will discuss one of the key ways of mobilizing the mind to cope with stress. Cognitive restructuring is an easily learned method to help us interpret what we are experiencing in a more practical way so that we, like Barbara, can respond positively to stress, instead of succumbing to it as Jim did.

Our Personality Shapes Our Perceptions

We each have our own unique personality. *Webster's* dictionary defines personality as "habitual patterns and qualities of behavior of any individual as expressed by physical and mental activities and attitudes." Personality involves the consistent way in which each of us perceives and interprets situations in accord with our values and beliefs.

Our earliest childhood experiences help to shape our personality. Who among us was brought up by such "perfect" parents that we have no irrational fears or expectations, no trouble experiencing situations without the slightest personal distortion, no vulnerabilities or sensitivities, and no bad habits? Obviously, to be human is to have quirks of personality. This helps make us the unique individuals that we are.

My years of experience as a psychiatrist have taught me the importance of understanding the personality of the individual who is suffering with a problem. For example, two totally unrelated people, Carl and Cindy, consulted me for the same problem—tension headaches.

Carl has an aggressive personality style. He experiences stress if he has to trust someone. He fears being taken advantage of or humiliated. Cindy has a dependent personality style. She needs to maintain the affection of others. She experiences stress if she perceives a loss of support. She fears confrontations. She submits and can't be assertive even when she wants to. Although they both have the same stress-related disorder—tension headache—their treatment is very different: Carl respects a strong authority figure guiding him; Cindy needs caring and supportive people around her.

Differences in personality also influence the types of stress-reduction exercises that will be most useful to the individual. People like Carl will often find meditation difficult. The need to focus passively in meditation is something that people with aggressive personalities often find hard to do. They do better with techniques like temperature biofeedback in which they can "keep score" of their progress by getting higher numbers as their hands warm. People with dependent personalities, like Cindy, often have trouble focusing on themselves. They need help and support to stop thinking of pleasing others, so as to relax during biofeedback. Imagery and visualization are useful ways to help them focus on self.

Each personality style brings with it advantages and disadvantages. The art of working with people is in understanding their unique personalities and helping them to be the best they can be in the context of who they are.

Each of us has a personality that is some blend of a number of the classically defined types. For example, some people have obsessiveness, or narcissism as the dominant mode of their personality. Remember that putting a label on a personality type does not imply pathology. Most of us function well within the normal range. As a matter of fact, the rational, logical, organized approach to life of a normal obsessive style can be very functional for getting things done. As with any style, problems arise when a dominant characteristic takes over at inappropriate times. For example, at a party, obsessive behavior, such as a host constantly cleaning up, isn't much fun. Mental health can be looked at as having the flexibility to respond appropriately to the situation at hand.

Helping Yourself

You can learn how to help yourself conquer stress. There are four major ways that you can break the stress cycle.

First, you can identify what the stresses are in your life. Then you can begin to develop ways to avoid or at least minimize your exposure to these stresses. Remember, successfully coping with stress is always a balance of forces. If you can minimize your exposure even a little bit, it will help.

Second, learning about your personality style is very useful in devising ways that you, as a unique individual, can make the adjustments you need to minimize the way you react to the inevitable stresses in your life. I emphasize learning about your individual self because that is often the crucial ingredient in helping yourself. Many of us have been given advice by friends and others about what is the right thing to do, but find it difficult to follow. Who hasn't had trouble losing a few pounds despite knowing that they should? By understanding your own unique personality and coping style you have a much better chance to make the changes in your life that you struggle to make but fail to achieve.

Third, you can learn specific mind-body skills that have been scientifically proven to reduce stress. Such techniques range from simply breathing in a more relaxed way to finding new, more positive ways to react to situations that bother you. These methods are easy to learn and put into practice in your daily life.

Finally, you can find ways to discharge your stress in healthful and pleasurable ways. You can learn how to make recreation and vacations work for you. You can develop an enjoyable, relaxing, and simple exercise program.

No matter where you are currently in the stress cycle, you can learn how to move in the direction of good health and well-being. You can learn to heal yourself by finding out how to get the most out of working with a stress specialist who will help you to help yourself.

The Brain Connects Our Thoughts and Feelings and Our Physical Health

The first step in the process is identifying a stressful event. As previously mentioned, a stressful event in the days of our caveman ancestors was an acute physical danger, such as an attack by a wild animal. Today, in our civilized environment, the stressful events are of a chronic psychological and social nature. A difficult boss, marital conflicts, money problems, traffic jams—all can trigger our stress response.

How we react mentally consists of two interrelated parts. The meaning we give to the experience is a thought process known as cognition. The feeling we have about the situation is an emotional process known as affect. The combination of this thinking-and-feeling evaluation of the incident results in our determining if the turn of events acts as a stressor or not.

In other words, our perception of the situation becomes the reality that we react to. For example, if we are stuck in a traffic jam and think, *I'll be late,* and feel enraged, then our perception of the situation will trigger the stress response. On the other hand, if we think, *I can't undo the traffic jam, but I can use the time to practice my breathing and muscle relaxation,*—and feel good about getting an unexpected opportunity to take a relaxation break, then our perception will help us to stay calm and centered.

You may be wondering, How can anyone relax in a traffic jam? I have helped many people learn how to stay in control, while others around them got stressed out by the traffic or other irritants. Ultimately, the mind controls the body. By focusing on your breathing and doing muscle relaxation, you can remain calm.

In our mind, our thoughts determine our emotions. As our thoughts change, our emotions change to fit our thoughts. It is our thoughts and feelings about a situation which color our perception as to whether it is a stressor or not. And our personality style plays a key role in how we think and feel about our experiences. For example, if we have an aggressive personality, we may easily experience a traffic jam as controlling us. We become angry and that triggers the stress response. However, we can change such personality traits with various mental techniques.

Our personality develops out of our personal history, including the rewards and punishments we have experienced from our actions. So even though we are all born with unique temperaments, or biological predispositions, key aspects of our personality involve learned behavior. What has been learned by experience can be changed and modified by new learning.

Specific anatomical areas of the brain are involved in our thought-and-feeling appraisal of situations. The highest thinking level of the human brain, the neocortex, is involved in taking in information from the environment. The frontal lobe of the neocortex is involved in such crucial human capacities as logic, imagination, understanding, remembering, solving problems, planning, and making decisions.

Just below and in communication with this highest level of human functioning is the emotional center of the brain, the limbic system. It contains a number of nerve centers involved in the biochemistry of emotions. The limbic system also directly communicates with the master gland, the pituitary, as well as being joined to the brain stem, which maintains such basic functions as breathing and heart rate. Thus, anatomically and physiologically, our emotional center directly connects to both our higher thought center and the centers for nerve and hormone regulation of our body's muscles and organs, such as the heart.

Our brain directly connects our thoughts and feelings to our body's functioning. Mind-body skills work because they enable us to affect this crucial process directly.

The Signs and Symptoms of Stress

Stress has many faces. This can be a blessing in disguise if you need the early warning signs that your life is out of balance.

The issue is not living forever. The issue is the quality of the life we live. We can either choose to join the fully living or ignore the warning signs of stress until the damage becomes unbearable. The choice is ours. We make the choice every day in what we do and how we react, and most important, in how we think and feel. Then our values, beliefs, and emotions determine our actions. We can accept the responsibility for directing our lives, or continue to merely respond to the turmoil that surrounds us.

Mental Symptoms of Stress

Psychological problems can be caused by stress and can linger after the stressful situation. There can be a decrease in our ability to perform mentally and to feel good emotionally. As with all signs and symptoms of stress, those listed below can appear in various combinations.

Anxiety, nervousness

Depression, hopelessness, crying, moodiness

Irritability, anger, frustration

Fatigue, low energy, apathy

Feeling trapped, pressured, tense

Feeling emotionally drained

Insomnia, oversleeping, nightmares

Trouble concentrating

Negative thoughts recur

Forgetfulness

Confusion

Disorganization

Indecisiveness

Overwhelmed by problems

Difficulty learning new information

Self-doubt

Low self-esteem

Loneliness

Fearing closeness

Suicidal thoughts

Obsessions

Poor judgment

Rapid thinking

Behavioral Symptoms

Stress-related behavioral symptoms involve self-defeating actions that we take in an attempt to escape, avoid, or relieve the stress. These misguided attempts to cope include:

Overeating, anorexia, bulimia

Alcohol and drug abuse

Tranquilizer and prescription
   drug abuse

Smoking

Withdrawing from friends and life

Blaming and criticizing others

Rushing around, pacing

Fidgeting, edginess

Garbled, fast speech

Suspiciousness, defensiveness,
   argumentativeness

Gambling, overspending

Trouble meeting commitments

Poorly done work

Lateness, absenteeism

Accident proneness

Impulsiveness

Urinating frequently

Vomiting frequently

Staring at television
   endlessly

Physical Symptoms

Bodily expressions of stress can involve the voluntary muscular system and/or the automatic nervous system. These symptoms can include the following:

Tension headaches

Back pain

Muscle tension and aches

Neck pain

Teeth grinding

Jaw pain

Trembling hands, lips

Stuttering, stammering

Tense body, frowning

Migraines

Chest pain

Diarrhea

Constipation

Decreased sexual desire

Heart palpitations

Cold, sweaty hands

Bloating, gas, belching

Panic attack

Heartburn

Colds, frequent and/or lingering

Chills, goose bumps

Rashes, hives

Swallowing difficulty

Dry mouth

Faint, dizzy, light-headed

Ears ringing, sound sensitivity

Light sensitivity, pupils widen

Blushing

Night sweats

Painful cold hands and feet

At this point you may be saying, Who doesn't suffer from one or more of these symptoms? Well, you're right. Stress is such an ingrained part of our daily life, that almost all of us have had some of these symptoms at one time or another. Of greater significance, over one hundred million Americans suffer from one or more stress-related symptoms every week! The sheer size and universal nature of the problem leads us to accept it almost as a "normal" part of daily life. But as we have seen, suffering from stress does not have to be normal. The earlier you face stress, the quicker your mind and body will respond to reverse its negative effects.

Burnout and Stress-Related Illness

Chronic buildup of stress can lead to burnout and stress-related illnesses. Burnout occurs when our mental and physical coping abilities can't handle chronic stress. Burnout is a progressive process that occurs over a period of time. Any of the signs and symptoms of stress can be present. Burnout is an end-stage of struggling with stress. This exhaustion phase is marked by a vicious cycle of despair, pessimism, and self-doubt. Feeling like a failure, with stress-related illnesses becoming increasingly incapacitating, the burned-out person feels like a helpless, hopeless victim who has lost control of life. Unfortunately, it is typically not until a person has progressed to this stage of burnout that he or she seeks professional help. At this advanced stage of being "stressed out" many different illnesses are often at various stages of development.

The list of stress-related disorders is large and continually growing as scientists learn more about the intricate links between stress and illness. These disorders range from the painful to the life-threatening. Stress affects the function of every organ system in the body. At the stage of exhaustion, stress is a major contributor not only to malfunction but also to the physical disease of the organ affected.

The New "Healing Partnership"

As noted earlier, the vast majority of illnesses we suffer from today are caused by factors relating to stress, especially our life-style. Regaining and maintaining health and well-being in the face of stress-related illness often involves the combination of the best of traditional medicine (wonder drugs, high technology) and harnessing the power of your own internal healing system. To give you an idea of the vast number of significant illness that have been scientifically documented to have a stress component and have been shown to be responsive to the new mind-body medicine, following is a partial list.

Stress-Related Illnesses

Coronary Heart Disease
High Blood Pressure
High Cholesterol
Hostile Heart

Ulcers
Colitis
Irritable Bowel Syndrome
Difficulty Swallowing

Tension Headache
Migraine

Back Pain Syndrome

Panic Disorder
Asthma
Chronic Fatigue
Severe Allergies
Multiple Chemical Sensitivities
Depression
Phobias
Pre-Menstrual Tension
Sexual Dysfunctions
Infertility

Alcoholism
Drug Abuse

Anorexia
Bulimia

Compulsive Overeating

Obesity

Dermatitis

Arthritis

You may be surprised to see some of the disorders on this list. Clearly, these are diseases involving known biochemical and pathological changes. Yet, scientists are discovering that stress plays a major role in these serious illnesses.

Healthy physiological functioning involves a delicate balance of forces. In all of the above-listed illnesses, learning to manage the stress in your life can tip the balance in favor of healing and health. Scientific research is rapidly documenting the benefits of mind-body medicine in startling new ways. Recently, a major study by Dr. Dean Ornish showed for the first time that coronary artery disease could actually be *reversed* using the mind-body techniques alone. Without surgery or drugs, existing coronary blockage melted away! (See page 245.)

Thus, taking charge of your life with these mind-body approaches has been shown to help not only the quality of life, but to prolong life as well and, in some cases, to help promote long remissions, and actual reversal and cure of the disease. Even in the area of cancer, recent advances in chemotherapy when combined with "turning on" your internal healing system have yielded remarkable results. Progress in AIDS is also moving rapidly. As we enter the 1990s, new hope is emerging both from studies of new drugs and from learning how to maximize our internal healing powers.

Monitoring the "Fight or Flight" Response

It is important to understand how quickly our body activates the stress response. Biofeedback devices measure the acute, moment-to-moment changes caused by the nervous system's emergency reaction to stress. Physiologist Walter Cannon's pioneering research showed that a combined neuroendocrine reaction occurs about a half-minute later than the initial neurological-only response. This "fight or flight" response can last ten times longer than the initial sympathetic nervous system effect. The adrenal catecholamines—adrenaline and non-adrenaline—responsible for the "fight or flight" reaction can be precisely measured by analyzing samples of blood or urine.

Hans Selye's research documented that the long-term effects of the stress response are carried out through the hormonal system itself. The corticosteroids, particularly cortisol, are the most commonly used quantitative measures of the chronic-stress response. Again, samples from blood or urine can be used to detect the different hormonal components.

The final effects of stress, especially the physical symptoms it causes us, are what typically motivates us to go to the doctor for help. Commonly, physical pain and dysfunction lead us to see our physician, who will use the diagnostic approach of traditional medicine, including physical exam and other tests and procedures. Physical diagnosis is a process of exclusion. A physician focuses, in his or her evaluation of your signs and symptoms, on ruling out as many possible causes of suffering as possible, finally, being left with what is the most likely cause of the problem. A diagnosis that indicates physical pathological changes may be given. For example, a person may be told he has ulcers. Among the contributing causes of ulcers is stress. More important, among the factors leading to cure is learning how to reduce the effects of stress on the stomach. Medication plays an important role in buying time for the internal healing system to work and heal the ulcer. Mind-body behavioral medicine techniques reduce the force of stress which maximizes the healing potential.

Some people suffer with a stress-related disorder that hasn't advanced yet to the stage of documented pathology. For example, symptoms may include abdominal pain, loss of appetite, nausea, diarrhea, and mucus in one's stool. Even though these symptoms have persisted for months, a physician may conclude after all the test results: "I can find nothing physically wrong. All the tests, including specific abdominal studies such as barium enema, upper GI tract radiography, sigmoidoscopy, and stool cultures do not show any organic disease, anatomical defect, parasite, or infection."

At this point, the physician might say, "I'm sorry I can't be of help. We call this irritable bowel syndrome. I recommend a consultation with a psychiatrist." Now we may become even more worried than before. Our relief that it isn't a "serious, life-threatening" problem quickly gets overtaken by the sense of panic that "It's all in the mind" and that the body is out of control.

The Mind-Body Link

Sadly, millions of people are left with the wrong impression that mind-body illness does not involve real, bodily, physiological process. The mind and the body are inextricably linked. They are two parts of the same whole being—you. As a matter of fact, scientists have discovered aspects of "mind" throughout the body. For example, the intestines have receptors for the same chemical messenger that goes to our brain to indicate that we have had enough to eat. Even more exciting are the scientific discoveries showing the biochemical and anatomical links among brain, mind, and immune system.

Irritable-bowel syndrome, described earlier, is a classic example of a mind-body or psycho-physiological process that is real and can be successfully treated with these new behavioral-medicine techniques. Previously, these disorders were called psychosomatic—literally meaning mind-body. However, the false belief that psychosomatic meant "all in your head" has caused this term to have an unfortunate negative label.

Chapter 6

Coping with Stress—Regaining Control

Staying in control of yourself is the key to handling stress successfully. How you react is the crucial factor in coping.

We all try to stay in control of our lives. Unfortunately, the stresses in our lives may overcome our abilities to cope. For example, Don, a successful accountant, suffered with terrible back pain every year around the fifteenth of April. Being highly responsible, he had to get out every tax return by the IRS-imposed deadline. Of course, being a responsible person is, appropriately, a highly regarded character trait. However, like any quality, under certain circumstances it can backfire.

Don did everything he could to avoid a pileup of returns at the last minute. As early as January, he urged his clients to get all their information to him. Typically, most of his clients didn't get around to doing this until late March. Don literally got hit with a back-breaking job, under the gun of a deadline.

How did Don cope? He hunkered down and worked twelve-, fifteen-, even twenty-hour days. Seven days a week, he labored as the deadline approached. His back began to groan in pain under the weight of this mounting physical and emotional abuse.

How did Don react to the early sign of stress overload, his aching back? He saw his only option as ignoring the pain and wishing it would go away so it would not interfere with what he had to do. He tried to maintain control by toughing it out. When the pain got so bad that he couldn't concentrate on his work, he popped pain killers. Soon, he needed more and more to get any relief; his back continued to scream for an easing of the burden, despite his attempt to numb himself. Eventually, Don couldn't think straight with all the pain killers.

This went on for several years. Don tried all the traditional methods, but to no avail. When the pain got so bad that he couldn't work, he discovered that he could derive some immediate release by getting a back massage. This was Don's first step toward recognizing that his body would respond positively if he cared for it. However, a few days later, the pain would return.

He saw many specialists for the pain; each specialist he saw had a different view of his problem. "Nerve involvement," the neurologist said; "Disc problem," said the orthopedist. But none of their remedies offered lasting relief. Finally, when surgery was suggested, Don resorted to giving me a call. He had finally found the motivation to address the real issue, which was stress.

Reframing and the "Worst Case" Scenario

In our work, Don discovered how to regain control by learning to be more flexible in his attitudes. He came to realize that his unspoken belief system was saddling him with an inhuman level of responsibility. He had been stuck in the need to see himself as responsible for getting every tax return out by the fifteenth of April, regardless of late input from his clients. The first step in reframing this situation was to help Don see that this concept of responsibility for clients was not productive. Through our talks he came to see that it was reasonable to expect their timely cooperation.

I asked him what was the worst possible outcome for his clients if their returns weren't ready by mid-April. To my surprise, it was even less of a problem than I had imagined. Not being an accountant, at the very least, I thought there would be automatic and severe fines for missing the deadline. But Don told me that if you pay what is due by the fifteenth of April, you can get up to a six-month extension for filing the actual return. No penalties, no fines, no nightmare scenes.

Sharing my misconception about stiff fines and my relief at hearing that there was an easy, painless solution helped Don to realize that he could dispel any irrational fears his clients might have about the situation. By giving them information, he could help his clients to stay calm and not panic if the returns weren't completed on time. Don was able to devise a more realistic approach that was consistent with his values of being responsible and respecting his own limits. He would begin to tell his clients that they had to get their information to him by mid-February. If they didn't, he would exercise his discretion to file an extension for them with the IRS.

Problem-Solving Replaces Fear

Another crucial consideration for Don in making this needed change was to work on quieting his fears that he would lose clients because he made a demand for timely data. An Achilles' heel of Don's personality was that he felt he needed to do extraordinary things to please others to gain their approval. He began to examine this situation when I asked him what was the worst case he could imagine happening. He thought for a while and said that if he lost one fourth of his clients he would have a real problem meeting his own bills.

I helped him devise an approach that enabled him to stay well within his needed margin of safety. Don would tell his clients one at a time about the need for timely data. That way, if he met opposition, we could reevaluate way before he felt the threat of losing one fourth of his practice. In addition, I asked him to make a list of his clients and to rank them in order of who would be most likely to go along with the request. To Don's surprise, his clients agreed that the mid-February due date for their tax information was sensible. By starting with the clients who were most likely to agree, Don gained confidence and his fears were lessened. He proceeded step by step, having successful experiences boost his self-esteem.

Finally, Don spoke with his few clients who were never satisfied, no matter what he did for them. True to form, they complained. One even threatened to find another accountant. But by now, Don had new confidence, based on his knowledge that everyone else had accepted his request for timely information. Don politely, but firmly, stood his ground. He could stand firm because he could accept one or two of them leaving. They were such a tiny part of his practice that he could go on without them, if necessary.

Calculated Risks

A key element of this problem-solving approach involves taking calculated risks. In Don's case, it meant talking to one client at a time instead of sending out a memo to everyone at once. This way, if the reaction was negative, adjustment could be made without Don's worst fears being triggered. In planning a calculated risk for positive change, ask yourself what step you can take that leaves you still feeling OK if it doesn't work. Try not to risk so much at once, since a bigger loss would obviously be more devastating than a smaller one.

The idea is the same as minimizing risk when investing money. Prudent financial advisors often suggest a 5 percent rule: Don't put more than 5 percent of your assets in any single investment. That way, if it turns sour, you won't be wiped out. As Don's example shows, the same idea can be applied to taking risks for positive change in your personal and work life.

What Is Control?

Don's story highlights some useful mind techniques. More important, it shows the need we all have to maintain control of our world. Like Don, all of us have "blind spots" in our personality that make it harder for us to stay in control in a healthy way. Don's need to please and to gain approval backfired under back-breaking deadlines. Learning to "see" new ways of coping resulted in a healthier solution, free of psychological pain so that he could become free of back pain.

Getting healthier control of his life involved Don's letting go of some common, mistaken notions of "being in control." Many of us, like Don, push ourselves mercilessly to try to control forces outside ourselves. Like Don, we don't stop to think about what this is doing to our health and well-being until we get sick. Doing the right thing for ourselves can be the hardest thing in the world. We tend to forget about ourselves under the pressure of demands and deadlines. It's as though we believe that we have inexhaustible supplies of energy and don't need to rest and replenish ourselves.

As noted earlier, stress occurs in our reaction to situations. It's not just the situation itself. No one can totally or even partially control the world he lives in. What we can do is stay in control of ourselves. Successful, healthy coping involves efforts at maintaining inner balance and calm—not in trying to control outside forces and people. As we have seen with Don, our perceptions, our ways of thinking and feeling, determine the "reality" we experience. Indeed, "perception is reality," as the old saying goes. In terms of control, the key is making the effort to do the best we can to influence the situation. We need to accept that no one can control events and people outside of themselves.

Look Inside Yourself

The solution is to look inside yourself for the answer to your problems. Don was confused, when we started, because he had been looking outside—at his clients and the IRS—as the source of his problems. I helped him to regain control of his life by looking inside—at his need to make superhuman efforts to please his clients.

Sadly, typically I don't see people until they are near mental and physical exhaustion. However, it is possible to self-correct at an earlier, less painful stage of stress. This may be hard to do alone, because of the blind spots we all have in our personalities. It is often a good idea to get the help of a guide, a therapist, as early as possible.

If you had a problem with any other part of your body, you would not feel any shame in seeing a physician. The legacy of shame about "mind and emotional problems" is a self-defeating, outdated relic. The lingering myth that having such problems means you are "crazy" or "weak" is a tragic error. Stress affects all of us. Our mind, emotions, and body are so closely linked as to really be different parts of the same whole—ourself, as a human being. Emotional pain is just as real from a biological, physiological, and biochemical point of view as physical pain. As a matter of fact, both are perceived and processed in the same area of the brain.

Getting professional help to heal yourself takes courage. There are practical and effective ways to convert that courage into real, solid gains in terms of your health and well-being. Especially with the help available from the new mind-body medical approach, professional guidance can be effective and short-term. The only shame, given our current knowledge, is in not taking advantage of the opportunity earlier to lead a healthier and happier life.

Understanding

Geniuses like Einstein have observed that we use less than one tenth of the powers we have in our brain. In this respect, our mind is like an iceberg. What is visible on the surface, in terms of consciousness, is a tiny fraction of what is there. Ninety percent is below the surface, in our unconscious. But we can learn how to understand this power stored beneath the surface, in our unconscious.

The genius of Sigmund Freud began the process of our understanding the unconscious and how to make it work better for us. The greatest insight of psychoanalysis is demonstrating the unconscious ways in which we adapt to the stresses of living. It is these adaptive mechanisms that make up the building blocks of our unique, individual coping style or personality.

No one likes to feel uncomfortable or threatened. We are aware of this anxiety on an unconscious, as well as a conscious, level. The unconscious ways that we try to resolve our discomfort are called defense mechanisms. Like immune system defense mechanisms, our ego defense mechanisms typically function out of our conscious awareness. Almost one hundred years of psychoanalytic insights have provided us with detailed road maps of our unconscious mental defense mechanisms. We can use this knowledge to help individuals become consciously aware of previously unconscious, automatic mental processes. While these defense mechanisms do keep uncomfortable feelings at bay, the defense mechanisms themselves can begin to interfere with our goals of health and happiness. Identifying defense mechanisms that add to an individual's stress, helping them resolve the underlying conflict, and redirecting their energy in more positive coping styles are major steps in alleviating stress in an individual's life.

Unconscious Conflicts

A major part of my initial session with clients is devoted to finding out how they are currently functioning in their personal and work life. I look for clues in their coping style that may be unconsciously contributing to their stress-related disorder. As I listen, I will usually hear one or two major unconscious conflicts that are out of the conscious awareness of the client.

For example, as Don talked about how he dealt with the mid-April IRS deadline, I was listening for the "unconscious music" hidden under his explanation of how he was trying to cope. What struck me, in listening to him, was his excessive need to please his clients, arising out of his unconscious fear of losing them. Don was only aware of having a deadline and being solely responsible for meeting it. His blind spot prevented him from seeing any other alternative but buckling down and getting the job done. He also was out of touch with the meaning of his back pain as a signal of a poor coping style. Initially, he could only see his back pain as a purely physical problem requiring medication and correct physical diagnosis and treatment. As a matter of fact, it was only his very conscious fear of undergoing surgery that propelled Don to call me, as a last resort.

I found a creative challenge in working with Don's defenses so that he could see the link between his coping style and his physical pain. The challenge then became finding ways to work with Don to overcome his other unconscious resistances, so that he could discover new and better ways of coping, by being able to face the fears that he had earlier unconsciously denied.

This is such a delicate, yet crucial process, that I have devoted the major part of this book to three major case studies that show how the process unfolds. I often find that the best way to teach is by example. As I did with Laura and Rick's case, I have included much of the dialogue in the cases coming up to make clear how the unconscious becomes conscious. In doing this, I hope to demystify the process. It is not magic. It is a combination of science and art.

As demonstrated in the detailed cases, note that my focus is always on using the energy that is freed up from unconscious conflicts to promote mind-body healing. Developing a healthier coping style not only relieves the immediate pain, but offers the long-term ability to maintain the gains because of a new ability to manage stress.

Mental Defense Mechanisms

With the national attention focused on cancer and AIDS, most of us know more about the different parts of our immune defense system than we do about our mind's mechanisms of defense. Now I'd like to explore with you some of the well-mapped-out means by which our mind deals with the world.

The term *ego* has a number of different meanings. In common usage, ego refers to the self. Psychoanalysts use *ego* as indicating the chief executive officer of the mind. The ego takes into account our unconscious wishes and fears and makes decisions about how we cope with stress. The ego is ultimately involved in our unique individual perception of stress.

The ego uses unconscious defense mechanisms to help us cope with the pressures of living. An analogy can be made with how we use a different lens on a camera to alter the reality we see. Our unconscious defense mechanisms act as filters that change our perceptions of what we experience, both inside and outside ourself.

Mature coping mechanisms enable us to master stress by helping to get and stay in control of ourself while at the same time enlisting the support of helpful people in our world. In marked contrast, immature coping mechanisms hurt us by furthering our sense of being out of control of ourself as well as by alienating those people who might be able to help us. As we increase our awareness of our defense mechanisms, we can bring them into our consciousness and can choose to change them. Thus, we can learn mature coping mechanisms that truly help us, and let go of immature defenses which frustrate us and actually increase our stress.

Harvard University Medical School Professor of Psychiatry, George Vaillant, M.D., did a major forty-year prospective study proving how different types of coping styles affect our health. A prospective study receives the highest degree of scientific respect from the most cautious and conservative researchers in the medical establishment. In a prospective study, a large number of healthy people are tested for a series of factors, then their health is followed for many years. Dr. Vaillant followed ninety-five healthy young men over four decades. He found that their unconscious coping style was the most important factor contributing to their continued health and well-being. The healthiness of their mental defense mechanisms was the most crucial factor of their physical as well as psychological health. The coping styles of these men were assessed during the first two decades of the study. In these first twenty years, almost everyone was in excellent health.

By their mid-fifties, the men's coping styles literally became a matter of life or death. The differences were astounding. Not one man died or had become disabled who had used mature mental defenses, such as a sense of humor. Yet, fully one out of every three men died or was disabled who had used more immature coping styles! These men could not take responsibility for themselves. They denied needing any help. They had personality disorders in which they put responsibility for their problems and their feelings onto others. Significant differences remained in physical health between these two different types of coping styles—even when such major factors as smoking, drinking, weight, suicide, and age of death of forebears were taken into account.

Dr. Vaillant's research offers confirmation that the key to health and long life in those studied was in the creation of loving bonds with others that arose out of healthy coping styles. In addition to a sense of humor, these men showed altruism. By serving others, they found gratification and health for themselves. Other mature ways of coping included the ability to anticipate in a realistic way how dealing with a conflict would feel. These subjects were also able to decide consciously when to put off dealing with stresses until they were ready to handle them. Also, these men had the capacity to sublimate. Sublimation is a mature defense mechanism in which basic instincts are transformed into socially acceptable behavior. For example, one could harness a basic drive like eating to pursue a socially useful career as a gourmet chef.

In marked contrast were the coping styles of those with immature defenses. They tended to alienate other people. They suffered greatly with illness and premature death. As Dr. Vaillant noted, these unhealthy mental mechanisms led to character problems. These men couldn't deal with their feelings, and often unconsciously blocked them out. Instead, they might have acted impulsively in destructive ways, without being aware of their feelings. Often, they projected onto others feelings that they couldn't acknowledge in themselves because they were unacceptable. For example, such men might be self-righteous and project onto others feelings of envy or jealousy. Many of these men were hypochondriacs. Every little discomfort would be exaggerated into a fearful life-threatening illness. As in a Woody Allen movie, such men could convert a minor ache into a fear that they were dying from a hidden cancer. These same men were often passive-aggressive. Not being able to be directly in touch with negative feelings such as anger, they would passively, indirectly, and ineffectively express their hostility to others. For example, such a man might forget to tell his co-worker about an important meeting. Some of them would create fantasy worlds in their minds. In these fantasies, they could accomplish what they couldn't in reality. For example, they might control others, or they might get the love they wanted, but couldn't get in their actual lives. They might fantasize solving problems that they couldn't solve in reality.

Obviously, such immature ways of coping have a high price in terms of both not being functional and in alienating others. Children and adolescents may cope in this manner as a part of their normal growth and development. This is why such coping mechanisms are termed immature. As adults, we need to develop the more mature coping patterns to stay healthy.

In his thorough analysis of defense mechanisms, Dr. Vaillant describes another group of mental defense mechanisms that are common to all of us. He terms them neurotic defenses. Functionally, the neurotic coping style lies midway between the healthy, mature style and the illness-producing, immature mechanisms. Neurotics feel their pain and seek help.

Among the neurotic defenses is the unconscious mental mechanism of isolation of feelings, which is found in people with obsessive coping styles. Don, the accountant, uses this unconscious way of coping. He did not feel the emotions that accompanied his experiences. Instead of feeling, Don overintellectualized everything.

Neurotic is a psychological term that has specific meaning, which is often obscured by its popular, everyday usage in our culture. Neurosis is a psychological disorder marked by such symptoms as anxiety, depression, unreasonable fear, doubts, obsessions, and physical ills. The symptoms result from unconscious conflicts.

Repression is perhaps the best known of the neurotic defenses. This unconscious mental process keeps out of our conscious awareness impulses, feelings, memories, or experiences that would cause anxiety. The repressed material, however, continues to seek expression. Our symptoms are often the visible signs of repressed wishes and fears. Repression is never totally successful at eliminating all anxiety; repression decreases the anxiety we feel.

We can identity many of our defense mechanisms by examining our experiences as children. The manner in which we were taught to handle uncomfortable situations can become part of our coping style. For example, the coping style of a patient of mine, Linda, involved a great deal of repression. She would often feel anxious. She grew up in a home where feelings like anger weren't talked about. She didn't even learn how to identify her anger. She repressed any angry thoughts.

Displacement is the process of unconsciously transferring feelings to a more acceptable substitute. Ed was taught that "big boys don't cry." He never cried when his mother died of cancer. When he saw a movie about a mother dying of cancer, he wept uncontrollably, much to his surprise. His powerful unexpressed feelings of loss of his own mother were displaced onto the dying mother in the movie.

Reaction formation is an unconscious process in which the attitudes and behavior we show are the opposite of ones we can't express. As a child, Diane loved to make mud pies. She enjoyed getting her hands dirty and her clothes messy. As an adult, she was excessive about cleanliness and neatness. She took three showers a day and became very upset if anything was even slightly out of place.

Dissociation involves splitting off a part of our personality so that we are not conscious of it. Dave's conscious self-image was that of a churchgoing man, faithful to his wife. Periodically, he would see a prostitute. This part of his behavior was split off from his conscious image of himself. The unconscious mental process of dissociation enabled Dave to avoid dealing with the dilemma of reconciling such behavior with his conscious self-image of himself as a very moral man.

Most mind-body problems can be corrected by focusing on the conscious part of the mind. Such techniques as behavior modification, cognitive restructuring, rational-emotive therapy, assertiveness training, and improving communication skills can be very effective.

The unconscious can be tapped quickly and effectively with such methods as hypnosis, imagery, visualization, and dream interpretation.

When these approaches are not sufficient, working with the underlying unconscious conflicts and unconscious defense mechanisms can lead to success. At this point, professional help is advisable. By definition, what is unconscious is out of our conscious awareness, and thus we need a professional to help us become aware of it. The goal of all in-depth psychoanalytic treatments is to make the unconscious conscious. However, you don't have to spend years in classic psychoanalysis to get the help you need for a mind-body problem.

Effective, brief psychotherapy methods have become well established. Many of the people I see have difficult and complicated mind-body problems. Therefore, I have created an approach that includes an understanding of the unconscious to effect mind-body change in a brief time period. The case histories in this book are good illustrations of how this process works.

Discovering the Motivation to Change

Developing healthful ways of living and loving is what each of us desires. Everyone who comes to see me is consciously well motivated to get relief from their pain and suffering and to regain their good health and well-being. They typically feel great relief in our first meeting, having found someone who understands that what they are going through is real and believes they can be helped. They easily see how the mind-body techniques can help them. They eagerly agree to practice what they learn so that their daily ways of living can change for the better.

Sounds easy. Here's the catch. By the next few sessions, I typically hear something like this: "I'm almost too embarrassed to tell you, Doctor, but I was really too busy to practice my breathing," or "I'm awfully sorry to say this, but I couldn't find the time to sit with the tape this week," or "It's useless. I got furious in the traffic jam again. Things will never change."

What I typically face, in all their countless variations, is the patient's unconscious resistance to doing what they know is right for themselves.

As has been humorously said: We have met the enemy, and "they is us." This is why I have created a treatment program that devotes the time and energy needed to identify and deal with the unconscious processes, including resistance and defense mechanisms, that block our progress.

How are we to deal with this hidden, unconscious resistance in us that prevents us from acting in our own best interests? Here is where I work together with patients to help them locate "the good mother within." I find this helps individuals to call upon their own inner unconscious resources to act in their own best interests.

The "Good Mother" and the "Second-Chance" Family

In my work with clients, I call it finding the "good mother" within yourself. No matter what our actual experiences were, we all have our own images of what being a "good mother" is all about. Good mothers having unending patience, love, and understanding. They are helpful and encouraging of our growth and development. They are always available for caring and comfort.

Clearly, no human being could be such a perfect mother. Yet, the ideal is valuable as a goal as we learn to be our own good mother. We need to treat ourselves with the same loving and healthy attitudes that our ideal mother would.

This crucial part of changing our inner attitudes toward ourself is the hardest thing to do. I find this part of my work with people to be the most challenging and most gratifying. A good working relationship with a therapist is like having a second-chance family situation. As human beings, we grow and change most naturally under the loving, supportive guidance of a good-mother figure.

In all good-mothering situations, the goal is the development of the self-confidence and self-esteem a person needs to face the world alone. The "good mother" role becomes internalized in our own mind and our own experience. We learn how to value ourselves through our experiences. Our primary caretakers—mothers and fathers—have provided the most important basis for this learning about ourselves. We have learned to react and to treat ourselves like they treated us. No matter what our experiences were as children, now we can learn how to value ourselves and love ourselves in mature, healthy ways. We need to treat ourselves with the love, care, and respect that a good mother would devote to her child. We need to create an atmosphere where we experience feelings as having value and worth.

How We Learn to Be Our Own "Good Mother"

In my experience, this is the most crucial part of all. Yet, how do we change ourselves? How do we learn to feel comfortable making our caring for ourselves a priority?

Throughout this book I show how people actually learned, step by step, to be their own good mother. This is a gradual process that unfolds over time. There is progress and there are setbacks. By showing the twists and turns of real-life changes toward healthy self-esteem, I demonstrate how it can be done. It is possible to make progress on your own, but due to blind spots in our personality and characteristic patterns of reacting, greater progress is made with the help of a guide, an experienced therapist in mind-body, self-growth. Laura and Rick's case was the first of several major cases being presented to give you a flavor of how this process between therapist and client can work to promote self-development.

As is evident in these studies, I focus on building on a person's strengths. I have found this to be the quickest and most effective way to promote the growth of healthy self-confidence and self-esteem. Most of us have something from our current life or a memory from our past that we're proud of doing well. I find that helping a person to recognize and transfer those good coping skills to other areas of his or her life can be a very effective way to maximize self-growth.

Note how this is just the opposite of the "knock them down, to build them up" school of thought. Unfortunately, just focusing on what is wrong does not automatically uncover what is right. What's more, focusing exclusively on failures and the negative is demoralizing, and contributes to lower self-esteem, as well as a further sense of hopelessness and helplessness. This leads to a vicious cycle of "victimization."

Sadly, many well-meaning psychotherapies take this approach. This has often led to years of work with the result of knowing "twenty more reasons why I'm neurotic" but still being unable to change for the better.

As a board-certified psychiatrist, I have a deep respect for the analytic understanding of mental-emotional conflict. Such understanding can be very helpful as part of a mind-body treatment approach that focuses on what a person can do right for himself. As these case studies show, I make use of analytic understanding of psychological dynamics. I help patients to identify their important unconscious patterns of behavior, to help them see that there are different ways of coping, and I encourage them to experiment with new approaches to get to a better place for themselves.

Using Visualization

Here is how you can tap into your inner, unconscious healing system. Imagine the ideal mother you wish you had. Picture her in your mind. How does she look? How does she dress? Try to make her as real a person as you can. Getting in touch with her physical characteristics can make it easier for you to communicate with her.

If you can't visualize her, it's all right. You can still benefit by focusing on the next crucial step. Make mental or written notes about how she is as a person, especially how she treats you. Is she kind, understanding, loving, considerate, warm? Remember this is your ideal mother, not your real, biological mother.

Obviously, no one can live up to an ideal. However, ideals help guide us to doing the right thing. By feeling the encouragement of our ideal "good mother" within, we can harness powerful untapped energy to help us do the right things for ourselves. A good mother, for example, would encourage us to do our "homework," practicing our newly learned mind-body techniques.

If we make a mistake, a good mother is supportive and understanding. If we are hurting, a good mother reaches out, offering comfort. A good mother doesn't add insult to injury. Yet, how often do we punish ourselves with guilt when we make an error? By calling on the good mother within, we can interrupt such unconscious, self-defeating habits.

A good mother encourages us to look at our troubles as problems to be solved. Good mothers don't spend their time trying to assign blame.

Most important, good mothers help us to learn to love and respect ourselves. Good mothers encourage our spiritual growth and ability to take good care of ourselves. Good mothers give their love freely out of the joy of nurturing. They neither sacrifice themselves, nor do they selfishly demand that their children sacrifice their growing selves to pay them back.

At this point, you may be saying to yourself, *this sounds like work*. Well, you're right. However, it is effort well spent. You will directly benefit in feeling better about yourself and your life. Though we don't often think about it, the one person we will spend every minute of our life with is ourself. It makes sense to learn how to like the person you are going to be with for such a long time.

Calling on Your "Good Mother"

Rita, a patient of mine, found a very creative way to call on her good mother to help her. First, Rita would tune in to her own thoughts about what the mother inside her was like. She found it helpful to look into a mirror and focus on listening to what she would say to herself. For example, when looking at herself in the mirror, Rita would hear herself say, "I hate my nose." She recalled that as a child, her older sister would run her finger over Rita's nose and shout, "ski slope, ski slope!"

Now Rita looks in the mirror, imagines her good mother standing next to her, then focuses on what her good mother would say. Rita lets herself feel the warmth and love of her good mother. She knows that her good mother feels that Rita is a beautiful person, physically and spiritually. This enables Rita to experience a wave of relaxation throughout her body as she lets herself take in the warm loving feelings. She uses her good mother in other helpful ways. Her understanding of her good mother lets Rita give herself little gifts that otherwise she would feel she didn't deserve. For example, she often felt uncomfortably cold in her car during the winter months. Her good mother encouraged her to notice this and take the time to purchase a lovely blanket to be warmer. Now Rita gets additional joy from her two kids playing underneath the blanket when they are all driving somewhere. Rita now sees such gifts to herself as coming out of love, and therefore, she is able to share it with others.

Rita used to have trouble going to sleep at night. Part of the problem was that she didn't feel comfortable with the one thin pillow she had. Because of her upbringing, she had felt it too extravagant to provide herself with more comfort. Once again, Rita's good mother came to the rescue. Now she has four pillows on her bed. So everyplace she turns, she has a big, soft pillow to rest her head. Her good mother has given Rita permission to comfort herself through this "indulgence."

Rita has found that calling on her good mother has been the most powerful way for her to change her life for the better. She experiences the added benefit of getting along better with others. As she feels loved and cared for, she no longer experiences feelings of resentment and jealousy toward others.

Even small steps can add up to a big difference in the quality of our life. Each little affirmation of our self-worth makes a big contribution to permitting ourselves to make our life a little easier. Or as Rita likes to say, "Now I can give myself a break. Before I couldn't."

Self-Respect Is Not Selfishness!

Respect yourself!

If I am asked to say in just two words what we all need to do to live a healthy and happy life, the two words are: *Respect yourself.* This is the same as saying: *Love yourself.* Unfortunately, in our society, telling people to love themselves is often mistaken to mean that you are encouraging selfishness. I find it easier to get this healing message accepted by saying: *Respect yourself.*

When we stop to think about it, we discover that love and respect go together. When we love someone or something we show caring and give of ourselves and our time and energy. Love is the highest form of respect. When you look at it this way, it is clear that treating yourself with love and respect is just the opposite of being selfish. To be able to give love to someone else, we have to have the ability to treat ourselves with kindness, understanding, and compassion. We can't share with others what we don't have ourselves.

Selfishness is actually the opposite of self-love. Selfishness arises out of an unfulfilled hunger for self-respect and love. Selfishness occurs when we are feeling empty and need to grab for anything we can get. A starving person is too desperate to share a morsel with others. When we have plenty of love, then we can share the bounty with others.

Love Is Not Self-Sacrifice

It is important to recognize that to be able to give, you have to have enough to meet your own needs. Self-sacrifice is often mistaken as a virtue, just as self-love is often mistaken as a vice.

Jill's story is an example of how the stressful and unhealthful ways of a self-sacrificing love take their toll on us. Jill felt obligated to cater to others, even if it meant that she felt deprived. She was brought up to believe that she would get love from others only if she sacrificed her own feelings, wants, and needs in order to serve others better. Instead, Jill was left with disappointment as people came to expect her to cater to them, rather than make their own effort to do things for themselves.

No one benefited from Jill's self-sacrificing love. Neither Jill nor those she loved this way grew spiritually or in self-respect. Jill felt she was unlovable if she expressed her normal wishes and feelings. Those she catered to came arrogantly to expect being waited on, instead of learn-

ing how to do things on their own. They became selfish in response to
Jill's self-sacrifice.

Like the sadist and masochist, the truly selfish and the self-sacrificing
make an unhealthy pair. The selfish uses the self-sacrificing, who gets
used. Both are losers. Neither learns the true meaning of healthy love.
Both need to learn that self-respect is the foundation of all love. The
selfish person gains self-respect by learning that self-reliance is the road
to truly meeting one's own needs. The self-sacrificing person gains self-
respect by learning that one has God-given worth as a unique individual. Out of self-respect, we can find the strength to live a healthy, happy
life that encompasses truly sharing with others the love we feel for ourselves.

Self-Respect and Relaxation: Changing Your Cholesterol Level

Paul was a patient who was concerned about his eating habits and
excess weight and how it increased his potential for a heart attack. Two
of Paul's uncles and his father had experienced heart attacks, so he was
extremely motivated to change. As studies have shown that cholesterol
levels could increase 65 percent while under stress, Paul was determined
to keep his body in a state of relaxation. He also wanted to change his
eating habits, but this he found more difficult to accomplish.

Paul described a childhood filled with daily candy snacks and evenings
of ice cream in front of the TV. Breakfast wasn't breakfast without fried
eggs, buttered toast, and bacon. Paul craved these foods and often mentioned how deprived he felt when he tried to stay away from them.

Together, we identified how Paul interpreted these foods as acts of
caring for himself. When given information about the dangers of high
cholesterol, Paul realized he needed to change his interpretation of what
these foods meant. Paul made a conscious choice to become responsible
for caring for his body. He made a decision that good health was more
important than the instant gratification these foods offered. He focused
on increasing his self-esteem by taking pride in the manner in which he
cared for his body. As he switched to more nutritious foods, he imagined his arteries clearing up as his cholesterol level lowered. This positive visualization made the reality of eating properly very vivid for Paul.

Paul was able to hook into the good mother inside himself. This was
especially necessary when he slipped up. He discovered that berating
himself for the dish of ice cream made him feel so discouraged that he
felt like he would never get back on track again. By offering himself

understanding—"It's going to take time to learn new habits," his "good mother" would tell him—Paul was able to recommit himself easily. Understanding and hope came to Paul as he visualized the support of a caring parent.

Similar to Paul's situation, many of the people I've worked with have learned to maintain their ideal weight by practicing relaxation techniques to control anxiety and depression. It's common practice in America to medicate ourselves with out favorite foods when we're upset. By focusing our attention within ourselves, we can learn to achieve a physical state of relaxation. Then we can question ourselves as to the source of our anxiety or depression. Often, our emotions improve simply as we identify them and relax. Cravings are reduced and food can become more functionally related to real hunger.

My clients are often skeptical when I suggest they focus on relaxation instead of raiding the refrigerator. But the motivation can be found within us, as we all are aware of how bad we feel when we step on the scale the following day after being on a binge. By using relaxation instead of food, there is an increase in self-esteem rather than an opportunity for self-depreciation.

Where to Begin Proper Breathing

The first step in caring for ourselves is so simple that its often overlooked and unacknowledged. I find that proper breathing is the single most useful body technique to break a stress attack and restore the body and mind to a calm peace. Typically, this occurs in less than sixty seconds.

Like most of us, I never thought about my breathing until I began my work with stress. We breathe automatically, without the need for conscious awareness. Typically, we only notice our breathing when we temporarily get short of breath. This is all quite normal and unremarkable. What is significant is that we can change our everyday breathing pattern and reverse the chronic stress response. Proper breathing turns our body physiology back toward a calm state.

The emergency stress response gears the body for maximal physical effort. Our breathing becomes rapid and shallow. Our chest heaves to take in air quickly. We have all temporarily experienced this extreme of the chest breathing pattern, during a peak effort of rapid physical exercise. In our average daily routine, most of us are also doing a chest pattern of breathing, at a rate of sixteen to twenty breaths per minute. This happens automatically and outside of our conscious awareness.

At any rate, chest breathing is stressful breathing! Most of us are in this chronic, stressful breathing pattern all day long. It's like parking your car, but leaving the motor running. You're wasting gas and causing unnecessary wear and tear. If you did this to your car all day, pretty soon different parts would begin to break down. A similar deterioration occurs in the human body, under chronic stress.

However, we can quickly learn to shift our breathing pattern and turn off the stress response. Healthy, relaxed breathing is "belly" breathing. Ironically, we are all born as belly breathers. Abdominal breathing allows ten times more volume of air into the lungs than our usual chest breathing. This vast increase in air supply enables much more oxygen to get into the bloodstream, so the heart can work easier. Having more oxygen in the blood permits more efficient metabolism. The cells of the body are better nourished. The blood supply doesn't have to be pumped through the lungs so quickly, since there is much more oxygen to pick up on each trip. Thus, the heart can slow down to more restful rate.

As both respiration rate and heart rate slow, this sends messages to the brain that the emergency is over and the body's physiology can return to a normal, resting rate. The nervous system shifts from the alarm mode to the restful, as does the hormone system. Our muscles begin to relax as inner calm is restored.

While we were all born as belly breathers, society made us self-conscious about letting go of our belly muscles. Women are taught that a flat, immobile stomach area is necessary for fashion's sake. Men are trained in the sports ideal of a tapered, immobile waistline. Thus, the culture conspires to turn us toward the chest pattern of breathing. We literally have to relearn a skill we were born with to help restore inner peace and calm.

How to Learn Belly Breathing Quickly

You can easily determine your own breathing pattern. Sit in a straight-backed chair. Put one hand over your chest. Place the other hand over your belly. Breathe in. Note which hand moves. If you're like most people, you will find that your chest expands as you breathe in. When you master the skill of belly breathing, you will note that only the hand over your abdomen moves forward as you inhale.

The way to doing belly breathing is as follows: First, exhale through your mouth as much air as you can. As you exhale, feel your belly flatten. Squeeze out the last particle of air! Now just let air passively flow in through your nose. Feel your belly rise! The key is to let your belly go. This may take some practice.

Another way to master belly breathing is by lying down. You can use your hands as before to note if you're belly breathing. Alternatively, you can gently rest a tissue box over your belly to see if it moves up and down as you breathe.

As will all stress-reduction techniques, practice is essential. The goal is to develop a slow, deep, rhythmic, belly-breathing pattern. Ideally, you want this to be how you breathe all the time. But remember, coping with stress involves tipping the balance of forces back in your favor. You will get significant relief from consciously focusing on proper breathing several times a day. We have wonderful natural restorative powers if we just give our bodies a chance. Take a stress break for a couple of minutes every few hours. You will feel the sense of calm being restored, as you literally breathe easier.

Using belly breathing to help restore inner calm is the first step in preparing yourself for mastering other stress-reduction techniques. Meditation, visualization, and imagery all depend on belly breathing to establish a base of inner calm to start with.

Proper breathing also has positive effects on our emotions. As we all know from common experience, negative emotions such as fear and anxiety lead to rapid and shallow chest breathing. Belly breathing helps break the stress cycle and restore emotional calm.

Biofeedback

Biofeedback enables us to monitor our progress in reducing stress within the body. An initial lack of knowledge about what biofeedback is causes more anxiety-filled questions being asked of me by patients than about muscle relaxation, breathing, and meditation combined.

Are there electrodes? Will I be stuck with needles? Will I get an electric shock? Does it hurt? These are some of the typical questions I often hear when I first mention biofeedback. The answer to all of these questions is a resounding *NO!*

Actually, we are all quite familiar with biofeedback in our daily lives. It's just that we don't think of it by that name. When you take your temperature you are doing biofeedback. All you do is place the thermometer under your tongue. A few minutes later you read the scale. The column of mercury in the thermometer moves up the scale, in proportion to your body warmth that it measures. The *bio* or biological process here is your body temperature, calibrated to an accuracy of one tenth of one degree. The thermometer is just an instrument to detect more subtle and precise measurements than you could determine by just feeling your forehead. You might sense you were warm, but not know how warm. The *feed* is the information itself—in this example, body temperature. The *back* part of biofeedback is getting the information back to you in a form that you can recognize. Thus, you will be able to make an appropriate response. If the thermometer reads 98.6 degrees, you know your temperature is normal. If it reads, let's say, 100 degrees, you know you have a fever. You may take an aspirin and get some extra rest and fluids into your system. These actions will help move your temperature back toward the normal range. In this example, you used your eyes to read the result. You have done visual biofeedback.

Learning How to Do It Yourself

Clinical biofeedback works exactly the same way. Just as the thermometer functioned as a sensor, there are different sensors to monitor different biological processes. For instance, a temperature device can be applied to a finger and held in place with some tape. Hand temperature is a good indicator of the amount of stress our body is struggling with. Our core body temperature always stays in a narrow range around 98.6 degrees. This is essential to maintain life. Powerful mechanisms deep in the brain maintain this level. However, the temperature in our extremities, hands and feet, can vary widely. When we are chronically triggering the stress response, blood is being shifted away from the extremities to the major muscles of the arms and legs for fight or flight. I've seen people with icy-cold hands, who initially barely registered 70 degrees in their fingertips.

Temperature biofeedback enables ongoing, accurate measures of how stress is affecting us. Sitting in a comfortable chair in a quiet room is the optimum setting for the practice of belly breathing and muscle relaxation. As the stress response is turned off, the hands naturally begin to warm. The sensor feeds information back to the person in the form of a tone. As the hand warms, the tone decreases. Therefore, it is possible to begin to link doing the relaxation exercises with actual, measurable stress reduction. Each individual learns to be able to tune in and monitor his or her own progress.

We don't use visual display, because it's possible to get to deeper states of relaxation by keeping your eyes closed, rather than having to focus on reading your score. It's the same as playing tennis, or any sport, for that matter. When you focus on your score, it makes you more tense and distracted from playing the game at your best. Actually, focusing on the ball is the way to do your best. The score will take care of itself. The same is true in using biofeedback to monitor your stress. Focus on your breathing and muscle relaxation; the score, as recorded by the instrument, will take care of itself.

I commonly see many of my hard-driving patients initially make a characteristic mistake of setting up a competition between themselves and the machine. They turn the machine into the opponent that they have to beat. Again, this causes increased stress and results in worse scores. This typically serves as a good opportunity to help these overly competitive people to see that there is a better way of achieving what they want. They soon learn that by shifting their focus to their own breathing and muscle relaxation, the score starts moving in the desired direction. We've already seen how this shift of focus benefited Rick in his biofeedback sessions.

The great advantage of biofeedback is that it enables us to tune in and monitor important biological processes that normally go on outside of our conscious awareness. The feedback enables us to make adjustments to return these biological processes to healthy harmony and balance. We begin to associate certain voluntary activities, such as belly breathing and muscle relaxation, with both subjective feelings of calm and objective biofeedback readings of return to normal balance. After a while, we no longer need the biofeedback equipment to tell us how we are doing. We have achieved our own sense of the different levels of letting go of stress.

It's like learning how to prepare a new recipe. The first few times you need to monitor all the objective measurable quantities carefully to make sure things go right. You make sure there is just the right amount of each ingredient, and that each step goes for just the right amount of time. After a short while, you begin to develop a feel for the right amounts and can judge by your own senses when the dish is ready, better than by the absolute measure of the exact amount of time it has been cooking. Soon you can do it right comfortably, on your own, without all the objective measuring devices.

The same is true in learning how to turn off your stress response. You soon learn the knack of the techniques and the feel of decreasing stress and increasing calm. The biofeedback devices serve as a temporary bridge, enabling you to monitor the process of how the techniques you practice lead to the calm you experience.

In fact, the entire treatment process is able to succeed in a short-term, about-ten-session program, for the very same reason. Right from the start, individuals are learning how to regain control of the parts of their life that have gone haywire. My role as coach is to help them to help themselves. They can maintain the gains on their own after the brief treatment process. All they have to do is to keep applying what they learned during the training. If you are a self-starter, you can use this book and do it yourself. Most of us, however, benefit from having someone experienced to guide us.

Taking the Training into Daily Life

The crucial point is bringing the training into your daily life. This is the key to long-term success. Right from the start, the focus is on this part of the process. We are all creatures of habit. We need to develop and use good habits to replace the old, bad ones that got us stressed in the first place.

The same transfer to daily life is even quicker and easier for belly breathing. As soon as you feel upset, consciously focus on your breathing. In a few breaths, you can restore inner calm and then focus on what's upsetting you in a problem-solving manner. The same transfer to daily life occurs with all the techniques you learn. Some take a little longer to integrate because we tend to repeat old habits. This is particularly true for the mind side of the stress equation. We tend to have emotional buttons that get pressed, causing us to become stressed. It usually takes longer to learn how to react emotionally in ways that work better for us by leaving us feeling calm. Helping to change perceptions, emotional reactions, and behavior is the hardest part of my work. It's also the most challenging, and therefore the part I most enjoy.

There are many ways to build helpful reminders into your daily life. For instance, you can stick a little blue dot on your telephone. This serves as your reminder to take a deep belly breath before answering the phone. This can be very helpful in putting you in a calm mental set before responding to the caller. As we all know, some phone calls can be stressful. At work, people often call because they want something as of yesterday, or they're upset over something. Even at home, calls from certain family members and friends can be upsetting. The blue dot helps remind you that you can stay in control of yourself and your stress response regardless of who is calling.

Another popular gadget that can be useful is one of those sensors that changes color according to the stress in your fingers. As part of an overall plan for decreasing stress, it can serve as a useful quick indicator of the amount of stress you are under at a given moment. Like all feedback, it can give you information so that you can make whatever adjustments you need to restore calm.

Making a Choice: Good Health or Cigarettes

On a daily basis, all of us make choices about how to act in our own best interest, according to the knowledge we have. By now, all of us have heard the warnings of the Surgeon General of the United States. Smoking cigarettes is by far the number-one hazard to our health and well-being that we can do something about all by ourselves. But, as we all know, it isn't so easy to quit and stay away from cigarettes for good.

The first warnings about the dangers of smoking began to appear in newspapers in the early 1950s. I can still remember my dad coming home from work one evening and showing my mother the headline. In capital letters, it proclaimed one of the first medical warnings about the cancer-causing capability of cigarettes. My father and mother had been lifelong smokers—two packs a day, on average. During and after dinner, they talked about the reported cancer link. They were both very health-conscious and very positively motivated. Late that night, they resolved that they had smoked their last cigarettes. They kept their promise to themselves.

As a child, witnessing this dramatic behavior change of my parents had a major effect on me. The "good mother" or "good parent" principle discussed earlier operated here to my benefit. I was able to absorb their values of taking positive action for their health and, as an adolescent, I was able to resist peer pressure to smoke.

Years later, when I began helping people to quit smoking, I thought about what useful lessons I could take from my parents' experience. Looking back on it, with my current knowledge of the powerfully addictive properties of nicotine, this achievement seems even more impressive to me. They had just quit, cold-turkey! The key to their success was that, as free people, they made a choice about what they were *for*. They were *for* their body. They were *for* their health and well-being. Therefore, even when faced with such a powerful, addictive, lifelong habit as smoking, they were able to succeed in stopping when they learned that cigarettes caused cancer.

Help Through Hypnosis

"That's nice," you may be saying to yourself, "but what about all the rest of us who need some help with self-motivation and willpower?"

I have found that hypnosis, together with other mind-body stress-reduction techniques, helps smokers to quit and stay away from tobacco. Hypnosis helps to program our mind positively to act in our best interests. The other stress reducers help to decrease the daily anxieties that tempt us to light up a cigarette.

Most of us have unfounded fears about hypnosis. The main fear is the false notion that being hypnotized means losing control and being under the power of the hypnotist. This misperception has its roots in popular culture. I can recall the typical movie version of hypnosis. Usually a scene will appear in a late-night rerun of a grade-B movie. The hypnotist is portrayed as a Svengali-like character. He is dressed like a magician. The subject is usually a sweet, innocent-looking young woman. The Svengali will pull out a pocket watch dangling from a chain. He will order our heroine to follow the movement of the watch back and forth, back and forth. In a sinister voice, he will say something like, "You cannot resist any longer. You are falling under my power." Well, this may create a thrilling, diabolical scene to watch. Unfortunately, it presents a totally false picture of hypnosis.

Plainly and simply, hypnosis is just a means of focused concentration. The power to enter into this state of mental focus is totally within ourselves. In reality, the hypnotist is just as benign as the biofeedback devices. The hypnotist merely provides a method for us to tap into our own inner potential for focused awareness. The power to get into and out of this state of focus is entirely within one's own control.

A false fear many people have relates to hearing that hypnosis has been called an altered state of consciousness. Many of us associate bad things such as being in a coma or in a crazed, drug-induced state with the term altered state of consciousness. While such mental states are indeed frightening, they have nothing to do with hypnosis. Most significant, being in a coma or experiencing the mental effects of taking drugs are indeed out of our control. This is totally opposite to the changes due to hypnosis, a process which we can totally, voluntarily, control instantly.

Hypnosis is best described as similar to daydreaming, where we let our mind wander into pleasant thoughts. At will, we can immediately switch our focus back to our present environment. Daydreaming itself is considered to be a totally harmless altered state of consciousness, and does have some useful purposes. It is a way of reminding us about people and experiences that we find enjoyable. It often provides an opportunity to turn away temporarily from a boring situation in which we may find ourselves. Remember being in a classroom with a dull teacher instructing on a topic you had no interest in? You were able to escape and find relief by allowing your mind to wander to more pleasant places.

Hypnosis is a way of shifting mental gears. Our attention shifts from the outside environment around us to our inner conscious and unconscious mental world. We can harness this power of focused concentration to help us do things we want to do, but are finding difficult, like quitting smoking. The therapeutic use of hypnosis goes back more than a century. Sigmund Freud, himself, began his study of the mind using hypnotic techniques. He used hypnosis as a means of facilitating his patients' ability to get in touch with their subconscious world of memories, experiences, beliefs, and feelings. He soon gave up using hypnosis as he found an easier method of getting his patients in tune with their unconscious. We all instantly recognize the classic image of the patient lying down on the couch, talking about whatever passes through his mind. Freud found this method of "free association" an easier means to use than hypnosis in order to tap into the world underneath our conscious awareness.

Doing Self-Hypnosis

Sit in a comfortable armchair. Let your body feel relaxed. Take a belly breath. Ease your awareness to slow, deep, rhythmic, relaxing breathing. Look straight ahead. Without moving your head, let your eyes roll up toward the ceiling. As you are looking up, slowly close your eyelids. Let yourself relax even further. In this state of relaxed, inner awareness, simply focus on your positive commitment to care for your body. Note how this sense of self-responsibility includes not putting poisons, like cigarettes, into your body.

I have found that when you create your own short, positive message, you are maximizing the power of your own strongly held beliefs and values. Self-hypnosis is a way of programming your brain. It's just like using a software tape to program a computer. In my work with hypnosis, I encourage patients to focus on three key points: First, smoking is harmful; second, I care for my body; finally, I will do what is healthful for me. I have found that by creating your own version, you will make the message most personally meaningful and effective.

My experience with people who have quit smoking for good is that they have been able to use the mind-body skills in their daily life to cope with stress effectively. They have developed new, healthy habits to deal with the physical, psychological, and social needs for which they previously used tobacco. The processes involved in developing a healthier life-style by stopping smoking are the same as in making the changes needed to maintain an ideal weight and cholesterol level. It's important to know that weight gain does not have to occur when smoking ceases. The mind-body techniques can be used to provide the stress relief. Food doesn't have to become a substitute for tobacco to ease your stress.

Part III

Healing: Restoring Your Physical Well-Being

This section is devoted to the healing of serious stress-related disorders.

Chapter 7 shows how Steve learns to change his hostile personality and maintain a healthy heart. As in Steve's example, changing a lifelong personality trait like hostility involves a fundamental change in the way we experience ourselves and our world. His story reveals how, in fewer than ten sessions, he was able to learn to change his angry personality and find new personal happiness.

Chapter 8 is designed to show how scientific understanding and medical treatment have evolved to include a significant role for mind-body treatment methods in a major field of medicine, heart disease.

Among the topics covered are:

> The Role of Stress and Personality
>
> Cholesterol
>
> Type-A Personality
>
> Hostility
>
> Learning How to Lower Your Blood Pressure
>
> Controlling Hypertension Without Drugs
>
> How to Deal with Chest Pain
>
> Reversing Heart Disease Without Surgery
>
> Preventing a Second Heart Attack

Chapter 9 shows how Susan worked together with me to overcome life-threatening multiple stress-related problems: a combination of an eating disorder that was starving her and a state of chronic fatigue and allergic chemical sensitivity.

Chapter 7

Healing a
Hostile Heart—
Steve's Story

Recently, I have noticed a hopeful sign of the times. With all of the media attention appropriately being given to new revelations about hostility and heart disease, I am being consulted by aggressive, hard-driving Type A's before they get the first signs or symptoms of heart disease or high blood pressure! They realize that they harbor inner hostility that robs them of happiness, as well as hangs over their future health. I am pleased to have the opportunity to work with them while they are still in relatively good health.

In working with a variety of people over the years, I have noticed a significant difference between those who suffer from a hostile heart and others who deal with any number of other stress-related disorders. The hostile-heart patients typically have normal physiologic measurements when initially monitored with biofeedback equipment. For example, their hand temperature, before even starting treatment, is often in the ninety-degree, or relaxed, range. In addition, these people often had tried to implement the behavioral changes recommended by leading researchers in the field, but had no success in changing their hostile patterns. I realized that I had to modify the mind-body approach that I had devised to help these people successfully cope with their stress-related disorders.

Hostile-heart patients need less emphasis on biofeedback training, while they do benefit from an increased awareness of their body's response to stress. Before an individual is in the act of rage, there is an increase in heart beat, sweating of the palms, shortness of breath, and a tightening of muscles. By becoming aware of these changes, patients can stop and take account of the situation. By choosing to breathe in a more relaxed pattern, they can stop the emotional escalation and regain control. Therefore, hostile-heart patients need to grow in awareness of their bodies' messages. While it is essential to learn proper breathing, less time is often spent using biofeedback equipment, as patients' bodies do not register stress unless they are in a situation that triggers their hostility.

I have found it necessary to target issues of self-image to promote healing in patients with hostile hearts. Often, these people have a deep-seated sense of the unfairness and injustices in life that date back to damage to their self-esteem in their formative years. They didn't feel the love that children usually receive just because they are lovable little beings. They felt they had to work hard to win love, and harbored deep scars of resentment. Remarkably, I have found that often in fewer than ten sessions, by focusing on working through their self-esteem problem, the hostility melts away. Then, with newly acquired self-confidence, such people can interact with the world without carrying a chip on their shoulders. Steve's story is a good example of this.

"Hello, I'm Steve Anthony," the telephone caller began. "I was given your name by Herb Miller. He said you deal with stress. He thinks you can help me. What's your method of working?" he asked emphatically.

The words came through the phone as rapid fire. I found myself reflexively moving the phone away from my ear, as one would recoil from a sudden burst of noise. I immediately recognized the aggressive, clipped speech pattern of a Type A personality. Recovering from my startled reaction, I replied, in a calm and measured tone, "I'll be happy to discuss with you how I work. It might save you some time though, if you told me a little bit about your problem first. If it's not something I can help with, how I work may be irrelevant to you."

Steve retorted, "I never met a doctor who didn't think he could help me, although no one ever has. Nobody wants to turn away a potential customer. It's bad for business."

"I can appreciate how frustrated and angry you feel about not getting the help you have wanted. Could you tell me a little about your stress?" I replied softly.

"Sure," Steve exclaimed. "I can tell you a whole lot about my stress!

But I'm interested in saving my time, so I'll get right to the point. I'm the ultimate cynic. People feel I'm too aggressive and hostile. I have to be, though, to be any good at my job. I'm a trial lawyer. I saw a discussion on television about the new research linking hostility to heart attack and I realized they were talking about me. I got scared. I had my secretary rush out and get me the book they were talking about, *The Trusting Heart,* by Dr. Williams. He's got good suggestions about becoming more trusting, but I just can't make the changes he recommends. I know he's right, but I just can't stop reacting with anger to everything. Herb Miller is a lawyer friend of mine who said he thought you could help me. Can you?"

"I have been able to help people to learn how to help themselves," I answered. "I say it that way because *you* need to be an active participant in the process of change."

Cynical Mistrust

"Look, Doc," Steve interrupted, "I've always been a hard worker. I'm a self-made man. I've always done whatever is necessary to get the job done. I'm looking for someone to show me how to make the changes. I haven't found anyone yet who can, and I've seen a number of highly recommended so-called experts."

"Mr. Anthony, I don't doubt your determination and work ethic," I replied. "I was going to say what being an active participant meant when you interrupted me."

"Don't let that bother you, Doc," Steve interrupted. "That's just how I am. I like to cut right through to the heart of the matter when I hear something. By the way, please call me Steve. It takes less time than saying Mr. Anthony. So, how do you work?" he asked in his emphatic fashion.

I explained to Steve how the mind-body treatment program works. I also let him know that being an active participant would involve his working in a way that was different from what he was used to. "We'll be working with your feelings, attitudes, beliefs, and perceptions," I said.

"I hope you don't mean psychotherapy," Steve shot back. "I've tried that. What a waste of my time and money. I didn't like it. Just a lot of talk. I need a goal-oriented course, not an exploration of my childhood."

"We do focus primarily on the here and now," I said. "We only get into the past, as it might be relevant to helping with a current logjam."

"OK. Just give me the right tools, Doc. I'll do the work. If you do your job right, I'll do mine," Steve declared.

We made an appointment for an initial session. After the phone call, I thought about the difficult road ahead for us to travel in journeying from a hostile to a trusting heart.

Steve arrived exactly on time for his appointment. I greeted him in the waiting room and said I would be right with him. I went to the bathroom and returned a few minutes later. He had a scowl on his face. Pointing to his watch, he said, "Weren't we supposed to meet at five o'clock sharp? I left work early to get here on time."

"Yes, our appointment was for five o'clock sharp," I replied evenly. "I just went to the bathroom. I won't cheat you on the amount of time you're due."

"People have cheated me out of more," Steve shot back. "Promptness is very important to me. It's rude to waste someone's time, starting late. But I can make an exception when nature calls," he added with a smile.

I smiled briefly and invited him into my office.

Back Pain

After we sat down, I asked him to talk more about how he suffered with stress and what different treatment approaches he had tried.

Steve told me that he had first noticed the effects of stress five years ago, when he was forty-five years old. The first episode began during a long and difficult trial. He described suffering from back pain intermittently for months. X rays showed no abnormality. He did not have a disc problem. He did have very tight muscles in his back when he was in pain. He found relief initially from a muscle relaxant. He soon discovered, however, that he needed increasing doses of Valium to get relief. He began to feel dulled mentally. He was less sharp and alert in the courtroom. He tapered off his use of the drug and got relief from massages and by using a heating pad at night. After the trial ended successfully, he was free of pain.

He found that over the next five years, pain in his back was a sensitive barometer of the amount of stress he was under. As burdens piled up, his back would literally cry out for relief from the weight of the world that it was carrying. Once, the pain got so bad that he had to take a day off from work to rest in bed. This was something he had never done before. As soon as he felt some relief, he began feeling guilty about what needed to be done at the office, and went back to work the next day. Recently, work was going well and he was free of pain.

Low Self-Esteem

Steve then shifted the focus back to his current concerns. "As I told you on the phone, I'm getting scared about this new research linking hostility and heart disease. I feel they're describing *me*. I know I'm blunt and stand-offish. I'm constantly finding myself enraged over incompetence and skullduggery. Even though my cholesterol is good and there is no history of heart disease in my family, I'm getting worried. I'm becoming obsessed with this. It's typical for me to be pessimistic. My mind is filled with negative thoughts and feelings. I guess this is my latest preoccupation.

"On paper, I have the perfect life," he continued. "I'm a successful attorney. I make a lot of money. I have a wonderful wife. She is the total opposite of me. She is caring and trusting. She is an Earth Mother. She brings out the positive in me. We have two lovely kids. But there is always this voice in my head that is looking for the bad." Steve's discouragement was revealed by the deepening of the etch lines on his face as he spoke to me.

I asked, "On the phone you mentioned that you have had some negative experiences with therapy. Could you tell me about that?"

"Sure," he answered quickly. "I've tried everything and nothing works. Three or four years ago, I saw a shrink for a few months. A lot of talk and no direction. I don't like all this free-floating, 'How are you doing today?' stuff. Last year I tried the cognitive approach twice a week for four months with a nationally renowned leader in the field. He had a very specific direction. He focused on examining the reasoning patterns that supported the negative feelings. I tried to do it, but it didn't work for me. I found myself turning back to my pessimistic thoughts. I've tried meditation, but found that more thoughts rushed in than rushed out when I tried to empty my mind. I've even done EST," Steve said with a wry smile. "So what's different about your approach from what I've already tried?" he asked in a skeptical tone.

"I can understand your cynicism," I began, "given your experiences with different therapies. The main difference in what we will do here is one of focus. We will be primarily concerned with your underlying attitude. Our principal goal will always be to help you improve your self-esteem. We will work primarily in the here and now to find solutions to your current problems that enable you to have a better sense of self-worth."

"You hit the bull's-eye when you mention self-esteem," Steve said. "Mine is in the doghouse. No matter what I achieve, I can only feel good about myself for a fleeting moment. I know that I'm afraid to feel good about myself. I'm afraid that I'd lose my competitive edge. People can hardly acknowledge what you're doing for them today, much less how you helped them yesterday!" he exclaimed. "I've got to produce everyday. I can't rest on my laurels."

Working Smarter

"You're suffering from a common misperception," I replied. "Hard-driving Type A's think they're successful because they constantly push themselves to the limit. The reality is that they are successful despite the energy they waste in constant overdrive. When your car is stuck in a rut, racing the engine just digs you into a deeper hole."

"So what am I supposed to do? Just throw up my hands and walk away?" Steve asked with exasperation.

"The answer is in working smarter, not harder," I replied. "For example, if you put some cardboard under the wheel, the tire can grip against it when you start the engine, and you can get out of the rut. Similarly, by taking a problem-solving approach, you can be productive and decrease your stress at the same time. I realize that I'm only giving you a general outline about how this process will work. Obviously, we will soon get into specifics as we deal with the nitty-gritty of your current problems. But before we plunge into that, it will be helpful for me to get a little background on your personal habits. The purpose is to find out what is working and not working for you. This can guide us as to what needs encouragement and what needs changing."

"Well, I have to admit I'm not proud of this gut of mine," Steve said while patting his protruding belly. "I could lose fifteen to twenty pounds, but who couldn't?" he added defensively. "I guess I'm like your average Joe. I eat a big dinner, and have some wine with it. Then I'll have a beer and some junk food while watching the eleven o'clock news. A couple of years ago, I was drinking more when the kids were just screaming babies. I curbed the whiskey because I found it dulled me at work the next day. My hard-driving work ethic prevented me from getting a serious drinking problem," Steve concluded.

I replied, "Your appropriate concern about being able to be mentally alert at work will continue to exist without your being in overdrive. Actually, the overdrive all day leads to wanting to relax at night by numbing out with alcohol. We will show you better ways to relieve your stress through tuning into your own body and feelings."

"I already know some better ways," Steve countered. "I feel great when I play tennis regularly. But I'm so busy I can't make the time for it."

Improving Self-Esteem

"I realize you're a busy professional," I answered. "There's a natural tendency to have all our time consumed by our responsibilities. We forget about ourselves, our health, and well-being. Self-esteem is really just our awareness of having a personal worth as human beings. It involves an inner feeling of self-respect. Unfortunately, it doesn't even appear on our 'things to do' priority list. As a human being, you deserve to pay some attention to your own well-being. A person's self-worth is much more valuable than his net worth. What's the use of all the material goods if you literally make yourself sick in striving for them?" I paused for a moment then continued, "Our body is a wonderful piece of equipment. It will give us great service with just a little time out for rest and rejuvenation. Minimal exercise, such as walking, can reduce physical and mental stress. The time spent is more than repaid in clearer thinking and more efficient working. It's part of investing in yourself that enhances your self-esteem. By considering yourself, you can have the best of both worlds. You can do well and feel good about yourself."

Steve shook his head in agreement. "I know you're right. Years ago, when I was single and didn't have any responsibilities, I worked hard and played hard. Sports was a great outlet for me. I relaxed with friends and felt fit, mentally and physically. But now I'm married with two kids. I don't have the free time I had when I was single."

I assured Steve, "You can achieve the same result of mental and physical well-being by using the simple and effective techniques you will learn here. As you practice them, they will become positive habits that will enable you to deal with stress before it builds up."

Steve responded, "As I told you on the phone, give me the right tools and I'll do the job."

"OK. Here's your homework," I said. I gave Steve my relaxation tape and instructed him in its use. I showed him how to do abdominal breathing and explained how it could be used to overcome a stress attack quickly. I demonstrated how biofeedback works by monitoring his hand temperature and having him see the display dial. I concluded the session by emphasizing the need to practice and integrate these techniques into daily living.

At the beginning of our second session, two weeks later, I asked Steve how he did with his homework. He reported that listening to the muscle-relaxation tape daily helped him to break up his tension at the end of the day. He confessed that he still was having trouble finding the time to do the tape in the morning. He also found the belly breathing a helpful way to start the process of regaining control of himself when he felt stressed. He was pleasantly surprised that it improved his alertness.

"These body techniques are helpful, but I'm in a typical 'no win' situation at the office and it creates more stress than the breathing and relaxation can take away," Steve concluded.

"Mental conflict is the greatest stressor of all," I replied. "Breaking old habits of mind and finding new ways to cope is the most challenging part of this work for both of us. Tell me what the 'no win' situation is."

Whose Fault Is It?

Steve recounted the problem. "My law partner's secretary isn't doing the job. She was hired as a favor to a big client of mine. She's the client's girlfriend. She's an OK worker, but she and my partner are like oil and water. They just don't mix. I'm caught in a no-win situation. My partner says to me, 'You hired her, you fire her.' If I do that, I'm in trouble with my biggest client. But I figured out a way to minimize the damage. My client's main concern will be that his girlfriend not think it was her fault. He doesn't want her to be upset with herself. I guess she's no fun to be with at those times. So I'll play the heavy. I'll do the face-saving for everybody else by taking responsibility—as the managing partner of the firm—for things not working out. She can get angry at me rather than at herself. Everyone knows I'm tough and that I take the heat."

"I can foresee a problem with that approach," I responded. "How will you feel inside yourself after you have set yourself up for her to vent her anger at you?"

"I'll bristle. I'll resent it. I'll feel it's unfair. But I've handled worse attacks from opposing attorneys in the courtroom. How else am I going to get off this hook, without taking some heat?" Steve asked challengingly.

"Remember," I said, "we've added a new factor to the equation: your self-esteem. Your feeling that resentment is too high a price to pay.

Smoldering anger is a chief culprit in causing heart disease. You won't feel the damage to your heart while you're steaming, but it will add up and could kill you over time. What if there isn't any fall guy in this situation?" I asked.

"How is that possible?" Steve asked in reply. "Somebody's at fault when something goes wrong," he said as though belaboring the obvious.

"That belief of yours involves a misperception that is unfortunately quite common," I explained. "More important, it leads to an attitude of looking to find who is to blame, with all the energy going into anger, resentment, and guilt. All these negative emotions cause stressful changes in our bodies and ourselves."

"What's a better way?" Steve shot back at me.

"Taking a problem-solving approach," I began, "which focuses the energy on how to make things better and resolve a situation as best as possible. This approach involves positively mobilizing ourselves and restores a sense of being useful and constructive, which reduces our stress."

"How could I do that in this situation?" Steve asked.

"Take a neutral stance in terms of fault and blame," I suggested. "Basically, things are not working out. There is a difference in personalities between your partner and your client's girlfriend. Nobody did anything wrong. Both of them are uncomfortable working together. Both will be relieved to go their separate ways. Focusing on resolving the problem frees each of them to make other arrangements. This minimizes the agony and avoids the toxic effect of trying to blame someone for things not working out. Finding solutions instead of culprits is both more productive and less stressful."

Steve listened intently and after a pause replied with a smile, "I've got nothing to lose and a lot to gain trying it this way. You've solved my problem. I guess I can go home now," he concluded with a laugh.

"Not quite yet," I replied with a smile. "Now that we don't have another crisis to deal with, we have an opportunity to understand better how your belief system developed. This will guide us in what needs to change and how best to do it. We all learn patterns of thinking and reacting from our experiences with our families while growing up. The usefulness of having a general sketch of how life was with parents and friends, at home and in school, is that we often repeat patterns we learned then in situations we are in now. Often, we are unaware that we are reacting with that baggage from the past. For instance, many of us grew up with parents who focused on finding out which kid was to blame when something went wrong and punishing the child."

"I hope you're not one of those permissive shrinks, who says, Do whatever you want to, kids," Steve interrupted. "What about the saying, 'Spare the rod and spoil the child'? Parents need to provide discipline. Look how everything has gotten so wild today."

"Either extreme creates problems," I replied. "Just focusing on punishment encourages avoidance behavior. Kids, like adults, will try to avoid punishment. But for healthy curiosity, growth, and creativity to have a chance, kids also need support to experiment, to try things, and even to fail—without being punished. What were your parents like when you were a child?"

Steve was thoughtful for a moment. "You know, I've talked about my childhood before, but I never made the connection. My mother never referred to me as a boy. I was always her 'hero.' I don't think she wanted me to be childish. I was to be the successful man that Dad wasn't. Often during dinner, she would criticize my father's lack of ambition in front of my younger brother and me."

"How did your father react to that?" I asked.

"She only put him down when he wasn't there," Steve replied. He was a watchman and often worked the four-P.M.-to-midnight shift and missed dinner at home with the family. My father's a football player, who never made the pros. He's the strong, silent type. When he was home, he was the boss. He didn't feel comfortable in social situations. My mother ran the show in dealing with the world outside our immediate family. She came from a well-to-do WASP background. Her parents disapproved of her marrying my father. They kept tight control of the purse strings and doled out dollars to my mother only for necessities that my father couldn't provide for us kids."

Doing It For Dad

"What was your relationship like with your dad?" I asked.

"Love-hate, very intense, still is," Steve answered. "He taught me sports—football, tennis. He was a natural athlete and a tough competitor. My 'wonder years' growing up were in junior high school because I excelled at the sports my dad taught me. I was popular then since I was the star lineman on the school team. That led to be my being chosen the team captain. When I got to high school, values changed. The clothes you wore had a lot more to do with your popularity. I hated Dad then for not being as good a provider as the other kids' fathers. I remember one incident in particular. I needed some money to go to the shopping center with my friends. He wouldn't give me any. We literally got into a fistfight. My mother sprained a finger in trying to break it up. I was so mad at him that I hardly talked to him after that." Steve paused for half a second and continued talking more and more quickly. "The high school had students from another junior high as well as mine. The competition in sports was tougher. I was no longer the football star. My father wanted me to win so badly. He would say, 'How did you do?' I'd say, 'OK.' He'd say, 'But did you win?' I already was really upset that I wasn't winning. To this day, when I'm playing tennis, if he's watching, my game falls apart. He's such a perfectionist when it comes to sports. When he's there, I become self-conscious and lose my concentration."

"Your father sounds like he's still an intimidating presence for you on the ball field," I interjected.

"He's also irritating to me when he visits my home. My oldest son is twelve. My dad gave him a football and wanted to take him out to do practice drills. I just want my kids to have fun with sports. I had to remind my dad that I was the father now, not him."

Pleasing Mom

"I can see where some of your cynical mistrust comes from," I said. "You've been struggling long and hard to gain control over your own world. Your father is quite set on having his own way. I appreciate all of the information you're giving me. I'm also aware that right now, you're breathing rapidly. How are you feeling?"

"Tight," Steve replied.

"Well, how about taking a few deep breaths. You will get a more relaxed mind, enabling a new, less stressful perspective," I encouraged. As Steve inhaled deeply, I continued, "You told me earlier that your mother referred to you as her 'hero.' Could you tell me more about her and her relationship with your father?"

His deep breathing completed, Steve responded, "My mother's always been frail and emotional. When my brother and I were teenagers, she went back to work as a secretary to help us all out financially. She would often come home from work and go straight to bed with a blinding migraine headache. On the plus side, my parents were always very affectionate with each other. My father's a very passionate guy and I'm sure that's what attracted my mother to him. They loved to dance. I certainly got that from them. I love disco dancing. But my mother has always catered to him. Despite his confidence on the dance floor, he's basically a loner. He never had any of his own friends. She deals with the outside world for him."

"I get the sense," I said, "that your mother wanted you to go out and conquer the world, in ways that your dad didn't. You certainly have succeeded in becoming a man whose accomplishments your mother can be proud of."

Steve looked thoughtful for a while, digesting what I had just said. Finally, he replied, "I never looked at it that way. I always just resented the burden of being her 'hero.'"

"That helps us understand why your self-esteem is low, despite your achievements," I observed. "You seem to experience your successes as fulfilling an obligation demanded of you by your mother, rather than owning your achievements for yourself."

"This is really surprising me," Steve stated quizzically. "It seems so clear to me now that you say it. I talked endlessly with my prior shrink, but he just listened and I felt like he never said anything to me."

"Perhaps he wanted you to explore your feelings more," I replied.

"I used to leave exhausted. I felt that I left *more* tied up in knots, not less. I felt I was doing myself a favor by not continuing," Steve added.

Lessons Learned from a Brother's Death

"Earlier you mentioned a younger brother. How have the two of you gotten along?" I asked.

For the first time, tears began to well up in Steve's eyes. He fought them back and said in a voice choked with emotion, "He's dead. He died of a drug overdose as a teenager." With these words, Steve couldn't stop his tears from flowing. After a moment, trying to regain his composure, he added apologetically, "God, I hate it when I break down like this."

I replied softly, "Your tears are the natural response of love for your brother. They are not a sign of weakness or lack of strength, Steve."

He looked at me with appreciation. "I really miss him." As he continued, I could hear the bitterness in his voice, spoken through clenched teeth. "Jim just wasn't strong enough to survive in our family. He was shy and not good at sports. He hated all the competitiveness." Steve paused again and sighed as he slipped back into his seat. "He withdrew into himself and street drugs."

"I hear you saying that in this world only the tough survive?" I asked. Steve shot back, "How else is there to see it?"

Reexperiencing Allows New Learning

I replied, "You and your brother always were two different people. Different personalities, different gifts, different vulnerabilities. As you have mentioned, you were always competitive and athletic, he wasn't. In your reaction to the meaning of his death, you have found justification for never letting your guard down. You have gone to the other extreme of cynical mistrust. We now know that this can kill you through wearing down your heart. A moment ago, you expressed some heartfelt emotion when you cried over your brother's memory. Getting back in touch with your emotions, especially the seemingly vulnerable ones, will actually save your life. You will never be a 'bleeding heart'—so don't worry about that. The risk that tough guys have is that 'hearts of stone' lead to heart attacks."

"I always thought that 'hearts of stone never break'," Steve said seriously.

"But they become so brittle, so clogged up, that they can't function properly," I replied. "They get hardening of the arteries. This leads to high blood pressure, chest pains, and eventually heart attacks, strokes, and sudden death. We now know that the constant outpouring of adrenaline into our system when we have a 'hostile heart' is the biochemical output leading to tragedy. By developing a more 'trusting heart' we turn off the outpouring of adrenaline and switch back to normal, healthy, physiological and biochemical pathways."

Steve looked at me with rapt attention as I spoke. When I finished, I could see he was still digesting my words. Finally, he said, "You've convinced me. I have a much better picture of what I have to do and, more important, why I have to do it."

"I'm glad to hear that," I responded. "My most important task is to help you to get properly motivated to make the changes you need to make to survive. As the old saying goes, 'You can lead a horse to water, but you can't make him drink.' Only you have the power to change yourself. You have to *want* to make the changes for your health and happiness—not because some doctor tells you that you should do it."

"That was the problem I had," Steve said. "Even after reading Dr. Williams's book, in which he clearly lists the steps to take, I still couldn't make the changes. I knew he was saying the right things, but I just couldn't do it."

"We all have that problem," I replied. "We know, intellectually, what is the right thing to do. But it takes an emotional experience to motivate us to do the hard work of changing old habits. Our talking about your brother's death was such an emotional experience for you that you were open to hearing things on a basic gut level, not just as mere words passing through your head."

"You're right," Steve said. "I really felt emotionally connected to what we were talking about. I think I kept pushing my feelings for my brother away. What good does it do to dwell on the pain, anyway? Did you do something to me? How did this happen?" Steve asked, half smiling and half mistrustful.

"No," I replied. "No magic, no tricks, no hypnosis. What happened is called catharsis. It simply means that an atmosphere of trust between us has developed, so that you can feel safe bringing to the surface old hidden wounds to be healed."

"I still have my work cut out for me," Steve mused. "Changing a lifetime of habits is no piece of cake. But I do love a challenge. My motivation is in gear. I'm a strong-willed S.O.B.," he said proudly.

"Good," I replied. "It sounds like you're making a commitment to care for yourself a top priority. You're in touch with your desire for peace and happiness."

"What do you know? I'm beginning to feel my 'self' as a real thing, not just some 'psychobabble' concept," Steve said with a laugh.

"Since we're both into having fun with old clichés today," I said, "let me conclude our session with the old truism: Where there's a will, there's a way."

Family Problems

I felt that Steve's new enthusiasm would be quickly tested in the contentious courtroom world in which he lived. The nature of the immediate problems, however, proved to be in his current family life.

"I've got some good news and some bad news," Steve began our next meeting. "My wife and I have two youngsters. We've decided that they would have a better life growing up surrounded by grass and trees rather than in the concrete of the New York City streets. So, we decided to sell our co-op to buy a house in the suburbs. That's the good news. The bad news is my wife, Mara, and I have been getting into arguments about where to move."

"What have the two of you been disagreeing about?" I asked.

"Mara wants to move to Connecticut," he answered. "I think people are too snooty there, like they are in Greenwich. I don't want my kids to get lost in petty competitions concerning possessions. I don't want my kids exposed to that."

"Is that the only reason you have reservations about Mara's choice?" I asked.

"What do you mean?" Steve questioned defensively. "Did you grow up with a silver spoon in your mouth so that you can't see my point?"

"I'm not disagreeing with or negating what you're saying," I replied. "Major decisions like moving involve lots of changes. I'd like to find out more about how you feel personally, about such things as the commute and the financial burden you'll be taking on yourself."

"Honestly, both those things bother me," Steve answered. "Right now, we live near both my office and the courthouse. I hardly have any hassles in getting to work. I really don't look forward to fighting traffic or dealing with the railroad crowding and delays. Also, I'm worried that it would be a stretch financially. I'm the sole breadwinner and I absolutely hate to be in debt. This move would require me to take a big mortgage. I guess I can't forget my childhood, when money was scarce. I don't want to get caught short if my business turns down."

"Have you shared these concerns with your wife?" I asked.

"No," Steve replied sheepishly. "I guess my old macho self wouldn't let me."

"How do you think your wife will respond to your concerns?" I asked.

"My wife? No problem with that," he answered. "I know she's very considerate about my comfort and well-being. I believe she would live in a shack with me if we had to. She's not hung up on possessions."

"Perhaps you overreacted to your shame about your father's inability to provide. Maybe you're pushing yourself by going to the other extreme and silently shouldering excess burdens," I suggested.

Steve thought for a moment and replied, "You've got something there. My motto has always been, Don't complain, don't explain."

"That truly is a tough way to live," I replied. "It's not being caring of yourself. Expressing feelings is not the same as complaining. Ignoring your feelings just leads to a harder heart."

"You're right," Steve said. "I'll talk to Mara about my feelings. She has another beef with me that's related to her wanting to move. She feels that I don't spend enough time with the kids because of the pace of city life. She feels I'd relax more out in the country and enjoy being with the kids more."

"How do you see that situation?" I asked.

"I think she's right. I'm so wired when I get home that I don't have the patience to play with the kids. Even if I do, I try to do something else, like an exercise routine at the same time, to be productive. They complain about not having my undivided attention."

I suggested, "Maybe you need some transition time for yourself to unwind at the end of the work day; it would benefit you before interacting with the family. Many people use the commute to the suburbs as time to shift gears and start relaxing, getting away from the hectic pace of the city. Even computers need 'down' time. People certainly do," I said with a smile.

Steve nodded in agreement. "Another related problem is that the kids hear us talking about moving and they get upset. They have established their network of friendships and don't want to lose them. What can I do about that?"

"Have you all sat down together as a family to discuss your plans to move?" I asked.

"No, it never occurred to me. We never did that when I was a kid. My brother and I were just told what would be happening, after the fact. No discussion. Our views didn't matter," Steve replied.

"How well did that work?" I asked.

"At the time, I just accepted it. Now I can see that it's part of the legacy I need to change to get to a better place," Steve replied.

"Family meetings on a regular once-a-week basis can provide a healthy forum for sharing information and feelings," I offered. "Kids know that parents still make the final decision. They just want to be heard and have their feelings taken into account."

"OK. I'll give it a try," Steve responded.

"Before we stop today, I want to ask how are you doing with your relaxation techniques?" I said.

"They're helping—when I remember to do them," Steve replied. "The breathing really helps when I feel angry. By shifting focus to calm breathing, I can feel how I shift emotional gears back to neutral. It's giving me a new chance to take a problem-solving approach, rather than just stew in my own rage."

I agreed with Steve. "Your experience is typical. Focusing on calm, slow breathing is the fastest way to shift back to neutral."

Testing the New Resolve

Steve began our next meeting in obvious distress. "Unexpected problems with moving. I'm trying my hardest not to blow up, but it isn't easy," he began.

"Is it what we talked about last time, or something new?" I asked.

"Something new," Steve replied. "Things are going great with what we talked about last time. Mara was very understanding about my concerns, as I knew she would be. We drove up to Greenwich and I fell in love with it. We are going to be able to have our dream house. We saw a home that has everything we want. I'm thrilled. Mara and I even went over our finances again. I feel more comfortable now that I know I can handle it. We met some people up there and they're down to earth, not highfalutin at all. The kids came up with us and we had some family meetings. They feel good about moving. We're planning to arrange for them to visit with their old friends in the city to maintain contact while they're in the process of making new friends in the suburbs. That reassured them."

"Sounds great, so far," I replied. "What's the clinker that's messing up the works?" I asked.

"The board of the co-op we live in is the clinker," Steve said with evident exasperation. "We have a buyer. A young couple. Both are professionals and make good money. They can afford our apartment."

"So, what's the problem?" I asked.

"There's a new board in power. They just decided to make the building more exclusive. They changed the house rules to require one-hundred-percent cash. They won't allow any mortgage. It's crazy. This couple has seen similar apartments in the neighborhood that allow eighty-percent financing. They need the tax deduction that they'll get for mortgage interest on the apartment. What particularly galls me is I helped elect the new board. The new board president has been a personal friend of ours for years. He knew I was planning to sell and he assured me my apartment would be 'grandfathered' under the old rules, permitting a mortgage. I got into a shouting match with him the other day. I told him, 'You talk out of both sides of your mouth.' He exploded back at me. He told me he's doing the best he can to push my deal through under the old rules, but that he's running into problems with the other new board members."

"Co-op boards can be difficult to deal with, even for board presidents," I said. "It's like the Supreme Court—every member has his own opinion."

"Who's side are you on anyway?" Steve replied angrily. "You wonder why I have what you call cynical mistrust." Well, I've just been shafted by my good friend who broke his word to me."

"Steve, I *am* on your side," I replied evenly. "This situation is a classic example of the kind of dilemma that poses a creative challenge to your new way of looking at things and reacting. Getting mad as hell and blowing up at the board president just does more damage to you and your cause. You don't have the power to intimidate him just because you are furious with him. You know, as a lawyer, that co-op boards can do what they want."

"I'm being squeezed to death!" Steve shouted. "I'm locked into buying the new house. I'll be bankrupt if I can't sell my apartment quickly. You'd be mad as hell if your chestnuts were in the nutcracker as mine are!"

I couldn't help but smile at Steve's graphic analogy.

"Now you're laughing at me! You think I'm pathetic, huh?" Steve's voice boomed at me.

"No. I was smiling at your graphic reference to 'chestnuts in the nutcracker,' " I replied, consciously striving to maintain a calm and even tone.

Finally, Steve's face broke out into a smile. "I'm glad you've got a sense of humor," he said.

"I'm glad that you can maintain yours during a crisis," I replied. "Sometimes we have to laugh a little over our troubles, so that we don't go ballistic. You have every right to feel hurt and angry. That's not the point. The point is that while it's normal and healthy to feel these emotions, they serve best as a signal of distress, not as a way of coping. Getting mad is simply not a good way to deal with a problem. You need to use your head to plan out a strategy and tactics to achieve your goal and thereby eliminate your anger by solving the problem that led to the anger in the first place."

"Sounds great in theory, but how can I do that now?" Steve shot back.

"Let's problem-solve this together," I said. "First, establish what your goal is. In this case, the goal is obvious. You've said you need to get the board's approval for financing to be able to sell your apartment quickly. The next step is to assess the situation to devise a workable strategy to achieve your goal. Since you can't force the board to do what you want, your best shot is to try to understand what their legitimate concerns are. Then you can try to satisfy them, so you can sell your apartment."

"Easier said than done," Steve retorted. "They won't accept anything less than one-hundred-percent cash from new purchasers."

"I understand that," I replied, "but even the board president thought your situation could be 'grandfathered' when he spoke with you earlier. Perhaps if you could provide solid evidence for the board of the future financial strength of this couple by documenting their good future prospects, the board might let them be 'grandfathered.'"

"You seem to be assuming that the board might listen to reason," Steve said.

"Yes, I do," I replied. "What's more important, you have nothing to lose by this approach. The worst they can do is say no. But perhaps the board president could appeal to a majority of the members, especially those on the slate he brought to power. Currently, your screaming at him just serves to alienate him from you."

Steve was thoughtful for a moment. "I guess you're right. It's worth a try. But I'm going to feel like I'm kissing ass," he said with a faint grimace.

"It doesn't have to," I replied seriously. "When we get what we want from life, we are winners, not losers. I'm glad to see you shifting gears and putting this into more of a management perspective. Your initial reaction was one of rage. Your belief that you were betrayed was so strong that I wonder if this situation triggered some old memory of being dealt with unfairly?" I asked.

Steve thought for a moment. "OK," he replied reluctantly. "As a matter of fact, it does. I can recall what was probably the most painful experience of my adolescence. I felt totally betrayed when my best friend wasn't able to prevent me from being blackballed from the fraternity I was pledging. It was so unfair. One frat brother didn't think I was 'cool' enough and used his blackball to keep me out. The S.O.B. thought I wasn't with it because I didn't wear expensive enough clothes. God, the humiliation was unbelievable. I was the only pledge to be blackballed. I was furious with my parents for not providing the attire I needed. I closed myself off from them. I didn't talk to them for months. I really gave them the silent treatment. I would even make my own TV dinner and eat alone in my room at home."

"Did you get into another frat?" I asked.

"The next year, my friends voted me into the same frat. The blackballer was gone. He had been a senior and graduated. But the scars never healed. First of all, I was so defensive that the year I got in, I lied about what my father did, to appear more acceptable. I said he was a detective because I was too embarrassed to say he was just a watchman."

"It's sad," I said. "It's not uncommon to create a false self to gain acceptance into a group. But to continue to live in this false self requires a lot of energy and is a major cause of stress. It's the kind of stress that leads to heart attacks and other ailments."

"In addition, the stigma I felt from being initially rejected spoiled my enthusiasm. I was never as active in the frat as I could have been," Steve concluded.

"It sounds like you couldn't get past the initial rejection to see that you were accepted," I said.

"Well, in the long run, I got a tiny bit of justice," Steve said with satisfaction. "A few years later, the guy who blackballed me lost a finger in a boating accident."

"That makes you feel better?" I asked.

"Well, I'm not ready to give up the good feeling of an eye-for-an-eye type of justice," Steve replied defensively.

"But an-eye-for-an-eye type of justice is costing you," I said. "It's not a harmless, good feeling—there is a reaction of adrenaline on your body. Gloating over the misfortune of adversaries is causing damage to you. But I guess forgiveness is a sign of weakness to you."

"Damn right it is!" Steve exclaimed. "Why should I excuse someone who has hurt me?"

"That's not what forgiveness is all about," I replied. "It doesn't mean excusing the person who hurt you. Forgiveness means stopping your own hating so that you don't become consumed by it and let it poison the rest of your life. It's true that living well, being happy, is the best revenge."

"I hear you!" Steve replied emphatically. "I'll give it some thought."

Steve saw my look of skepticism.

"I really will give it some thought," he said. "It makes sense when you say it that way. But as you've told me, I have to accept and feel something for myself if it's going to have true meaning for me."

"I can't argue with that," I said, as we ended our session.

"Good" Stress

Steve was tied up with a trial and I didn't see him for six weeks. From the moment he arrived, I could see he was in good spirits. "I won a tough case in a jury trial," he beamed. "I love performing, being the center of attention—having the fate of my client in my hands. When I'm 'on' I feel exhilarated. I can feel the adrenaline pumping. Now don't tell me that's bad for me. I won't accept that, not even from you!" he declared.

I smiled and replied, "Not to worry, Steve. The excitement of successful achievement is healthy. We call it 'good' stress when we are challenged and can marshall our resources of mind, spirit, and body and feel the satisfaction of performing at our best. It's energizing in a positive way for our whole system as well as for our growth and development. That's why playing sports is so healthful. We not only benefit from the physical exercise, but also from the joy of doing our best."

Steve smiled and said, "I'm relieved to hear that. As you know, sports always has been a great outlet for me, except when my father was intimidating me."

"You bring up a good point. The healthiest way is just to focus on the game and do your best. Unfortunately, some of us get caught up in having to prove something to a parent, or we hate to lose so much that we just generate negative stress for ourselves," I responded. "I'm glad to see you in such good spirits. Is it just winning a tough case, or are there other things you're feeling good about?"

"There are other things I'm feeling good about," Steve replied. "It was the *type* of case, not just winning any case, that feels great to me. I get a kick out of taking the side of the underdog. The contingency-fee system enables people to get justice, people who otherwise couldn't afford to pay a lawyer out of their pocket. I know what it's like to be there. I'll never forget my childhood and the deprivations that a lack of money can cause."

"It's wonderful how you've been able to use your painful early experience in a very constructive manner to identify with the little guy," I said. "What you're doing is using a healthy defense mechanism called sublimation, to convert your instinctual rage at injustice into a socially acceptable form, as well as a personally gratifying one."

"That's a new one on me," Steve said with a smile. "I thought all psychological defense mechanisms were neurotic."

"Not at all," I replied. "Much of human creativity comes from transforming primitive instincts and drives into culturally acceptable passions. Your love of being at center stage in the courtroom drama is an example of healthy narcissism."

Steve looked pleasantly surprised. "I always heard that narcissism was just selfish and bad for society."

"Every personality trait can be either beneficial or harmful to the individual or society. It all depends on whether we do things in an infantile or adult way," I replied.

"Well, hearing that makes me feel better about the other thing I've done since our last meeting," Steve replied. "I put my performing skills to work to help get the board to approve my buyer with financing," he said proudly.

"Congratulations!" I exclaimed. "How did you do it?"

"I thought about what you said and decided to treat myself as I would treat a client of mine. My job is to act in whatever manner helps advance my client's case. So I decided to eat some humble pie and apologized to the board president for my previous outburst. He was very receptive to my overture. He apologized back to me for his reaction, and now that we were out of the heat of the moment, he even admitted that he felt guilty about letting me down. He wanted my help in figuring out a way to get my buyer in with financing. Since we were on the same side now, I asked him what it would take to convince the board that the buyers were rock solid financially. I gave him all the information I had about the stability of their high-paying positions and the references I had received about their financial conscientiousness. He said that was just what he needed to get the board's approval. The problem had been that on the papers they submitted, it only asks for current income and current personal assets. As they are just starting out, the application didn't accurately reflect their true earning power in the future."

"So you weren't just being blackballed all over again," I said.

"No, I wasn't. I feel a lot better toward this guy, the board president. I feel I can enjoy his friendship again," Steve beamed.

"It sounds like you've forgiven him," I offered.

"Yeah, I guess I really have," Steve replied, a little surprised.

"You're getting straight A's in this course," I said with a smile. "Pretty soon you'll be ready to teach it."

"I appreciate hearing that from you," Steve said. "I feel I am doing well and don't need to be here much longer. But I kind of thought you guys never let someone go," he said with a smile.

"Your comment, like all humor, has a basis in reality," I replied. "Actually, I see my self-interest in a broader perspective. If you do well and graduate from here quickly, it helps me. I'm not losing a patient, I'm gaining a spokesperson who will talk to others about what can be done in a short period of time. Having people see the positive changes in you is the best advertisement for my work."

"I don't want to leave and immediately lose it. How will I know I'm ready? Will you tell me?" Steve asked.

"We'll both know. You're ready when you find yourself reacting in a healthy, problem-solving manner rather than just stewing with rage. You are growing and feeling better about how you are valuing yourself on a day-to-day basis. The test is being able to handle setbacks, without them throwing you for a loop."

"I feel I'm at that level now, but I'm a little worried about keeping it together on my own," Steve said.

"You've been doing the job. I haven't even seen you in six weeks. If something goes wrong, you can always give me a call. How about we schedule a final meeting for two months from now. That will give us some time to see how you're doing on your own."

"OK," Steve said. "I'll see you then."

Understanding Why the Program Works

When I saw Steve for our final meeting, he appeared tanned and relaxed.

"Just get back from vacation?" I asked.

"From the best vacation I've ever had!" Steve exclaimed. "We took the kids to visit my parents in Arizona for a week. They retired there because my mother developed asthma. For the first time, I saw myself in a different role in relation to my father. He's no longer the boss intimidating me. I see him as he really is these days—a frail old man who still has his cantankerous ways about him. I realize there's no reason for me to react to his suggestions. When he talks incessantly now, I just humor him like a good son. I no longer take his telling me how to raise my kids as orders to be carried out."

"I guess you have gone from being the 'last angry man' to becoming a diplomat," I said with a smile.

Steve smiled back and said, "I feel good about my life now. I'm a lot happier with myself. I'm even enjoying being fully involved when I spend time with the kids. I find getting into their world with them a relaxing break from mine. At work, I'm reacting more reasonably. My anger doesn't rise so quickly. I'm seeing another side to things more often. I'm feeling more secure within myself, and therefore less threatened by others." Steve paused for a second and continued, "I don't feel so tossed about, because I don't feel the need to react to everything. I feel a sense of stability. I'm thinking more about my actions, and in return, getting pushed around less," Steve concluded.

"It sounds like a fundamental self-perception of yours has changed," I said. "You used to see yourself as the perpetual outsider. Now you correctly see yourself as an insider. You're aware you can be a leader of a team, not just a rebel. It's great how you're able, at the same time, to let the sensitive and caring side of yourself show more now when you're with your kids. You can let yourself really be with them."

"You're right," Steve said, nodding in the affirmative. "Important perceptions of mine have changed. In addition to what you noted, I now feel that a nice guy *can* finish first. I don't hold grudges the way I used to."

"That's because you no longer see yourself as a powerless victim who can be easily blackballed," I replied. "Now that you have a more realistic sense of your own power, you can indeed be kinder and gentler."

"I really appreciate all the help you've given me," Steve said with evident gratitude.

"Thank you," I replied. "I'm glad I didn't disappoint you. Before we call it a day, I'd like to hear your understanding of why you think this treatment worked better for you than your prior experiences did."

Steve was thoughtful for a long moment. "Two main things stand out in my mind. First, your helping me to see my 'self' issues in the way I lead my life. I hadn't the foggiest notion of what self-esteem was before I came here, except to know that I didn't have any. The problem with the cognitive treatment I had before seeing you was that it didn't deal with my underlying attitudes. It was too mechanical a formula telling me to eliminate 'should' from my life. The other key for me has been the role you've played in giving me feedback and encouragement. You shared your ideas with me, offered suggestions I might try, and were always supportive of me. I think the difficulty with my prior analytic psychotherapy was the lack of feedback. I didn't get the encouragement I felt I needed. I really need the direction of trying different approaches to solve a problem. You have been able to help me focus on a new reality: that I have choices in how I respond when I'm upset. Instead of just getting mad, I can act in a way that helps me to get what I want and feel better about myself at the same time."

I wished Steve well. We shook hands and said good-bye.

Postscript

Steve Anthony is typical of this new type of patient I'm beginning to see. As you may recall, Steve, having just turned fifty, was a smashing success in his highly demanding profession. While still in good health, with a good marriage and two beautiful children, Steve was not happy. In fact, he was miserable. He would focus on whatever went wrong, no matter how minor. If his secretary made a single typo, he was furious. He tried to hide his rage, but it burned within him.

Steve had tried everything before calling me. He had been in psychotherapy, but found that after a year he hadn't changed, despite working with a highly regarded analyst. He sought help from a world-renowned behaviorist, again without being able to turn off his hostility.

Through our work together, Steve learned how to let go of his hostility. He also learned how to hold on to the positives in his life. Above and beyond the benefits of the integrated mind-body method, I found a particular key to help Steve unlock his own inner "prison doors" behind which he was holding himself hostage. Specifically, in working with his unconscious, I helped him to get in touch with the level of his emotions just beneath, but hidden from him, by his rage. I have found that tapping this hidden reservoir opens up the inner healing forces for "hostile-heart" patients like Steve. Buried beneath the rage was the vulnerable, idealistic child in Steve. Covered over by cynicism, this "scared little boy" inside still believed in fairness and justice. Helping Steve to get back in touch with his buried inner child helped him to release himself from his defense of hostility.

Steve found new ways to create a place in his life for values that he always cherished, but had long ago buried deeply, for fear that they weren't practical for his ambitious climb to the top. Now he could truly breathe easier by being true to his best self. He learned that he could turn his sword of cynicism into a plowshare for helping others and feel good about himself at the same time.

Chapter 8

Heart Disease— Treatment and Prevention

There is great news for tens of millions of Americans. You can reverse existing heart disease with today's mind-body healing techniques! One of every two deaths in the United States is caused by heart attacks, strokes, or high blood pressure. The toll on patient and family in terms of pain and suffering is enormous. In recent years, a number of different, well-documented studies have clearly shown how you can learn to heal your heart. A review of some of the major scientific research clearly shows the value of a behavioral-medicine approach to health.

Starting in the 1950s, several thousand people near Boston were studied to learn what factors play a role in getting a heart attack. In this prospective study, a large number of healthy people were tested for a number of factors, and then followed for many years. This type of study is necessary to show that the presence of certain risk factors really does predict an increased likelihood of later getting a heart attack. The results of this classic Framingham Study proved that high blood pressure, high cholesterol, and cigarette smoking are very reliable predictors of increased risk of getting a heart attack and dying from it.

The study also opened up some important pathways. It showed that the traditional medical model of looking for one specific cause for an illness, while useful for infectious diseases, needed to be replaced by a larger model taking into account many factors, including human behavior. In adding the human element to chronic illnesses such as heart disease, the study served to motivate physicians to develop techniques to help people improve their health by changing some of their behavior.

The Role of Stress and Personality

In the late 1950s, the idea that emotional stress and personality could cause a heart attack just wasn't taken seriously by the medical community. The breakthrough in linking mental stress and heart disease was made by two physicians, Meyer Friedman and Ray H. Rosenman. In their 1973 book, *Type A Behavior and Your Heart,* they talk about how they came to look at personality as a factor causing heart disease. As busy heart specialists, they saw lots of people. Their focus was on urging their patients to exercise, avoid smoking, and eat low-cholesterol food. Yet, they knew a major piece of the puzzle was missing. Too many good studies showed that you couldn't explain heart disease by cholesterol and fat alone.

They now joke that the answer was literally right in front of their eyes. The chairs in their waiting room had become worn thin. The repairman remarked that only the front edges of the chair seats were worn out. This clue to the behavior pattern of their heart patients, however, hadn't registered yet in the doctors' minds. It took a comment by a housewife to get them started in the right direction. She told them her belief that it was the stress at work that caused men to have heart attacks.

The doctors then sent a questionnaire to one hundred and fifty businessmen to get their views. Over 70 percent replied that excessive competitive drive and meeting deadlines were easily identified characteristics of friends who had heart attacks. Interestingly, less than 5 percent thought that their friends' heart attacks wee triggered by too many fatty foods, cigarettes, or no exercise. (Early studies were predominantly with men. Recent studies show women just as prone to Type A problems.)

Significantly, Friedman and Rosenman concluded, "We know quite well that no medical editor would publish just these data." So they surveyed one hundred heart specialists. Most of the doctors also thought that excessive competitive drive and pressure to meet deadlines most frequently accounted for heart attacks.

The supreme irony of the situation struck the researchers. Both the general public and heart doctors recognized that personality and behavior were influencing the body and causing a heart attack. Yet, no medical journal would publish such information! The ruling dogma of the time within the scientific establishment refused to consider such factors. Only purely biological factors were considered to cause disease. The role of the mind and emotions was dismissed. One could not measure mental processes in a test tube. One couldn't prove a direct cause-and-effect relationship in the laboratory. Therefore, according to the scientific logic of the time, the effects of the mind on the body were not looked at.

Friedman and Rosenman knew that they would be going up against the ruling scientific establishment. They said, "As for us, we knew quite well that there now could be no turning back." They knew they had to pursue the truth. Their carefully documented studies opened up a new era. Their work literally revolutionized the scientific study of health and disease. Now, it is universally accepted that personality and behavior are major causes of heart attacks. Their pioneering efforts demonstrated the need for a mind-body approach to health. As they said so well in the preface to their book, "If the crippling and deaths caused by heart disease are to be prevented, the average American must himself become involved in the process of protecting himself. The doctor alone cannot possibly do the job."

They went on to present their conclusions.

> The major cause of premature heart disease is the specific behavior pattern that we have designated Type A. In the absence of Type A Behavior Pattern, coronary heart disease almost never occurs before seventy years of age, regardless of the fatty foods eaten, the cigarettes smoked, or the lack of exercise. But when this behavior pattern is present, coronary heart disease can easily erupt in one's thirties or forties.

They went on to state that this harmful behavior pattern could be stopped by an individual's effort. In essence, you could keep your heart healthy by changing parts of your personality.

They noted that you should pay attention to diet, exercise, and not smoking. However, only one third of heart attacks could be avoided by attention to all of those factors. Over one half of heart attacks occurred in people for whom neither smoking, poor diet, nor lack of exercise was the cause.

Friedman and Rosenman described the Type A Behavior Pattern as "an action-emotion complex that can be observed in any person who is aggressively involved in a chronic incessant struggle to achieve more and more in less and less time, and if required to do so, against the opposing efforts of other things or other persons." They noted that such behavior is not only socially acceptable, but is indeed praised as the competitive spirit, observing that people with this pattern had a "free-floating but extraordinarily well-rationalized hostility." This hostile component is one of the most significant traits that has stood the test of time as a cause of heart attack and early death. Significantly, they reported that this Type A pattern was a reaction to challenges in their environment. A fuse was necessary for these patients to explode. Lacking confrontation or challenge, they didn't get into the Type A pattern.

Opposite characteristics marked the Type B Behavior Pattern. The B Type was more calm, confident, and had an inner sense of security. B Types didn't get caught up in life as a constant battle. They were more easygoing and steady. B Types were tactful, not hostile. B Types were as smart, as ambitious, and often more successful than Type A's.

Cholesterol

Cholesterol is an important factor in heart disease. Diet alone is not the answer to lowering cholesterol in your blood. What matters is how the body handles whatever cholesterol you eat. As Friedman and Rosenman noted, "Perhaps the most common and certainly the most medically neglected cause of an abnormally high serum cholesterol in man is the particular complex of emotional stresses we have designated as Type A Behavior Pattern."

Right from the start, they looked for biochemical evidence that Type A's, who were still seemingly healthy, showed changes similar to patients with heart disease. A dozen years of research showed: "First, there is no question about the fact that the serum cholesterol level may vary directly with the intensity of Type A Behavior Pattern." These apparently healthy Type A patients showed free-floating hostility as one of their personality traits. This characteristic has proven to be crucial in causing heart attacks. The Type B personality, lacking such Type A traits as hostility, has much lower blood cholesterol levels even when eating the same foods as Type A personalities. As we shall see later, only certain aspects of Type A behavior pattern account for the damage to the heart.

Studies by others have shown that accountants who maintained their usual pattern of behavior in relation to eating, smoking, and exercise, showed marked increase in cholesterol levels as the April 15 tax deadline approached. The accountants' changes in their serum cholesterol could only have been caused by emotional stress.

As Friedman and Rosenman note, "Here was the first completely documented and controlled demonstration that the brain and its functions could alter the blood or serum cholesterol level." Yet, when they spoke at the American Heart Association in 1957 they were met with stony silence. The experts were not ready to accept the fact that what a man feels can be more important than what he eats!

The "experts" wanted even more proof. They wanted a study of men without any detectable trace of heart disease. Over thirty-five hundred healthy men were studied for more than a decade. Over two hundred and fifty suffered coronary heart disease. As the researchers note: "Did the dietary data we obtained at the beginning help us to predict who was most apt to succumb later to coronary heart disease? Not at all! Did the amount of physical exercise they took help us to discern those who later fell prey to heart disease? Not at all!"

The personality pattern most accurately predicted future heart disease. Not even one man in the study who had Type B personality and normal blood pressure, serum cholesterol, and fat level developed heart disease. Most of the risk factors established by the American Heart Association at about that time (1960) did not appear to affect such Type B men. Such men did not get heart disease even though they may have been eating diets high in cholesterol and fat, even though they were overweight, even though one or both parents had heart disease, even though they smoked heavily!

The ability to predict future heart disease by Type A Behavior Pattern led the researchers to see if the Type A personality also was largely responsible for causing the heart trouble. To show a cause-and-effect relationship in a scientifically valid way, they had to show that a laboratory animal would get heart disease from emotional changes. Otherwise, the scientific community would say that it was only increased serum cholesterol that was the cause of heart disease. Emotions and personality would be considered as merely an associated factor, unless this cause-and-effect relationship could be proved. So the doctors changed the emotional center in brains of rats to create a viciously aggressive Type A behavior pattern. This emotional change directly caused a marked increase in serum cholesterol! This proved the direct causative chain linking emotions, cholesterol, and heart disease.

Type A Personality

Looking at the different aspects of Type A personality sheds light on how your feelings and behavior affect the health of your heart. The importance of some traits of the Type A have since been shown to be more significant than others in causing heart disease. This ongoing process of change in accepted scientific knowledge is useful to observe. We can see how even expert opinion shifts over time. It serves as a useful reminder that one's health is too important to be left just to the experts.

Resistance to accepting a link between personality and heart disease existed at the highest levels of the scientific establishment in the 1950s. Friedman and Rosenman were turned down for federal research funds several times. Puzzled by the rejections, they asked a friend at the National Institutes of Health why he thought their proposed research was being turned down. He told them that requests to study a "coronary-prone personality" wouldn't be funded. The decision-makers didn't want to hear about personality affecting heart disease. So Friedman and Rosenman changed the title to Type A *Behavior*. Although personality obviously dictates behavior, the word substitution worked. They then got the needed funds for their study.

For the first time, observable behavior patterns had medical significance. Type A habits led to heart disease.

Freidman and Rosenman felt that the most significant trait of the Type A was ongoing struggle against time. They termed it "hurry sickness." Time was the enemy. There was not time to smell the flowers. Type A's created deadlines for themselves to cram more work in faster. Speed became more important than the quality of creative thinking and judgment. This resulted in a loss of adaptability to life's everchanging circumstances.

Another identified trait of the type A was an obsession with numbers as a mark of achievement: numbers of dollars made, numbers of papers published, numbers of widgets produced—quantity instead of quality of life, work, and experiences. This reflects an inability to maintain an inner sense of self-worth. The Type A's inner sense of security is based on the pace at which he climbs the ladder of success, achievement, and status. Ignoring his human need for love and affection, the Type A is a man on a mission, isolated form the solace of friends and family. Superficially confident and eager, the Type A seems so much like the man in the gray flannel suit in corporate America in the 1950s. Indeed, this type of behavior has been observed in thousands of middle managers, dying to please their superiors and get that promotion! Medicine has its fair share of Type A's. The researcher obsessed with the quantity, not the quality, of his work. The physician glorying in the number of patients he can see in a day, not in taking the time to be more helpful to each individual. Sadly, such people do not generate any sympathy from those around them. Tragically, even if they did, they wouldn't know how to respond to love and concern from friends or family.

The final important trait of Type A's is their hostility. Typically Type A's are not aware of their hostility. Such feelings are kept in hiding, even from themselves. Yet, the hostility can be observed in the competitive and challenging nature of these people. Everything from a simple discussion to a friendly game becomes an opportunity for aggression. Type A's are provocative. They look for an argument, rather than passing over a point of contention. Friedman and Rosenman noted hostility as a sub-theme in the Type A. Later researchers have shown that hostility is a main component leading to heart disease.

Type A shows itself in an aggressive manner of speaking, an explosive rhythm of speech, and hurrying at the end of sentences. An impatience at waiting for someone else to finish talking is another mark of the Type A. These aspects are at the core of the structured interviewing technique used by Friedman and Rosenman to spot Type A's. This type of interview brings out the Type A behavior. Questions are posed in a deliberately challenging manner. The vigorous and explosive replies are the hallmark of Type A's. Written questionnaires don't differentiate well between Type A and B, because they both may give similar answers. It is the way the type A verbally engages in battle that distinguishes him from the more matter-of-fact style of the Type B.

Dawn of a New Era

Other researchers began confirming the same findings about Type A personality and heart disease. By the late 1970s, the highest levels of the scientific establishment added their seal of approval. The National Heart, Lung, and Blood Institute created a special review panel to judge the merits of this new scientific work. The conclusion was a landmark. Type A behavior was officially recognized as a greater risk for causing heart disease than high blood pressure, high cholesterol, and smoking!

A revolutionary change was taking place. For the first time, the medical research establishment was saying the mind *does* affect the body. Mental phenomena such as emotions and personality *can* cause heart disease. A new era in behavioral medicine was opening up. Scientists would be encouraged to study how the mind affects the body.

Our understanding of the ways the mind and body work together has deepened in the area of heart disease. Whole new fields have opened up. Studies of how the mind affects the nerves, hormones, and immune system have begun in earnest. Termed psychoneuroimmunology (PNI), this field has shown how the mind can affect other serious illnesses such as cancer. These discoveries have led to the development of short-term, effective, mind-body treatments.

Among the important fruits of this new emphasis on how the mind affects the body has been the discovery that not all of the Type A's behavior is bad for his heart. This ongoing modification of knowledge is a constant feature of science.

Hostility

The new possibilities for research opened up by Friedman and Rosenman resulted in major modifications of their own findings. Ironically, just as the medical research establishment was proclaiming Type A Behavior Pattern as a cause of heart disease, new data began to question the validity of two of the described aspects of the behavior pattern. In his book, *The Trusting Heart*, heart researcher Redford Brown Williams, M.D., tells how new scientific information came to light. Dr. Williams's own research at Duke was crucial in determining that it is hostility, anger, and mistrust that are the personality traits which cause heart disease.

From his own research and the work of others, Dr. Williams began to doubt the validity of the harmful effects on the heart of two major traits of Type A behavior: He called into question why being ambitious, and being in a hurry, should harm the heart. Instead, he began to focus on hostility as the main element of Type A behavior that damages the heart.

Hostile people show their rage in everyday situations. I remember Tim, an angry man, bursting into my office. In a booming voice, he declared, "You won't believe what just happened to me." With hatred in his eyes, he shouted at me, "Some jerk cut me off on the highway." Trying to calm him down, I quietly asked, "What did you do?" With a look of triumph, he shot back, "I raced after him, honking all the way, until I passed him." Holding his chest, he explained, "It's guys like that driver who give me a pain right here." In our work together, Tim began to realize that the real enemy was within—his own hostility waiting to spring forth with the slightest provocation. As part of learning how to take charge of his health, Tim mastered techniques to turn off his hostility.

We can learn how to change our cynical beliefs, angry feelings, and our hostile behavior. We can learn how to heal our heart. The road of scientific knowledge is beginning to link up with the wisdom of two thousand years of religious and spiritual teaching. Science is learning the biological paths by which love, trust, and hope provide healing to the body.

The Stress Connection

The stress response is the link between negative thoughts and feelings and damage to the body. The stress or emergency response is an automatic reflex to danger. This fight-or-flight response served our cavemen ancestors well in the jungle. An irony of modern life is that a biological response that helped save our ancestors is now killing us. Darwin, who wrote about the survival of the fittest, would appreciate this dramatic shift. Survival depends on the ability to adapt to one's environment.

We now know a great deal about how chronic stress wears out the body. Our understanding of how the prolonged stress response wreaks so much havoc owes much to the pioneering work of physician Hans Selye. He is universally and justly regarded as the father of stress research. Starting in the mid 1920s, this hormone specialist made many valuable discoveries that laid the groundwork for the later advances of Friedman and Rosenman and others. His book *The Stress of Life,* published in the mid-1950s, is still a classic. Selye was the first to show the pattern of bodily processes triggered by stress. Our entire system, not just isolated parts, gets caught up in the stress response. He gave a name to this specific series of bodily processes: the General Adaptation Syndrome (G.A.S.). Any source of stress, mental or physical, can trigger the syndrome. Selye's years of research led him to conclude that there were three phases to this reaction: alarm, resistance, and exhaustion.

The first stage is the most dramatic. In this alarm phase, the body rapidly prepares for fight or flight. The mind, through the nervous and hormonal systems, instantly mobilizes the body to deal with the emergency. Adrenaline pumps through your system. Your heart races, your pressure rises, sweat pours off you. You gasp for air as stored energy floods the bloodstream.

If there is no immediate resolution of the conflict, your body enters the second stage. In this phase of resistance, the body digs in for the long haul. We try to learn how to adapt to the stress. A tug-of-war develops. All our energies are focused on survival. Eventually, this takes its toll by grinding us down. For example, the angry, hostile, mistrustful person is on a constant vigil. All his energies are focused on struggling with a world he sees as posing constant threats. The constant triggering of the stress response with the repeated outpouring of adrenaline causes physical damage. The chronic release of stress hormones raises blood pressure and cholesterol and promotes damage to the blood vessels. Plaques begin to form in the blood vessels. As the vessels are narrowed, less blood can get through. This leads to a vicious cycle of even more stress on the system, as reserves get depleted.

The final stage is exhaustion. The body becomes worn out and breaks down. When the body fails in the battle with stress, the result is disease. Signs and symptoms of illness become apparent. Chest pain and heart attack may herald this final stage for the hostile person.

The Relaxation Response

The relaxation response is the body's natural alternative to the stress response. The calming effects of this alternate branch of our system enable us to heal.

Heart specialist Herbert Benson and his colleagues at Harvard have done the pioneering work in establishing our knowledge of this inner healing force. Starting in the late 1960s, Dr. Benson began studying the effects of meditation on the body. This led to his discovery of bodily changes opposite to those caused by stress.

The relaxation response involves slowing heart rate, blood pressure, breathing, and metabolism. As we calm down, blood flows more evenly throughout the body. Our brain waves shift to enable more creative thinking and problem solving. This relaxation or calming response is nature's way of reestablishing peace and harmony. Our mind and body function at an optimal balanced level. Our energy flows smoothly. Equilibrium is reestablished. This set of coordinated changes can be triggered by a number of different techniques. Learning the different approaches to restore calm is a crucial part of taking charge of our health.

High Blood Pressure—the Silent Killer

Stress raises blood pressure. Emotions like anxiety, anger, and fear can increase blood pressure. Normally, blood pressure is kept within a narrow range by internal feedback mechanisms. This happens in a way similar to maintaining a specific room temperature by setting a thermostat. If the room gets too warm, the release of cool air brings the temperature back down. If the room gets too cold, the release of warm air raises the temperature up to the preset level.

Chronic stress ruins the sensitivity of the body's blood pressure "thermostat." The body reads the chronic stress and associated increase of blood pressure as the new level to maintain. It's like resetting the thermostat in your home to maintain a higher room temperature.

The walls of the arteries are muscular and elastic. The walls stretch as the blood pressure rises when the heart muscle contracts. The walls contract as the blood pressure goes down when the heart is filling with blood. This natural ebb and flow occurs with every beat of your heart.

Chronic stress causes the muscular walls of the arteries to contract and thicken, resulting in a hardening of the arteries. This loss of elasticity increases resistance to blood flow. We can measure this as an increase in blood pressure. We can't feel it. We don't experience pain or other symptoms to call our attention to it. Yet, hypertension kills hundreds of thousands of Americans each year. High blood pressure is a major cause of heart disease and stroke.

The heart functions like a pump sending blood into the arteries. As blood flows, it exerts a pressure against the walls of the vessels. Blood pressure devices provide readings of the force of the flow at two different phases of the heart cycle. For example, a doctor may take a blood pressure reading and tell a patient that it is normal at 110/70. The larger number is called the systolic pressure. This reflects the pressure at which blood is forced out of the heart as the heart muscle contracts. The smaller number corresponds to the phase in which the heart is filling up with blood prior to its next contraction. This smaller number is called the diastolic pressure.

Generally accepted guidelines exist for distinguishing high from normal blood pressure readings. The World Health organization considers the ranges for normal resting blood pressure to be 100–140/60–90. This means that normal range for systolic pressure is between 100 and 140. Again, this reflects blood pressure when the heart contracts. Normal range for diastolic pressure is between 60 to 90. This reflects blood pressure when the heart is filling. Borderline hypertension is when the range is between 140–160/90–95. High blood pressure is anything over 160/95.

Systolic pressure normally fluctuates a great deal, as it reflects the force exerted when the heart contracts. However, diastolic pressure reflects the average pressure the system must bear continually, since it reflects the baseline pressure while the heart is filling before the next contraction.

Thus, even small increases in diastolic pressure can have serious consequences. This is reflected in classifying the severity of hypertension according to diastolic pressure alone. Diastolic values between 90 to 105 reflect mild hypertension; numbers between 105 and 115 indicate moderate hypertension; any diastolic over 120 shows severe high blood pressure.

Learning How to Lower Your Blood Pressure

As we have noted, the chronic triggering of the stress response causes high blood pressure to develop. Mind-body techniques that turn off the fight-flight response and trigger the relaxation response can lower blood pressure.

Studies began to appear in the early 1970s showing that people already suffering with high blood pressure can learn to lower it. Most of these studies, however, used highly motivated volunteers, as Chandra Patel, M.D., has noted in the introduction to her *Therapist's Manual for Training Hypertensive Patients in Relaxation and Stress Management*. In addition, many of these earlier studies had other shortcomings. As Dr. Patel points out, often no control group of patients was studied. A control group has characteristics similar to the group being tested. The one difference is that patients in the control group would not learn methods to deal with their stress response. The control group is important because it would clearly show that triggering the relaxation response was the factor that enabled people in the test group to lower their blood pressure. Another shortcoming of these early studies was that in addition to being highly motivated, the volunteers were often taking blood pressure medication at the same time as learning stress-reduction methods. This makes it difficult to tell just what was causing the decrease in blood pressure. A final problem common to much of this early research was a relatively short period of following up on how patients did after learning the relaxation skills. Could the benefits really last or were they merely short-term?

Throughout the 1970s and 1980s, Dr. Patel extended the frontier of the effectiveness of relaxation and stress management in lowering blood pressure. Her work has continually set the standard in the field. A British-trained physician, she is based in London. She talks about how her growing up in India gave her an appreciation of the benefits of yoga training for calming the mind and body. At the time, she didn't think of the breathing and meditation aspects of yoga as having medical treatment value. Instead, she looked to training in the latest developments of scientific, technological Western medicine to guide her treatment of patients. However, she began to see that even the latest advances in drug therapy were not helping many of her patients with the stresses in their lives. These stresses both contributed to high blood pressure and made it more difficult to deal with the hypertension.

The turning point in her approach to helping her patients occurred one night when Dr. Patel was the physician on call at the hospital. This means that she was responsible for any problems that might arise during the night. One of her patients was in distress. Following standard practice, she prescribed more drugs to ease the situation. Every few hours through the night, the distress would break through stronger than the medication. Dr. Patel realized that something more than drugs was needed. This patient had to learn how to deal with stress before it got to be a medical crisis. Dr. Patel recalled the soothing effects of yoga breathing and meditation. Her insight proved helpful to the distressed patient. She soon found that many of her patients could quickly learn and benefit from these ancient practices.

Dr. Patel began to study how effective relaxation training could be for lowering her patients' blood pressure. In the early 1970s, she showed that relaxation training enabled the majority of patients to lower the amount of blood pressure drugs they took. Given the troublesome side effects of these drugs that we have noted, needing less of them permits the enjoyment of a fuller life.

By the mid 1970s, Dr. Patel developed methods enabling people to use relaxation and mediation in their daily lives. Patients learned new habits for dealing with stress. Dramatic reductions in blood pressure resulted. As noted earlier, systolic refers to blood pressure when the heart muscle contracts; diastolic refers to pressure as the heart fills with blood before its next contraction. Both are measured in millimeters of mercury (mmHg). Patients using stress-management methods lowered systolic 26 mmHg and lowered diastolic 15 mmHg! In this study, Dr. Patel used a control group of patients who rested on a couch for the same amount of time as the stress-management group did their training.

Significantly, the patients who merely rested hardly had any decrease in their blood pressure. Rest alone did not significantly lower blood pressure, because just resting does not turn off the stress response. It's important to note that the patients in the study were chosen randomly. This eliminated the bias of earlier studies that used only highly motivated volunteers. In addition, the study was conducted as a crossover trial. This means that the experimental group doing the stress-management training and the control group just resting were interchanged during the course of the study. This showed that it was the training, not any characteristics of the particular people, that caused the dramatic results. All the patients in the study had moderately severe hypertension (diastolic of at least 110) and all the patients received a constant dosage of blood pressure drugs.

Dr. Patel then began to think about what significant points still needed to be determined. She decided that her next study needed to answer five questions.

First, she knew that one of every five adults suffers from mild hypertension. Could they, as well as the moderately severe hypertensive patients, benefit from stress management?

Second, she noted that the previously studied patients were taking blood pressure drugs. It was possible that patients were taking the drugs more consistently when they reduced their stress. It was important to rule out increased patient compliance with the prescribed medication regimens as causing the dramatic results. This could be tested by a new study with patients not taking any medications. Could benefits of the stress-reduction methods be confirmed in patients not taking blood pressure drugs at the start of the new study?

Third, Dr. Patel was concerned about delivering the most effective treatment at the lowest cost to the patient. Could people learn in a group setting, rather than by more expensive individual treatment?

Fourth, would people who worked at jobs full-time find it acceptable to take the time to practice the needed skills?

Finally, Dr. Patel wanted to demonstrate that the effectiveness was due to the method and not due to any unique aspects of her relationship with her patients. Would the methods work with people whom she had not known previously?

Dr. Patel's next study, published in 1981, answered all five questions with a resounding YES!

In the study, more than one thousand workers were screened. Over two hundred were selected for having at least two of three risk factors: hypertension, high cholesterol, and smoking more than a half-pack of cigarettes a day. They were randomly put into treatment or control groups. Both groups got health-education literature with advice to decrease fat intake and stop smoking.

The treatment group learned stress management. Significantly, the total time required was just one hour once a week for eight weeks, plus three lunchtime meetings. Training in breathing, relaxation, meditation, and biofeedback usage was given. Follow-up results were documented after eight weeks, eight months, and four years.

After four years, the gains were maintained! The effectiveness of stress management for lowering blood pressure had long-lasting value. In addition, greater reduction in cigarette smoking, as well as greater decrease in cholesterol, occurred in the group trained to deal with stress. Diet was not a factor in these changes.

Within eight weeks of starting relaxation training, blood tests showed decreases in components related to both stress and hypertension. The body's blood pressure "thermostat" appeared to be resetting back to a lower, normal level.

Another significant result emerged from the study: a strong trend of lower morbidity (rate of sickness) and lower mortality (death) from heart disease for the stress-management group. After four years, not even one fatal heart attack occurred among those trained in triggering the relaxation response. Unfortunately, the same could not be said for the control group, which did not learn how to turn off the stress response.

In addition, after four years, the trained patients reported one-quarter the number of episodes of chest pain and heart attack as did the untrained patients. Finally, EKGs were done and coded "blindly." This means that the technician didn't know whether the person who got the cardiogram was in the treatment or control group. This independent verification helped to rule out the possibility of a bias in the self-reports by the patients. Five times as many patients in the untrained control group as in the stress management group showed documented EKG changes indicative of heart attack.

Controlling Hypertension Without Drugs

Dr. Patel noted that while the results of the study were very encouraging, she saw the need for an even larger and more definitive trial. By the mid 1980s, she realized that four more questions needed to be answered by her next study.

First, since her prior study had shown that she could teach people to lower their blood pressure even though she hadn't worked with them before, could general practitioners be trained quickly in the techniques so that they could successfully teach their own hypertensive patients?

Second, Dr. Patel was concerned about patients being on long-term drug treatment for mild hypertension, given the previously discussed side effects of the drugs. Could these people stop taking drugs and control their blood pressure just with relaxation training?

Third, she knew that some patients would need to continue taking drugs because of the severity of their high blood pressure. Could relaxation training let them have a better quality of life by enabling them to lower their blood pressure with less medication?

Finally, Dr. Patel wanted more evidence about the ability of relaxation training to lower the rate of sickness and death from heart disease. She hoped that the doctors and patients in the study could shed more light on the ultimate question of achieving a healthier and longer life.

Once again, all the questions were answered with a resounding *yes* in Dr. Patel's study published in 1988. The study involved a huge number of people. All the patients had previously been part of a treatment trial of mild hypertension in which over seventeen thousand patients and almost two hundred physicians took part. The patients selected for this study had already been treated for six previous years with blood pressure drugs.

Their medical doctors were trained over a weekend. These general practitioners then taught the relaxation techniques to their own patients. The total time used to teach patients was just one hour a week for only eight weeks. Patients were taught in groups of ten. They learned general stress-management techniques and specific ways to trigger the relaxation response by using meditation, breathing exercises, muscle relaxation, and biofeedback. Using these techniques to decrease stress in daily life was the prime goal of the training.

Follow-up examinations of the patients occurred after eight weeks, three months, six months, and one year. The results showed that physicians quickly learn and effectively teach relaxation techniques. This is important because "Most heart attacks occur among the large number of people with mild to moderate levels of risk factor. General practitioners are in a key position to help prevent coronary heart disease." This quote from Dr. Patel's conclusions once again shows the powerful benefits patients can get from working with their doctors to take charge of their health.

The study documented that patients who had required medication for six years to control their blood pressure could stop taking the drugs! Using relaxation therapy only, these patients could maintain their pressure at the level that had been achieved previously through drugs. In addition, those patients who continued to take their drugs got to even lower pressure readings with the use of relaxation techniques.

Thus, the results showed that quality of life could improve by using safe and effective relaxation training to replace or decrease the amount of drugs needed to control blood pressure.

The study also showed the benefits of relaxation training for maintaining a healthy heart. No patients got a heart attack. No patients showed any EKG changes even suggestive of blood shortage to the heart. No patients reported any episodes of chest pain. Unfortunately, the control group members who did not learn how to handle their stress experienced various serious symptoms.

Heart Disease—Often Silent Until Fatal

Severe damage can result from prolonged hypertension. The higher blood pressure required to force blood through the narrower vessels can cause the vessel walls to weaken and tear. Arteriosclerosis is the medical term for hardening of the arteries. To repair the damage, scar tissue forms. This mass often includes cholesterol and is called atherosclerosis.

The blood vessels that nourish the heart muscle are named coronary arteries. Coronary artery disease occurs when these blood vessels are damaged by atherosclerosis. These thickened blood vessels provide less blood supply to the heart. This blood shortage to the heart proceeds silently. As Friedman and Rosenman note:

> Not even an electrocardiogram (EKG) taken after the severest sort of physical activity will necessarily reveal the presence of those potentially dangerous plaques. This is so because the EKG records nothing but the excitatory electrical stimulus coursing along the fibers of the heart. Thus, unless a plaque cuts down the blood flow through a coronary vessel 85 to 95 percent, its presence will not show up on an EKG. To be noticed, it must block 90 percent or more of the artery through which the blood is flowing.

It is possible not to experience any pain or show any evidence of heart disease until only 10 percent of the usual blood flow is being used to nourish the heart muscle. Without any prior warning, it is possible to have a fatal heart attack.

Chest Pain

When angina pectoris or chest pain occurs, even the bravest person can be overcome by fear that he is having a heart attack. Chest pain is a warning sign to be taken seriously. However, an attack of chest pain is not the same as having a heart attack. As Friedman and Rosenman remark, chest pain is "just a form of 'body language' whereby the heart indicates it temporarily lacks oxygen." They note that it is a sign of danger that says, "See a doctor." However, "No permanent or significant damage is done to the heart during or following the attack" of chest pain.

They point out that heart specialists use the term angina pectoris to designate chest pain when decreased blood flow to the heart causes a lack of oxygen to the heart muscle. This state of oxygen shortage is termed ischemia. As previously noted, by the time one experiences this type of chest pain, he may have only 10 percent of the usual blood flow going to the heart muscle. Even with such minimal blood flow there may be enough oxygen going to the heart while sleeping. The experience of chest pain does not occur until there is more activity and an increased demand on the heart. Emotional stress can tip this delicate balance as easily as trying to digest a heavy meal. The experience of anginal pain is the heart's way of screaming for more oxygen.

How to Deal with Chest Pain

Immediately stop all physical activity! Rest, sit down, or lie down. This is the way to react to chest pain. As the previous discussion shows, anginal pain screams, "More oxygen." The only way to get more oxygen to the heart immediately is by decreasing the demands from the rest of the body.

Unfortunately, many people do just the opposite. They immediately react to chest pain by testing their bodies to reassure themselves that they are not having a heart attack. Let me give you an example of this common reaction by a patient of mine. Jim is in his early forties. He exercises regularly to keep fit. He started working with me because of chest pain. I asked him to describe his first experience of the pain.

"I am in the gym, pedaling on the exercise bike," he began. "I'm just doing my normal routine. Suddenly, I get this tight feeling in the middle of my chest. I get scared. I notice I'm sweating more, too. I say to myself, 'This can't be. I can't be getting a heart attack.' "

"What did you do?" I asked.

"I rubbed my chest where it felt sore and kept pedaling to work through the ache. You know what they say, no pain, no gain," he added with a smile.

"But you said you were worried that you were getting a heart attack. Why didn't you just stop your workout?" I asked.

"I guess I wanted to reassure myself that it was really nothing serious," Jim replied.

At that moment, Jim couldn't deal with the possibility that his chest pain might indicate serious heart trouble. He used a common psychological defense mechanism known as denial. Denial operates on an unconscious level. Denial enables us to avoid facing a personal problem by not consciously acknowledging the reality of the situation. Denial permitted Jim to avoid confronting his deep-seated fear of death. He reacted in a way to counter the existence of his fear. He needed to prove that nothing serious was happening.

Jim was lucky. His chest pain was being caused by tension in the muscle wall of his chest, not by a shortage of blood to his heart. He was able to work through the sore muscle in the gym. Our discussion of the episode enabled him to begin to see that he was avoiding looking at important areas of his life that were causing him stress and muscle spasms in his chest wall.

Jim's experience points up the fact that when chest pain occurs, it is not possible to know if it reflects serious trouble inside the body. It is of utmost necessity to respect the signal of the pain and stop to rest, whether the pain indicates heart trouble or not. Chest pain can be the first sign of a developing heart attack. A blockage of one of the coronary arteries that supplies blood to the heart muscle causes a heart attack. The area of the heart muscle that loses its blood supply of oxygen dies. This is technically termed a myocardial infarction.

Even when someone has already suffered a heart attack, he or she can use the mind-body technique to assist in reversing existing hardening of the arteries. Thus, one can help prevent getting another heart attack.

Reversing Heart Disease Without Surgery

Most heart doctors would say it could not be done, even as recently as the late 1980s. The medical establishment did not believe that it was possible to reverse existing heart disease by just making changes in your life-style. The standard approach to deal with hardening of the arteries was major surgery. If the arteries going to the heart were clogged, the accepted treatment was surgery. Coronary bypass surgery became standard operating procedure.

It was one thing to show that hostility, stress, and high blood pressure led to heart disease. By the late 1980s, the medical establishment accepted the evidence that it was possible to prevent the buildup of fatty deposits in arteries by learning how to change personality traits, trigger the relaxation response, and lower blood pressure. It has even become accepted that it is possible to lower cholesterol by learning how to deal with stress.

But once the arteries to the heart became seriously blocked, it was considered a different matter entirely. For example, symptoms of heart disease, like chest pain, don't usually appear until the arteries feeding the heart are over two-thirds blocked. Cineangiography is the test used to document the extent of blockage. A dye is injected into the bloodstream. Motion-picture photography records the passage of the dye through the blood vessels.

Surgery was considered the only way to deal with existing blockage. Coronary bypass surgery is a long and complicated major operation. The chest is cut open. Healthy vessels are surgically removed from other parts of the body. They are sewn to the heart to bypass the blocked coronary vessels. By the late 1980s, a less radical surgical procedure was being used, when possible, before resorting to major bypass surgery. This type of surgical repair of a blood vessel is called angioplasty. The procedure involves threading an inflatable tube through the circulatory system until it gets inside the constricted artery. Then the tube is inflated to compress the mass of plaque against the wall of the blood vessel. Although less risky than bypass surgery, angioplasty involves risks such as rupture of the wall of the artery when the cholesterol mass is compressed against it.

The only possible alternative to surgery that the medical community saw was new and powerful drugs. The idea was to develop a chemical that acted like Drano, cleaning a clogged sewer pipe. The search was on for something corrosive enough to dissolve clots while sparing the vessels. Indeed, in 1987, some small progress in this direction was reported. A new drug, colestipol, used in combination with large doses of niacin (a member of the Vitamin B complex) showed some decrease in artery blockage but only in 15 percent of the patients in a study.

Clearly, something else was needed. To the surprise of the medical establishment, the breakthrough came not from a newer drug or surgical procedure. The breakthrough came from people taking charge of their health by changing their life-styles. Learning how to cope with stress was a key element.

Created by Dr. Dean Ornish, the "Opening Your Heart Program" focused on stress management exercises and helped over 80 percent of the people in the program to open up their blocked coronary arteries! These dramatic results were presented to the American Heart Association in late 1988.

The "Lifestyle Heart Trial" study built on over ten years of research by Dr. Ornish. In his recent book, *Dr. Dean Ornish's Program for Reversing Heart Disease,* he describes in detail how patients can help heal their hearts. His stress-management exercises include meditation, breathing, relaxation, and mental imagery. Dr. Ornish's program includes a low-calorie, low-cholesterol diet and moderate exercise such as brisk walking, but "he puts unique trust in his meditation/relaxation exercises. He believes they bring in deeper changes of the spirit." This quote from a special mind-heart issue of *Psychology Today* (January 1989) comes from an interview with Dr. Ornish by Editor-in-Chief T. George Harris. In the same article, Dr. Ornish reveals his concerns about how carrying around negative mental baggage can weigh down the heart.

Dean Ornish . . . talks privately to friends about a problem that troubles most of his heart patients: the need to support a "persona," a presented self that does not jibe with the real self. One of the individuals in his experimental group claimed to have been an Olympic athlete, though the man had never been anywhere near a champ's role.

Cholesterol levels plummeted in the treatment group. This further quote from T. George Harris once again reveals the power of taking control of your health.

The successful patients in the experimental group reduced their total cholesterol level by 40 percent and the level of the harmful kind of cholesterol (low-density lipoprotein) by 60 percent. These were the biggest drops ever achieved without drugs in an experiment. Patients also brought down their blood pressure, enough in most cases to reduce or go off medications.

Such a powerful reduction in cholesterol is even more impressive in comparison with the control group. Those patients had only tiny decreases. Average total cholesterol dropped less than 10 percent. Harmful cholesterol dropped less than 15 percent. These poor results occurred even though the control group was given the best of today's traditional medical care. This included advice on lowering their cholesterol and blood pressure, as well as stopping smoking. Yet 55 percent of the patients in this control group got measurably worse. Their heart disease problems progressed. Interestingly, the men "who improved proudly admitted cheating. They had wanted to get into the experimental program so badly, they made some of Ornish's lifestyle changes on their own," noted Harris.

Preventing a Second Heart Attack

Recent scientific research has documented that learning how to cope with negative emotions, such as hostility and depression, can prevent a second heart attack. A landmark eight-year study has also shown that emotions are more important than extent of heart disease, cholesterol, and diet in predicting who lives and who dies from a second heart attack.

The principal researcher, Dr. Carl Thoreson, professor at Stamford University, noted that the basic problem involves low self-esteem. In men, this manifests itself in hostility and anger. In women, this gets expressed in anxiety, fear, and phobias. In both men and women, underlying these negative emotions were depression and low self-esteem. More important, the research documents that learning how to change such self-defeating behavior could prevent a second heart attack. Even after eight years, the emotional changes protected them against suffering another heart attack.

The study was funded by the National Heart, Lung and Blood Institute. The findings confirm other recent research, indicating that chronic stress and negative emotions affect many serious illnesses ranging from breast cancer to immune disorders.

Sudden Death from Stress

"I still can't believe it," she cried. "It happened so suddenly. I was getting more groceries while my husband Ted went to get on the check-out line. He got into an argument with another man about who was there first. No blows were exchanged, just shouting. All of a sudden, Ted turned blue in the face, keeled over, and collapsed. I rushed to him. Someone got smelling salts. Nothing helped. He died in my arms." Barbara wept inconsolably. Through her tears she added, "He seemed in good health. Just the day before he saw our doctor and everything, including his heart, seemed OK."

Ted's sudden death was triggered by stress. Sadly, his is far from a unique case. Every minute of every day, others die suddenly, usually without warning. In an earlier book, *Stress, Diet, and Your Health*, Dr. Dean Ornish notes that close to two thirds of people "who die from coronary heart disease do not die from heart attacks (myocardial infarction)—they die from what is called, quite appropriately, sudden cardiac death. Most of these people are in the most productive phase of their lives, seemingly healthy men in their forties and fifties."

What is happening to these people, that they die so suddenly? In most cases, the rhythm of their heartbeat suddenly becomes wildly irregular. The heart muscle can't contract effectively to such a chaotic rhythm. Not enough blood gets pumped out of the heart. In a few minutes the brain dies from lack of blood and oxygen. Ventricular fibrillation is the medical term for this deadly process. The left ventricle is the chamber of the heart that contracts to push blood out into the arteries. Fibrillation is the rapid irregular contractions that can result in the heart ineffectively twitching instead of effectively pumping blood. The heart muscle becomes a useless quivering mass incapable of sustaining life.

The role of stress in causing sudden death has been recognized throughout history. Extreme emotional upset has often been the trigger. Intense anger, rage, and fear can trigger the stress response. The emergency messages go to the brain, which releases stress hormones that speed up the heart rate and may alter the normal heart rhythm.

All of us have experienced our heart skipping a beat. This variation typically quickly corrects itself. The danger occurs when, instead of self-correcting, the heartbeat spins out of control, leading to ineffective heart-muscle contraction. Dr. Ornish notes an interesting example in his earlier book. He recounts that *The New England Journal of Medicine* published a letter from a physician about a patient who was an avid Boston Celtics basketball fan. While watching an exciting playoff game on television, the patient's EKG was monitored. The frequency of irregular heartbeats increased as the game continued. The irregularities became more pathological. In the final minutes of this nip-and-tuck Celtics game, the patient had five episodes of ventricular tachycardia (a racing heartbeat), which in many cases leads to ventricular fibrillation.

The Celtics finally won by one point. Gradually over the next two hours, the irregular heartbeats decreased. Learning how to turn off the stress response can help return the heart to its rhythm.

Putting It All Together

You can learn how to heal your heart. The work discussed in this chapter created a revolution in medical thinking and practice. The evidence clearly showed that the mind affects the health of the body. Your emotions and personality, values, and beliefs—all affect your physical well-being. Science began to show, using its own methodology, the value of thousands of years of religious and philosophical teachings on how to lead a good life. By combining the wisdom of the past with modern advances, a new healing approach has evolved. Effective and easily learned techniques have helped individuals to tap their own inner resources for health.

One of the most feared killers, heart disease, has been giving ground to these new methods of mind-body healing. Studies have proven that cholesterol, hypertension, and heart disease itself are made worse by stress; and, more important, can be reversed by your own efforts.

Many heart specialists have been responsible for the research breakthroughs discussed in this chapter. They have developed similar treatment programs. They all emphasize turning off the stress response. They use different combinations of such effective techniques as abdominal breathing, muscle relaxation, and biofeedback to help restore calm to the body. Some help people tap into their mental powers with such techniques as meditation, imagery, and visualization. The training programs use education and behavior modification to help change harmful habits. These beneficial methods can help you control other ills, in addition to heart disease.

All the leading researchers realize that the most difficult roadblocks to healthier hearts can be found in the mind. People can easily learn what they need to do to improve their health. Unfortunately, many of us find it difficult to continue the new habits as part of our daily life.

My training and years of experience as a psychiatrist have given me the background and opportunity to help people remove the roadblocks and free up their willpower to take charge of their health. You can release the energy trapped in unconscious mental conflicts and use the power to develop a healthy self. You can learn how to find the inner strength to actually do what you know is right for you. You can take an exciting journey of self-discovery. Throughout history, religious and philosophical leaders have spoken about these hidden powers of the mind as the soul, and their energy, as the spirit. You can call upon these natural, God-given forces to take charge of your health.

Chapter 9

A Desperate Call for Help— Susan's Story

Eating Disorders

Eating disorders can be life-threatening. Stress plays a major role in all eating disorders from the most common—overeating—to the most feared—anorexia and bulimia. Although people suffer from different types of eating disorders, many share a common stressor: an inner conflict of being loved.

The earliest bond, between mother and infant, fuses together love, nurturance, and feeding. As the child grows and begins the process of developing its own self, the blissful earlier oneness with mother is broken. This normal process of individuation often becomes a power struggle between mother and child over the pace and extent of the development of the child's autonomy and separation of self from the mother. Often, the battleground becomes food. How much and what the child eats is sometimes the only area in which he or she feels able to assert any power of self-determination in relation to the mother. Thus, difficulties in the earliest relationship between mother and child can sow the seeds of an eating disorder. The form the problem takes—be it over- or undereating, or more serious disorders such as anorexia or bulimia—is influenced by the intensity, duration, and severity of the mother-child conflict.

Starting with the mother-child relationship, links are formed among love, connectedness, struggles for self-determination, and food. In addition, each new love relationship or lack of one has its own problems which can trigger emotional difficulties that become visible as an eating disorder.

In this chapter, I have chosen to write about Susan's story because her life-threatening difficulties in swallowing presented a baffling puzzle until it became apparent that it involved an unusual form of eating disorder. But first, let us review three other stress-related disorders that Susan also suffered from.

Chronic Fatigue, Severe Allergies, and Multiple Chemical Sensitivities (M.C.S.)

A growing number of people are going to doctors with chief complaints ranging from chronic tiredness, to severe allergies to many substances, to extreme sensitivity to various common foods and chemicals. Their symptoms can include fatigue, confusion, depression, nausea, headaches, difficulty swallowing, dizziness, rashes, trouble breathing, stuffed and runny nose, and eyes watering with tears. Typically, after a thorough medical evaluation, no known illness can be found as the cause of the symptoms.

Researchers have recently found evidence of chronic activation of the immune system in many of these patients. Yet, current laboratory tests lack the sophistication to identify the cause of overactivity within the immune system of these sufferers. Consequently and tragically, these patients are often dismissed as hypochondriacs. But much like canaries who have more sensitive systems, and therefore were used in coal mines to give early warning of lethal air, these people's sensitivities may be forecasting what problems will exist for all of us if we don't take heed of the chemical load with which we are polluting our environment.

Our physiology has gradually evolved over hundreds of thousands of years to enable us to survive in a relatively stable environment. But in the name of progress and gross national products, we are radically altering everything from the food we eat, to the clothes we wear, to the air we breathe. Now these drastic changes are taking their toll on uncounted victims among us.

Sadly, these patients are often dismissed as atypical of the human race because of some studies pointing to their histories of suffering from psychological symptoms such as anxiety, depression, and panic disorder.

Indeed they do, but the proper conclusion to be drawn from this fact is that these people are just more sensitive reactors than the rest of us are. Their mind-body reactions occur at exposure levels that are slightly lower than those that would affect the rest of us.

While there is not yet a generally accepted cure for this syndrome, my experience in working with people suffering from it is that they can decrease their sensitivity by learning how to turn off their stress response using mind-body techniques.

Perhaps the chronic-stress response itself is triggering a chronic activation of the immune system. We know that an allergy is an overreaction of the immune system to a substance. While these patients demonstrate a valid allergic response to chemicals, the extent of their symptoms may be exacerbated by the chronic triggering of the body's stress response.

The Common Cold and Stress

In a related development, a recent breakthrough study has documented for the first time that increased psychological stress leads to increased rates of infection by common cold viruses. The research showed a dose-related connection between stress and illness; the bigger the dose of stress a person experiences, the greater the likelihood of becoming infected when exposed to cold viruses. Interestingly, Jane Brody, the *New York Times* science reporter, notes in her August 29, 1991, article on the study that "no relationship was found between immune measures and the occurrence of viral infection or clinical colds." She then quotes the author of the study, Dr. Sheldon Cohen, as saying, "This does not mean the immune system was not involved, just that the factors we studied were not responsible for the observed relationship between stress and illness."

I find it significant that the current laboratory tests of immune function are not sophisticated enough to determine the specific mechanism responsible for the lowered resistance to colds in those suffering from stress. Just as with chronic fatigue, our current knowledge of the immune system is not able to explain exactly how stress causes the observed increased susceptibility to illness.

Dr. Cohen's study, "Psychological Stress and Susceptibility to the Common Cold," is considered so important that the world's most respected medical publication, *The New England Journal of Medicine,* chose to publish it. In addition, the editors of the *Journal* highlighted the importance of this study and other recent advances in our knowledge of how psychological stress affects our health in a separate editorial, "Stress and the Common Cold," by Morton Swartz, M.D., of the prestigious Massachusetts General Hospital (affiliated with Harvard Medical School). Dr. Swartz notes how Dr. Cohen's work continues the progress of our understanding of mind-body interaction that the emerging field of psychoneuroimmunology research has begun to reveal. Both the editorial and the original research article are in the August 29, 1991, issue of *The New England Journal of Medicine*.

The emerging field of psychoneuroimmunology (PNI) research may hold the answer. Aleady, researchers have shown that our emotions, nervous system, and immune system are directly interconnected. As our knowledge of these linkages develops, we may learn the specific biochemical mechanisms that underlly our clinical observations that emotional stress plays an important role in making sensitive reactors more allergic to common substances. Now to Susan's story.

I could hear the fear in the voice of the woman who said she was calling long distance from Texas. She was speaking just above a whisper. I had to strain to hear her opening question: "Can I please speak to Dr. Moskowitz? I read about his work with stress in the *Newsweek* magazine cover story." When I responded that she was indeed speaking to me, a note of surprise and relief came into her voice as she blurted out, "I feel like I'm dying. I'm totally exhausted all the time."

Now it was my turn to register surprise at her apparent sense of doom. I asked her to tell me why she felt she was dying. In her wispy voice, she said her problems with swallowing over the last two years had progressed to such an extreme that she was having difficulty just sipping water. She had grown weak from her inability to eat any solid foods for months. She continued, "I really became desperate when I found that I couldn't even swallow soup that I had put through a strainer."

I was mentally going through the different diagnostic possibilities of this woman's chief complaint as I asked her what medical evaluation she had received. She began her answer by remarking that she was a physician herself and gave me her name. (I will refer to her as Susan.) Susan proceeded to describe, in medical terms, an odyssey through the full array of the latest medical technology. This ordeal included: time-and-motion studies of her swallowing barium for an upper GI series under the watchful eye of radiologists; detailed medical workups by internists, gastroenterologists; and even consultation with an ear, nose, and throat specialist. No possible methods of examination from the most sophisticated to the standard battery of blood tests and X rays had been over-looked. Over the two-year period, many studies were repeated, both by doctors at the hospital where she worked and at a nationally renowned medical center. All the tests were negative. No one could find any cause for her continuing inability to swallow. She was becoming progressively more debilitated through her lack of normal nutrition and a mounting terror that her body was out of control.

Of course, as the "body" doctors continued to find nothing to explain or help Susan's problem, she was referred to a "head" doctor. The psychiatrist told her she was suffering from anxiety, and prescribed tranquilizers to "calm her nerves." Instead of helping, she described how the tranquilizers slowed up her mind as well as her body. She found it increasingly difficult to function in her work as a physician and had to stop the drugs, since she felt they impaired her further. The sessions with the psychiatrist didn't help either. While Susan found the sessions to be interesting discussions of her past, including her childhood, she did not gain any insight or make any association that helped her find relief. Susan concluded her detailed description of the treatment she received with a discussion of her search for help from a behavioral psychologist. Just as the other doctors before had done what they knew best, the behaviorist examined the problem from his unique perspective. Unfortunately, this failed just as all the previous treatments approaches had.

As soon as she concluded this detailed analysis of her prior treatment, Susan said with evident desperation in her voice, "I feel like I'm at the end of the line. I've tried everything and things are getting worse. My body is out of control and I hardly have any energy to work. I can't go on like this. Can you help me?"

I paused for a moment before replying. As I surveyed my own thoughts, I made a mental note of the fact that indeed Susan had been through every possible diagnostic and treatment approach in the standard and accepted universe of the most up-to-date medical and psychological practice. I also thought to myself that the techniques that I and a few other medical pioneers in the field of stress-related disorders have developed have helped people in desperate straits like Susan's. I also realized that she was a physician living and working halfway across the country.

I told Susan that there was cause for hope. I said that the possibility existed for her to regain control of her swallowing and of herself. I added that while there were no guarantees, she could learn how to reverse this progressive debilitation.

Susan's voice showed a trace of relief that there was hope for her. She told me she needed a few weeks to arrange coverage of her own medical practice and made an appointment to see me in my office.

Looking Like a Skeleton

Susan arrived half an hour early for our first meeting. Looking at her for the first time provided visual confirmation of the mental image I had formed of her from our phone call. I was immediately struck by her gaunt appearance. Indeed, she had been wasting away from chronic malnutrition. Her face had a haggard look and her slowed movement belied her low energy. Her eyes showed the fear she felt inside. However, as a thorough physician, she was insistent on beginning, in classical good medical form, with a detailed history of the events she had sketched out to me on the phone. She began by saying she was in her mid-thirties. Up until three years ago, she could eat anything. "I loved pizza, the stringier the cheese, the better," she said, as she recounted that seemingly distant time when she felt normal.

Susan recalled the first sign of trouble as beginning three years earlier when she began noticing that while she was on her usual one-hour drive from home to office, she began feeling that her throat was very dry. She started to carry water with her on the drive and soon found herself depending on it being there to allay the discomfort at feeling that she did not have enough saliva in her mouth. At about the same time, she noticed that elevators and airplanes made her feel queasy. With her medical knowledge, she termed this claustrophobia. Sometime between two and three years ago, she felt an increase in the frequency of these symptoms, but believed she could basically handle the situation. She began to experience a fear of heights, and for the first time in her life, felt hesitant about flying. She was particularly surprised by this symptom, she said, "because I had been flying in airplanes since I was nine years old." She particularly remembered that many times during college she flew in bad weather conditions, without any upset or fear, to and from her university in the Midwest.

At this point in her narration, Susan paused and let out a big sigh, saying, "Two years ago, things really started going downhill." She recalled receiving a phone call from her mother, who still lived in New Jersey where Susan grew up. Her mother told her that her grandmother was gravely ill. Susan's voice began to falter as she continued her story. "I was always very attached to my grandmother." When Susan's mother called, she told Susan that Granny was in the hospital and "it didn't look like she was going to make it." Susan knew that Granny had been suffering with a life-threatening lymphoma. So she immediately decided to go home to New Jersey from Texas to be with Granny in her final days. By this time, Susan's own fear of flying had progressed to such a paralyzing point that she took a train home. When she got to New York, she rented a car and on the George Washington Bridge was held up in a typical traffic jam. She found herself feeling trapped in her car, feeling everything in her life was spinning out of control. She felt her heart pound and sweat poured out of her body. She realized she was having a panic attack.

She barely was able to finish the drive to the hospital. When she got there, she rushed to Granny's room. There she was, frail and tired. Susan tried feeding her, but to no avail. Her grandmother had a mass in her neck that pressed on her esophagus making it impossible to swallow. Susan continued to describe how she felt a wave of nausea throughout her own body. She couldn't bear the sight of her beloved grandmother wasting away. Over the next few days, she went to the hospital religiously. However, she couldn't bring herself to go back into her grandmother's room to see her dying. Within the week, Granny passed away. Susan felt so anxious during this ordeal that she saw a psychiatrist, a friend of the family, who prescribed Valium, "which really didn't help," Susan said.

Soon after, Susan returned to Texas and her medical practice. She felt her own condition progressively deteriorating. Gradually, one type of food after another became too difficult for her to swallow. "First I couldn't eat steak, then veal, then chicken, finally even soups were too thick to swallow," she said to me. "Even food in liquid form had too much consistency for me to swallow comfortably—either things were too thick, oily, or greasy." Susan said she felt that she had no control over her swallowing and that terrified her. "The food would trickle down my throat. I couldn't do anything about it." Needless to say, Susan continued losing weight. As the symptoms worsened, her physician in Texas prescribed an increase in the dose of Valium to calm her nerves. Instead, she found herself getting more lethargic from the drug. She found it harder to work under the influence of medication that was making her tired and sleepy.

Six weeks before she called me, her fears had increased to the point where she believed that if she tried to swallow any food of a somewhat solid consistency, she could choke to death. Becoming even more desperate, she consulted a psychologist, who told Susan that she was hysterical. Unfortunately, the psychologists's treatment approach involving behavioral desensitization did not help. Two weeks before calling me, Susan even consulted an acupuncturist. Again, no relief.

By now, Susan had begun to lose confidence in getting any help. She began to "treat" herself by using alcohol to "enable me to eat better." At first, she would drink one or two martinis to lubricate the way for food. Quickly, Susan found that this home remedy of hers now required four to five martinis and did not facilitate smooth eating. "I began to get hung over and could hardly function; everything was causing me to panic more." A few days before calling me, Susan had gone to a diner for breakfast. "I ordered eggs and toast and was so scared that I would die if I tried to eat it. I felt my heart pounding and sweat pouring off my body. I knew I was losing control. I called a friend and begged him to pick me up. He did and that's when I decided my last option left was to call you. All I knew about you was the article I read in *Newsweek*."

Making Sense of the Mystery

Susan was obviously a good historian. I knew that she could continue right on giving me relevant past history. However, I realized that this was a good point to stop her narration to enable me to give her some information. I have found that it is crucial both to listen thoroughly to the patient and to begin treatment in the first session. This two-way communication helps clients to develop trust that I understand their troubles and also know how to help.

I began by complimenting Susan on her excellent detailed presentation of the history of her present illness. It was helpful to me in understanding her problem, and I wanted to continue the session by discussing it and reassuring her.

Her history and symptoms indicated a stress-related disorder. I told Susan that I, personally, as well as colleagues in this emerging field, had successfully treated patients with problems similar to hers. My initial comment brought a ray of hope to Susan's face. "So I'm really not just a one-of-a-kind case?" she asked. I understood her need for reassurance that she really could get help, as implied by her question. I repeated that indeed others had presented with similar problems and learned how to heal themselves. "Well, what's gone wrong and how does the healing process work?" she asked.

First, I explained to Susan how the stress response triggers an outpouring of adrenaline and the gearing up of mind and body. Then I described how we all face a chronic bombardment of psychological and social demands. "Different people show strain in different ways. For a variety of reasons which we will explore, you manifest the stress in your swallowing difficulties."

As I spoke, I could see that Susan was intently focused on my every word. Signs of relief of strain appeared in Susan's face as she listened to me and began, for the first time, to hear information about her problems that would enable her to picture her difficulties in an understandable framework. The first step toward healing involves being able to transform our mental set, changing our view from one of terror of the unknown forces plaguing us, to one of hope that learning about the known factors will enable us to deal with them.

Susan said, "That's the first time anyone ever put this into a meaningful context for me. I'm relieved to know that what's going on in me makes sense in some way. But I still don't understand how I can get better."

The New Mind-Body Method

I smiled as I told Susan that she had anticipated the next part of our conversation. "The process of healing involves a combined effort of the mind and body. We now know a lot about the connecting links between the brain and the rest of the body. We have a new unique treatment that combines learning how to change our bodily physiology as well as our mental thought processes, emotions, and behavior patterns."

As I said this, I noticed Susan's eyes widen in amazement. She said, "I thought I was completely up-to-date on medical-treatment techniques." I assured her that she was not alone, that most of the medical community was still unaware of these new breakthroughs.

"Is there a specific formula for how this new approach works?" Susan asked.

"Not exactly," I replied. "It's more like a framework in which each part interrelates with the others. Instead of a rigid protocol, there is a meshing as each part contributes to the healing process. It's like a good team effort in which each player's role contributes to the team's success. For instance, we have already started the healing process today. Your learning that your problems are understandable in a known physiological framework replaces the misperception you had that you were the victim of mysterious, uncontrollable forces. This enables the beginning of an emotional shift away from panic toward hope. Decreasing panic lessens the triggering of the stress response that alters your swallowing mechanism. The next step will be on the physiological side. I want you to listen at home to this tape that I've prepared. Each side is approximately twenty minutes. The first side is called active relaxation; the other side is passive relaxation. Active relaxation involves contracting and then relaxing different muscle groups throughout the body in sequence. Many people are not aware of the amount of muscle tension they carry in the body and this exercise helps them get in touch with where they carry tension."

Continuing my review of work to be done with the tape, I said, "It's important, however, to practice the second side of the tape at least twice a day. This is called passive, or continuing, relaxation. It's a proven method for helping the body to get the break from ongoing stress that it needs to recuperate. The body is a wonderful self-healing organism if it's given an opportunity to rest from stress and return to normal functioning. I suggest that you sit in a comfortable chair and follow my voice on the tape, allowing it to guide you in letting go of the tension throughout your body. Doing the tape in the morning and the evening enables the body to get the break it needs. If you can also take half a minute a few times during the day to do some quick relaxation techniques that I will teach you, they will further help to restore your normal physiological equilibrium."

Shifting focus, I said, "Now I want to give you an overview of how the treatment processes will proceed. Today, we have concentrated on getting your history, understanding your problems, and beginning the healing process. Your second visit will be devoted exclusively to working with the biofeedback equipment and beginning to learn relaxed breathing and imagery techniques. The sensors in biofeedback merely monitor your physiological parameters—muscle tension, hand temperature, heart and respiration rate. The feedback is auditory. The machine beeps as it records tension. The sound you hear will decrease and eventually shut off as you progressively learn how to influence your physiology to return to normal. From the third session onward, each visit will have two parts. First, we will focus on the mental aspects of controlling your specific stress problems. We will examine your coping style, including your perceptions, emotional reactions, and actual behavior under stress. We will work to correct misperceptions, encourage the choosing of healthy emotions, and explore more functional behavioral responses. The second part of each session will be devoted to learning how to relax your physiology while using the biofeedback equipment to monitor your progress. Just as you would practice with a coach to improve and fine-tune your tennis strokes, here you will expand the range and sophistication

of your coping skills in dealing with the stresses in your life, both personally and at work. You will learn new habits of mind and body. Repetition will make them automatic. The old habits will recede into the
background as your energy flows into the rewarding new patterns."

"Sounds great in theory," Susan said, raising her eyebrows in question.

I smiled as I replied, "Yes, and it really works, as well. Of course,
progress never is in a straight line. There will be setbacks, plateaus, and
resistances. They will provide the challenges to us. We'll be working
together. Obviously, we have a lot more ground to cover in our upcom-
ing sessions, but before we stop today, I want to ask if you have any
questions about what we have discussed?"

Apprehensively, Susan replied, "What do I do if things get really bad
for me between our sessions?"

"Call me anytime you feel you need to. That's why I'm here," I said.

"That's a relief. Just knowing that, I probably won't have to call,"
Susan concluded.

"I leave that judgment to you," I answered, as we ended our initial
session. As Susan left, I made a mental note of how positively she responded to the reassurance that I would be available if needed.

The purpose of my asking if there are any questions before ending
the first session is to find out what may be most important to the patient, or not clear. Not only is the information gained valuable, but
asking for questions points up my wish to have give-and-take, active
participation by the patient as part of the healing process. Specifically,
Susan's question was typical of a frightened patient's need to know that
the doctor cares enough to be available. Her relief at my response showed
how important this would be to her healing.

Overall, I felt we were off to a good start. I thought her story about
Granny's dying and Susan being unable to swallow were related. But I
knew I needed to learn more about Susan and not jump to any hasty
conclusions.

Biofeedback and Breathing

Susan's second session was devoted exclusively to starting her physiological training with the biofeedback equipment. She had done her
homework, practicing with the relaxation tape I had given her near the
end of our first session. The beginning of the body training always focuses first on relearning proper breathing. The fastest way to shift gears
from the stress response to the relaxation response is through breathing

correctly. All of us tend toward shallow chest breathing, which correlates with the stress response. As stress increases, respiration becomes shallower and quicker. However, slow, deep abdominal breathing shifts our physiology toward normal. Breath retraining involves relearning to use that great internal muscular sheath, the diaphragm, which acts as a bellows, sucking air fully and deeply into our expanding lungs.

For most of us, it is initially very frustrating to try to control the diaphragm muscle voluntarily after years of ignoring it. Since proper breathing is so fundamental to learning how to control stress physiologically, we focus on this until it is mastered. Sometimes this requires four or five of the physiological training sessions. Susan got the hang of it right away. Perhaps, as she said, the fact that she was a good swimmer and had practiced using the full capacity of her lungs made it easier for her to shift to abdominal breathing on request. However, as with all these techniques, the need to make them function automatically, out of our conscious awareness, always requires practice over time.

Now that Susan could do the proper breathing techniques, it was time to introduce her to experiencing biofeedback. Seeing us demonstrate the equipment, Susan's response was, "looks fine to me. Hook me up." We started Susan with a sensor on a fingertip on each hand. The sensor is designed to measure changing skin temperatures. Skin temperature is important, as it correlates with the degree to which warm blood flows through the blood vessels in the extremities—fingers and toes. Stress causes blood vessels to the extremities to constrict. The common expression "His hands are as cold as ice" is descriptive of someone under stress. Susan's hand-temperature readings hovered between 89.5 degrees and 91.7 degrees during the first monitoring day. Her readings were good for someone hooked up for the first time, without any prior training. Susan's hand temperature was actually within normal range. This showed that the blood flow to her hands was OK.

Since her problem involved swallowing, Susan's digestive tube was probably being constricted by muscle tension. This would require using specific muscle biofeedback training to relax that area. That would be easier to do after the initial experience with the simpler hand temperature measurements.

Getting to Know the Person

As I mentally prepared for Susan's next visit with me, I realized that I needed to understand more about the significant people in her life. I wanted to get a picture of Susan's parents through her eyes. So much of our characteristic styles of living are shaped by our early experiences. It is important to get a handle on the themes that may be underlying present conflict and illness. These themes are often uncovered in discussions concerning the person's feelings about interactions with other family members. With this in mind, I knew I would inquire about Susan's past after I had given her an opportunity to tell me how she was doing since our first visit.

After Susan arrived and sat down, I asked her, "How do you feel?" She said, "I'm feeling OK. I had a mediocre week. I didn't go away to the shore on the weekend as I had planned. I'm a little disappointed about that, but otherwise I'm OK."

"Good," I said. "Today I would like to go back to discussing your grandmother and your relationship with her. Maybe we should start with your relationship with your parents, if that's easier."

"All right," Susan replied. "Well, my mother—she's OK. She tends to be a little hyper. I lived with my folks at home until I was seventeen, then I left for college. My father was a physician. He suffered a heart attack eight years ago. As a matter of fact, the anniversary of his death is just a few weeks away. He was your typical old-fashioned doctor. Totally dedicated to his patients. I hardly saw him when I was growing up because he was such a workaholic. We became closer as I was in medical school. God, I'll never forget the time I saved his life."

Susan stopped briefly, as she noted the look of surprise on my face. "Yes, I really saved his life. We were out together on a boat and he developed crushing chest pain. I realized he was having a serious heart attack and notified the Coast Guard. They air-lifted him to the hospital, where he underwent quadruple coronary bypass surgery. He died three years ago from lung cancer. He had to have a lung removed, and he had trouble breathing at the end. During his last years when I was in my medical training, we spent more time together and got closer. I think he really took pride in my following in his footsteps. At that point, we had a really good relationship. It gets to me that we weren't closer before, because he was working all the time."

Susan paused and then continued, "But in addition to my parents, as you know, I had a super grandmother. She lived nearby when I was growing up. She was always so alive and 'with it' as a person. She was warm and good-natured. She loved music—singing and dancing. One of the last happy memories I have of her was seeing her before she went out one evening. Here's this little old lady all decked out and excited— all charged up to go out dancing. She looked great."

In seconds, Susan's expression changed from one of happy reminiscing to one of pain.

"Do you want to talk about it?" I asked.

"My thoughts just switched back to those final days when my grandmother was in the hospital," Susan began. "I couldn't bear sitting at that deathwatch at the hospital. To tell you the truth, I spoke to her doctor and asked him to increase her morphine to kill her pain. I think I wanted to speed up the end of her suffering. I knew her death was coming. I just couldn't stand to see her that way." As tears began welling up in her eyes, Susan added, "I don't want to start crying."

"It's all right," I replied. "All of us need to cry sometimes. It's healthy to express our feelings and we all need to go through a normal grief process."

"Not me," she said. "I never cried about my grandmother before—not at the hospital, or afterward. Someone's got to keep it together."

"I can understand that," I responded. "But this is part of your problem. Mentally, emotionally, and physiologically, it's unhealthy to block the normal outflow of grief. The pain doesn't just disappear by not expressing it. As a matter of fact, the opposite occurs. We hold onto unexpressed feelings in our body. It produces chronic stress which causes us long-term suffering. We were meant to express our grief at the time so that we can properly mourn, letting go of loved ones' physical presence, while maintaining our memories and spiritual connection to them. By avoiding the grieving process, one is denying the new reality and it makes it impossible to go on in a healthy way."

"I never realized that," Susan said, looking somewhat astonished. "I learned all about the grief process in school. I guess I never realized I was denying myself that."

"You're not alone," I replied. "We all get so preoccupied with caring for others with all the latest medical advances that we lose sight of ourselves and forget that the most precious asset for healing is within each individual."

As Susan left, I sat by myself for a few minutes reviewing where we were. I had accomplished my session goal of learning more about her family. More important, Susan had been able to reconnect emotionally with a crucial experience: her grandmother's death. She began to experience her grief overtly for the first time, although it was difficult for her. This is clinically termed abreaction. The definition of abreaction is a release of feelings or emotions through reliving (in fantasy or action) a situation previously denied to conscious awareness. This process is necessary for the healing mechanism known as catharsis to occur. Catharsis is a release of tension and anxiety through abreaction. It often is a necessary step in healing.

I sensed, however, that this was just the beginning and there was more to explore. I felt that there was more to Susan's relationship with her mother than her two-sentence description. I also was impressed by the significance of her relationship with her father and wanted to understand its relevance to her present painful condition. Finally, I was struck by the fact that this articulate, talkative patient had not yet said anything about her current familiar and intimate social relationships. My intuition told me that all of these associations somehow held the keys to the cure.

Focusing on Muscle Relaxation

During the physiological training part of this session, Susan again progressed well. She was able to start at 92.0 degrees hand temperature and reached 93.0 degrees as she focused on breathing and relaxing. That the initial reading was higher than the prior session indicated a more relaxed baseline physiology. The early work had enabled Susan to be generally more physiologically relaxed. A narrow one-degree warming was typical of the difficulty in shifting gears physiologically at such an early stage in training.

We then simultaneously attached temperature sensors to a toe on Susan's left foot to observe the distal peripheral blood flow. Initially, this measurement was 91.5 degrees and rose later to 92.5 degrees. Both measurements were one-half degree less than the initial and subsequent hand temperatures discussed above. This noted difference between hand and foot blood flow is common.

Finally, we also added a sensor to her forehead to measure muscle tension. The forehead region is a good proxy for the amount of muscle tension that we have throughout the body. As with the temperature measurements, the patient hears a tone decreasing which tells her that she is relaxing. The actual measurement scale for muscle tension is a relative one, varying with each separate instrument, as opposed to an absolute standard scale like body temperature. Susan started at 2.5 on the relative scale and was able to relax down to 1.5 practicing breathing and letting her mind quiet down during the training session. This showed a good muscle relaxation responsiveness.

Severe Allergies and Multiple Chemical Sensitivities (M.C.S.)

At the start of our third session together, Susan declared, "I want you to know that I'm also seeing an allergist while I'm here. I'm leaving no stone unturned." After a pause she slowly added, "I hope that doesn't bother you."

"No," I replied, "you should certainly pursue all approaches that you believe may be of some help to you."

"Well, I admit I'm relieved that you have an open attitude and don't take it as a lack of faith in what you're doing," Susan replied, speaking a lot less defensively than her initial statement.

"Far from it," I replied. "You are the consumer. You have every right to explore alternatives. I wouldn't trust a doctor who objected to a patient doing that."

"Well, I haven't always encountered such an open attitude among physicians," Susan said. "But I'm really trying to look at all the possible contributing factors to my illness. I felt that I needed to examine if an allergic reaction could be a part of it."

"Did you have some prior experience that made you think there's a possibility of an allergic reaction causing your problem?" I asked.

"To start with, I have always wondered about a genetic predisposition to allergies, since my dad suffered from intense allergy attacks. When I was a child, he almost died. He was stung by a bee or wasp and his face blew up. His entire system went into anaphylactic shock. He couldn't breathe. His airway became obstructed because of the internal swelling. The venom was about to kill him. He got an emergency shot of epinephrine in time, which reversed the process and saved his life."

As she continued her account Susan explained, "I have had many different situations in which I suffered from allergic reactions. I remember going to the dentist and needing an anesthetic. He gave me lidocaine with epinephrine and I began breaking out in a cold sweat with my heart pounding. I was terrified. I felt claustrophobic. I feared going unconscious. That was it for me for that dentist. The poor guy couldn't handle it. He told me to find another dentist," Susan said, smiling. "Another incident occurred two years ago. I had a bad case of bronchitis. To treat it, I used an aerosol spray, Bronchosol. The normal adult dose is one-quarter to one-half cc. Thank God I was being cautious and took just one-tenth cc. Immediately, my heart started racing. I became 'speedy,' and I felt like I was jumping out of my skin."

I was glad to see that Susan was beginning to open up and trust me with the more personal-feelings aspect of her reactions, not just information. I said, "These two incidents definitely underscore your extreme sensitivity to substances. You're getting an exaggerated stress-response reaction from minute amounts of sympathomimetic agents. Most people don't realize that a significant minority of us do have this kind of biochemical super sensitivity. Unfortunately, as your dentist demonstrated, people who are sensitive are often dismissed as crazy."

"One thing all this has done for me is made me more understanding of the patients I see," Susan replied in agreement. Then she continued, "Anytime things are out of my control, I get really uptight. I can easily think of so many examples of this. I don't like tight clothes, especially sweaters with tight necks. I feel claustrophobic in them. Also, if I get anything on my skin that I can't immediately wash off, it continues to irritate me immensely. For example, two months ago I had a small blood clot under a fingernail. I realized it would take a long time for it to go away. That really upset me. I felt like it was controlling me. Even having a ring on my finger makes me anxious and panicky."

Susan noticed my smile at that last sentence and looked at me quizzically.

"I know a lot of *men* who have a reaction similar to yours to the idea of having a ring on their finger," I replied.

She had to think for a second before she got my quip. Then we both laughed together. Smiling, she retorted, "I appreciate that. I was really getting on an anxious roll. But that comment is a lot closer to home than you might think."

"Oh, really?" I asked.

"Yes, but," Susan hesitated, "I thought we were discussing what triggered an intense stress response in me. How'd we get here?"

"Yes, we were," I replied. "So how about you finish up what you were saying and then let's explore what's 'closer to home' about a ring for you? Perhaps there's something valuable in that as well."

"OK," Susan replied. "I know I haven't talked about my personal life. I just didn't think it was relevant to my physical problems."

"Well, just as you didn't rule out the possibility that an allergy may be relevant, from my experience in working with stress disorders, I don't want to rule out the relevancy of intimacy," I said.

"Fair enough," Susan rejoined. "We'll explore my anxieties, then intimacy, as you suggested. So getting back to what I was saying, a few years ago I asked a physician friend of mine to do a standard treadmill stress test on me. I was all hooked up and after about ten minutes, I was at a maximum level. I began sweating profusely, and found myself gasping for breath. I felt constricted with the wires around me, so I ripped them off. My friend feared I was having a heart attack and ran to get the emergency medication cart. It was nothing but a panic attack. Another incident I recall occurred at a fund-raising event at our hospital. Both to raise money and have fun, we ran a mock judicial system and had the local cops acting as arrest officers. The 'bail' you had to pay went to the charity. Well, one of my good friends, who is a cop, came over to handcuff me. I had to insist that he 'arrest' me without the cuffs because I could feel my fear growing at the thought of having something tight around my wrists."

Susan reflected for a moment and then went on. "This all started around four years ago. Actually, that dates it to be about one year before my current symptoms began. I remember, because I was feeling in a kookie mood that day and I went to the hairdresser. I told her I needed a change in my hairstyle. I wanted it to curl all over the place. So she began by wrapping tight rollers all over my head. Then she started pouring this hot, liquid, ammonia-based chemical over my hair and scalp. It felt like it started to seep into my pores. Well, I quickly went from kookie mood to cuckoo! I felt this hot liquid taking me over, burning my head off. The vapors were going through me. I couldn't breathe. I was convinced I was suffocating. My heart was pounding. Sweat was pouring out of me. I was a mess of panic. I screamed at her, 'Get these things off of me!' She had to remove the curlers one by one. It seemed like an eternity. I felt I needed cold water on me immediately. I jumped up and plunged my head into the sink and turned the cold water on full blast on my head and neck. Then I reached for the wash hose. The hairdresser was terrified. She wanted to call an ambulance. I know she thought I was nuts."

It took Susan a few minutes to continue. I could tell she had relived the experience, and felt at least some of it all over again.

"Over the last few years, I have noticed an increased sensitivity to chemicals," she continued. "One day on my way to work, I stopped at a convenience store for a newspaper. The floor was being mopped with ammonia. As soon as I realized that, it began all over again. I had to get cold water over me to wash away the chemicals. I drove back home, ripped my clothes off and jumped in a cold shower for fifteen minutes. I was late getting to my office but I didn't care. I felt I had no choice."

Fear Triggers the Stress Response

"Your experiences fit into a common reaction pattern," I said. "An initial stimulus like ammonia-based products will trigger an exaggerated stress response. Then future exposure to the noxious stimulus quickly triggers the memory of the past, and escalating fear drives another exaggerated stress response. So a vicious cycle occurs and by repetition leads to a habit of being vulnerable. It's like a reflex response to a chain of events."

"I never thought of it that way," Susan replied. "The reason I went to the allergist was to investigate it from a purely toxic-substance approach. However, my experience with the allergist tends to confirm your view. When I saw him the other day, I told him about my allergic history, just as I'm telling you. I also spoke about the problem I'm working on here. He said that, based on my history, there was no evidence of a systemic reaction like my dad had to the bee venom. He felt there might be a hypersensitivity, but no real allergy in my system. He didn't think it was necessary to test me for a reaction to venom. As for epinephrine, he felt my history showed a hypersensitivity. You have explained it better to me in terms of an exaggerated stress response. As for the procedure of allergy testing, it involves iodine preparation of the skin and twenty-seven injections. The shots are given in nine different sets of three each. Each set of three has a progressively stronger concentration of any potential allergen to determine at what strength I would react. After the first three injections, I noticed my anxiety increasing. I began thinking it was too late to remove them from under my skin. I began feeling out of control. 'It' was in control. By the end of the second full set of three, I could feel my heart pounding and my jaws tightening. I began to have a peculiar sensation upon swallowing. I felt as though I had a foreign body going down my throat. After the third set, I could feel my throat tightening up. I started saying to myself, *Don't give up.* I couldn't relax, however, and I began having a headache. I said to the allergist, 'This is getting worse as we progress up the line; maybe I can skip the rest. I'm feeling weak; maybe it's because I haven't eaten all day.' He responded, 'You can stop if you want. I know you're feeling anxious. If we can continue, however, we will get a definitive answer.' I said, 'All right, I'll go for it; but I am feeling light-headed. Do you think I could get some orange juice someplace?' He asked his nurse and she returned with chocolate milk. It was all she could lay her hands on. But after I drank it, I felt better. The nurse smiled at me guzzling it down and said, 'You look just like a kid!' I began relaxing and the symptoms started to subside. I could even feel my palms starting to dry out. I finished the test without any more problems. The allergist read the results as negative, as he had anticipated."

"I'm sorry that you had such a trying experience. There is a positive part to your ordeal, though. You were able to see your symptoms clearly, including the peculiar sensations when swallowing, and the tightening of your throat, all directly resulting from fear triggering the stress response. More important, you were able to correct the situation by triggering the relaxation response to get the symptoms to subside. You did this by communicating your concerns to a responsive listener—the allergist—and getting nurturance from him and his sympathetic nurse. They helped emotionally and concretely by bringing you the chocolate milk. Your experience encompasses all the elements of stress and resolution."

As I was speaking, I could see Susan looking at me with rapt attention. When I finished she said, "I never understood it conceptually before. But what you're saying makes sense out of what I experienced."

During the physiological training part of this session, Susan was able to maintain her hand temperature in the range she achieved in the prior biofeedback session. She was able to lower her muscle tension. She began at a lower level than the previous session and relaxed down to a new, more relaxed level than she had achieved previously. The insight she had gained in our discussion had obviously helped her to let go of some of the tension she was carrying in her body. Her growing understanding enabled her to let go of some of the body armoring. Susan didn't need to be so girded for battle, as she began to see that she could respond appropriately when the need arose.

Mother, Guilt, and Trouble Swallowing

As I reflected on the session, I noted that Susan still hadn't kept her end of the bargain about discussing her current personal life. I did have her commitment to do so and that would make it easier to remind her if she didn't get to it in the next few sessions. The experience with the allergy testing was fresh in Susan's mind and too good an opportunity for providing insight into her condition to have cut it short by pushing her to talk about things she was reluctant to discuss.

Susan began our next session saying, "I feel guilty as hell. I'm also angry, and my symptoms, including trouble swallowing, have flared up. It began last night with my mother. She has remarried and moved here to live with her new husband. I've been staying at their place while I'm up here working with you. Well, they had some friends over last evening and I went out by myself to a bar for a drink. When I got home about eleven o'clock, her husband took me aside and said, 'Your mother was having some chest pains tonight. One of our friends who was over is a doctor and thought it was probably tension or an upset stomach. He suggested she take Valium and an antacid, which she did. She gets this pain every so often.'" Susan continued, "When I heard this, I immediately got angry. I took one look at my mother, who is in her mid-sixties, and I could see that she looked pale and was sweating. I screamed at her, 'You should know better! You should go to the hospital emergency room for a workup to make sure you're not having a heart attack.' She said, 'Oh, it's no big deal. I've had these pains before. Our doctor friend who was here didn't think it was serious. Probably playing tennis tomorrow morning will help me loosen up and I'll feel better when I'm relaxed. Then I got really angry and shouted, 'You could kill yourself doing that if this pain is an early heart attack!' She started to walk away from me declaring, 'I'm OK. I'll stop if I'm not feeling right on the tennis court.'"

Susan concluded the account. "When I calmed down, I told her, 'Ma, you're putting me under stress worrying about you.' Well, I couldn't get to sleep for over an hour. I was worrying: Will she drop dead in her sleep tonight? If she does get sick and die, how will I ever get over my guilt at not insisting she go to the hospital now?"

After a long pause, Susan added, "I can remember when my dad used to have a reaction similar to mine. First, he would get angry and say, 'How did you get in that position?' It took a while for his compassion and caring to come to the forefront. His first reaction was to get angry. I guess he didn't want to seem to be too coddling and condoning of the irresponsible behavior that created the problem."

At this point I asked Susan, "Did you have any symptoms during this time when you were feeling both guilty and angry?"

"Yes," Susan replied, "my throat tightened up. I could hardly eat some soft ice cream that I tried to swallow. All night I struggled with the question, Should I wake her up and take her to the hospital? In the morning, when I told her of my sleepless night's thoughts, she said, 'I'm glad you didn't wake me. I needed the sleep.' Well today, I'm still struggling with my guilt. Should I have tried to make her feel guilty enough about my worrying so that she wouldn't go play tennis? Should I have said to her: If you die playing tennis, the guilt will put me under increased pressure, so don't do it, for me. Should I have insisted that I didn't want her to go? I just decided to push it away and not do anything."

I asked, "Well, how do you feel about not insisting?"

Susan replied indignantly. "I feel OK if no problem occurs. I'll feel terribly guilty if she dies playing tennis today. Sure, I know that she is an adult and I did tell her what I thought, but I'm still upset."

"Why?" I asked.

"I don't want to lose her," Susan answered. "But I make myself responsible for things even if they are out of my power. I'm too protective of her."

Insight Leads to Relief

"It sounds like you want to be Superwoman," I said. "You want to guarantee that only good outcomes occur. But this must make it very difficult for you to love anyone. If you're going to hold yourself accountable for everything that goes on in someone else's life, then loving someone is going to become a huge responsibility. Since you know you can't control everything, you're going to feel like a failure. This means that guilt, anger, and self-reproach are the result. These emotions trigger the stress response and your swallowing difficulties."

"I guess we've hit on a lot of heavy issues here," Susan said. "My need to control and my guilt feelings seem crucial. I guess I never let myself feel angry until I was furious, because I was trying to be a good girl. I never realized how these things affected my health. There's so much to learn," Susan moaned.

"Wisdom is knowing how much you don't know," I encouraged.

"Let me review with you what I think is happening, to see if it makes sense," Susan said. "My mother was always very strong-willed. I never felt close to her because of it. I resented her being so domineering. I think I really pushed my feelings away to be a good girl. I consciously tried to be different from her. I became quiet and reserved. You're saying that now I put guilt on myself about her playing tennis and maybe getting a heart attack. Yet, I never felt guilty about my dad. I knew I was a good daughter to him. I saved his life that time on the boat. I was there for him through his illnesses. There was nothing I could have done for him that I didn't do."

"That's the key," I said. "To feel guilty, one has to feel personal responsibility for something. You believed that you had the power to stop your mother from playing tennis and didn't use it. With respect to your father, however, you don't feel guilt, because you felt you always did everything you possibly could to help him. Your need to control and guarantee a positive outcome involves a mental perception that sets up a no-win situation for you. If you don't control your mother's actions and she has an attack, you're guilty; but if you do override her wishes and nothing bad happens to her physically, you're still guilty—this time for interfering and dictating to an adult against her wishes."

"That's my dilemma," Susan said. "Whatever choice I make, I lose. I feel guilty. How can I win in such a situation?"

"Your dilemma results from your asking the wrong question. Your idea that you need to figure out the right thing to 'do' leads to the no-win situation. Your need to control and guarantee a positive outcome unconsciously pushes you into this trap. The realistic and healthier approach to the situation involves your acknowledging that you can't play God and control outcomes for the good. This correct perception enables you to focus on the right question to ask yourself, which is: 'How can I express my concern, behave as a loving daughter, and feel at peace with myself?' By accepting your human limitations, you can focus on your appropriate role as daughter and not misperceive your role as omnipotent doctor. This frees you up to see that you did do everything you could by expressing your concern the night before and recommending a workup at the hospital and avoiding strenuous tennis. Being relieved of unrealistic self-expectations of guaranteeing her well-being, you can accept her adult decision based on her previous experience with similar discomfort, and the opinion of her doctor friend that she was probably suffering from tension and/or indigestion. He certainly is in a better position to see the situation more objectively than you do, since he is not her daughter. The reason physicians shouldn't treat their own families is because their perceptions are clouded by their emotional involvement. In this situation, you're feeling guilty because of your resentment at her not following your advice. And your anger at not being omnipotently in control frustrates you because you're feeling 'responsible' for guaranteeing her health."

"You know," Susan replied, "I'm just amazed at how what you're saying makes sense out of things I couldn't piece together before. As I'm thinking about what you're saying I'm asking myself, How did I ever get so mixed up?"

After a few seconds' pause, I said, "What are your thoughts about that?"

"Well, I bet both my parents have contributed. I guess that doesn't surprise you," Susan added with a smile.

I smiled back in acknowledgment. "You're right about that, but let me hear what you think is their contribution."

Susan began, "I can clearly see that my overactive sense of responsibility comes from my father and so does my choosing the profession of ultimate responsibility—medicine. It's my mother's influence that I'm still struggling with. A lot of things about her still upset me. For instance, I can remember when she stopped smoking a few years ago. As a reformed smoker, she banned smoking in her home. I noticed, however, that the cleaning lady chain-smoked and my mother never said anything to her. Well, I didn't comment on that until one day my boyfriend, Mike, was at Mother's house with me, and probably out of nervousness, started to light a cigarette. Before he could take a puff, my mother exclaimed, 'How awful. I don't permit smoking in my house.' I was taken aback my mother's rudeness, knowing how hypocritical it was in view of her letting the cleaning lady smoke in the house all the time. When I confronted her with this contradiction, she retorted, 'I need the house cleaned. That's important enough to me to overlook her smoking.' Her unsaid, but clear, implication that my boyfriend was of no importance to her further enraged me. Yet, I've always felt I had to be polite and respectful to her. I was raised to believe an adult is always deserving of respect."

"That incident illuminates an underlying pattern in your relationship to your mother," I said. "You understandably found her overbearing, but 'swallowed' your resentment. This both laid a foundation for your symptoms to develop and left open a possible way to retaliate by trying to control her behavior for her own good—as yesterday's chest-pain incident exemplifies."

"So you think I'm retaliating by trying to control her," Susan asked. "You don't know my mom. She doesn't mind being rude. She's so sure of herself. She doesn't listen, cuts you off, and talks over you. The smoking incident exemplifies all that. It's amazing how she can be so catty and cutting. I remember walking with her one day when she saw another woman wearing a dress like the one she had on. Her comment to me was, 'I have shoes to match— obviously that woman doesn't have the same taste as I do.' "

"That example shows your mother's insecurity," I replied. "She overcompensated by being domineering and disparaging."

Looking at Susan's face, I could see a light going on in her mind. "You think so?" she asked. "I always experienced her domination. I didn't see any insecurity underneath. The only time I can recall that I saw any insecurity was when Dad died and she showed her fear about finances. Then she remarried soon after Dad's death. Her current husband had lost his wife about the same time as when my dad died. Mom needed the security, I guess. Her husband is strong-willed, like Dad was."

As Susan got up to go for her physiological training part of the session, I reflected upon the new information revealed. In addition to Susan gaining insight into the dynamics of her relationship with her mother and how her symptoms were affected, she had finally opened up, indirectly, about a boyfriend. As the smoking incident showed, her mother obviously was threatened by this new power in her territory.

Susan began the biofeedback training at her most relaxed initial level yet. Her hand temperature was one half degree higher than prior baselines and she relaxed her body further through breathing and imagery techniques to achieve a new high reading one half degree above prior levels. Although these increases may appear small, their significance is that she was breaking through to new levels. Even more important, her muscle-tension readings showed results similar to the hand temperatures indicated.

Expressing Yourself Helps

Susan began our fifth session with some good news. "For the first time in six months, I was able to eat two scrambled eggs. I was able to finish everything on my plate. And, for the first time in ages, I felt comfortable in the shower. I was able to let the water run on my face without panicking about water running up my nose and cutting off my breathing."

"That's real progress," I replied. "It seems like you learned a lot from our last session that has enabled you to let go of some of the tightness in your throat and some of your apprehension."

"Yes," Susan replied, "I thought a lot about the session and I even made some notes for myself as a reminder. Are you impressed?" she asked, teasingly.

"Sure," I answered. "In this context, it can be helpful. It's like being back in school, except the subject you're learning about is yourself. Just don't hide behind the notes. Keep experiencing your feelings and thinking about what you're doing."

"I'm glad you approve," Susan said with a smile. "I already realized that I kept using the word *should* in describing the situation with my mother's chest pain. My language itself was focused on obligations!"

"That's very common in people who are overresponsible for others," I said. "They talk and think in terms of *should* and *ought*. Their focus is control, and necessities. You hardly hear any talk of wants or desires from such people. It's because they deny their own needs. But in doing so, they jeopardize their own freedom and their own self-control by being the martyr for others."

I could see the look of recognition in Susan's face. "That's me," she said. "I set up situations so that everyone else can be happy. I work long and hard to make things perfect for them. It's especially true in relation to both my mother and my boyfriend. But I am trying to change, to put into effect what I'm learning here. Yesterday, my mother wanted to have a 'mother-daughter' talk. She had been sensing that I don't like being told by her what to do. She started the talk by asking if she was in the way of my getting better? Since she asked, I told her, but I tried to pick the right words. I told her she was not an easy person to be with, that it was hard for me to relax around her. She expressed surprise at that and asked me to be more specific. When I said I didn't want to hurt her feelings, she insisted. So I told her about her rudeness to people, saying I believed it was unintentional and not out of malice. She asked for an example. I thought I'd start in the past and reminded her of the smoking incident with my boyfriend and her defense of permitting the cleaning lady to smoke because her services were necessary. To my surprise, she just blandly said, 'OK.' Then I reminded her that while I've been staying here, Mike—my boyfriend—calls often. Last night my mother picked up the phone during a conversation to say that she was leaving the house. I told her that type of interruption was rude to Mike and me."

"How did you feel about speaking directly to your mother about what upsets you in her behavior?" I asked.

"I felt good," Susan answered. "I know that because she didn't cry, and didn't seem upset, it made it a lot easier."

"I'm glad you could express yourself and find out that it does not always lead to a bitter rejection," I said.

"I also called Mike again before I came here today. I was terrified that he might be upset at me for my mother's interruption yesterday, that he would be distant," Susan continued. "But Mike was as warm and loving as he always is."

"It sounds like you were expecting Mike to react the way your mother would—that he would have been self-righteously angry," I said.

After a moment's reflection, Susan said, "I never realized that I might react to Mike in a way that would be anticipating the response my mother would give. I'm so used to her dominating the situation. I remember a little while back, I was going to dinner with her and her husband. We had reservations for eight o'clock. She always has to get to an appointment early. I was nursing a drink in the living room, when she said, 'Let's go,' expecting everyone to get up and obey. Instead of directly saying I wanted to finish my drink, I got defensive and said, 'Well, go without me.' Actually, her husband came to my defense and I finished the drink and we all left together."

"I think it's clear to you now that there's an advantage to being direct about your feelings, instead of being intimidated," I said.

"Yes, my mother isn't crumbling, even though I'm expressing myself," Susan rejoined.

"More important, you don't have to swallow things you don't want to swallow," I countered.

As Susan left to go for her biofeedback training, I thought about how the pieces of the puzzle were beginning to fall into place. Susan's relationship with her mother came more clearly into focus. The existence of Susan's boyfriend was acknowledged and that relationship needed to be brought into bolder relief. In addition, Susan was making good progress in decreasing the frequency and severity of her swallowing difficulties.

During the physiological training part of the session, Susan maintained her gain from the previous session. This was a confirmatory sign that she was maintaining the gains she had established.

Being Afraid to Love

Susan continued to display steady progress. She began the sixth session by describing how she was eating better. Since our last visit, she had been able to eliminate the need for a drink before meals. She also was able to eat chopped broccoli for the first time in years. She even went to the gym and exercised without triggering her stress response. The signs of progress were evident. To top off the good report, she noted that she didn't get a panic attack when she was stuck in traffic on the way to my office.

Susan continued the session by stating bluntly, "I want to talk about my relationship with my boyfriend, Mike. We have been living together for four years. I'm torn about whether to get married or end it. I don't know what I should do."

I could see the perplexed look on her face. "Tell me about the forces pulling you in such opposite directions," I said.

"Mike is the warmest, most loving man I've ever known," Susan replied. "He's loyally been there for me and with me throughout this long nightmare of my illness."

"Sounds great," I interjected. "So where is the problem?"

"The negative for me," Susan continued, "is that he can't make a living. He is perfectly content to sit at home writing poetry and working on writing a novel that no publisher has shown any interest in. You wouldn't believe how unproductive he is."

"What do you mean by productive?" I asked.

"How about having a real job or studying for a career. I just don't think it's healthy not to take care of oneself!" Susan exclaimed.

"That's one definition of being productive. There are other definitions that are less rigid," I replied.

"But I thought that everyone worked these days and that made for healthy self-esteem," Susan said.

"It is true as a general statement that meaningful activity is an important contribution to self-esteem," I replied. "It's only important that it's 'meaningful' to the particular person. In this situation, Mike finds real meaning in wanting to be a writer. What's wrong with that?"

"Isn't it healthier for Mike to be more self-reliant and work and make some money?" Susan asked.

"I think that possibly the amount of money Mike could make is insignificant in comparison to your earning power," I replied.

"That's what he says," Susan exclaimed.

"Let's continue along this vein," I suggested. "Can you describe your concept of marriage?" I asked.

"Sharing, communicating, loving," Susan replied easily.

"Well," I continued, "doesn't sharing involve each partner doing what he or she does best, or is it more important for both to do one thing, even though one is more efficient at it?"

"Yes, but if Mike has nothing to do all day long except play with words, won't he get bored and restless just staying at home?" Susan replied.

"It sounds like you're projecting your own possible reactions in that situation onto him. He appears happy living that way," I said. "Perhaps you have an underlying fear that he will become too dependent on you."

"What do you mean? I have no problem supporting the both of us. I don't need him working for the money. I thought it would be good for him," Susan retorted. "Maybe the discipline of holding down a job would help him to be a more productive writer. He doesn't even write anything for weeks at a time."

"I didn't mean financial support, I meant emotional support," I said. "Maybe there's a fear that he will make demands on your time and energy unless he's more occupied with things to do."

After a pause, Susan acknowledged my statement. "I see what you're saying. It is true that I like to be by myself a lot. I need a break from people around me all day. I resent the thought of having to do things just to occupy someone else's time. It's like being a nursemaid."

"I think there is another factor operating here outside your conscious awareness," I continued. "From your description of your experiences with your mother, you had to learn to function almost totally autonomously to protect against her intrusiveness and her dependency. Being self-reliant was a major way of coping. Obviously, it has worked for you professionally, but it's making personal intimacy a struggle for you. While you obviously desire the nurturance of a warm, loving man like Mike, you can't 'take in' the closeness, for fear of losing your independence."

I could see tears welling up in Susan's eyes. "That's what's been missing," she cried out. "I've been afraid to love."

"More specifically, you have been terrified of being loved." Speaking softly, I continued to encourage her. "You can love others, it leaves you in control. The feared vulnerability of needing someone else is what you have been struggling against. You have to see that you are an adult now, not a child. Mike is not your mother. Literally, the emotional distance that protected you from her intrusiveness is preventing you from taking in the love you need now. You are starving for love, but can't 'swallow it.' "

Breaking Through to New Levels

As Susan left for her biofeedback training, I felt good that we had found the key to the puzzle. Most important, Susan understood it with her feelings, not just her intellectuality. I knew we had reached the turning point and that although there would probably be some setbacks along the way, we had all the pieces in place now for healing.

Susan broke through to a new level of bodily relaxation during the physiological training. Not surprisingly, the mental breakthrough we achieved in our meeting carried through from her mind to her body. Susan's hand temperature was approaching 95 degrees in both hands simultaneously. This is a clinically significant level. It correlates with relief of symptoms in many stress-related disorders. More important in Susan's case of swallowing trouble due to muscle contraction and spasm, this warm hand temperature corresponded to a physiological relaxation response associated with muscle relaxation biofeedback readings approximating normal, nonstress levels.

Susan began our seventh session talking about planning to return home. This confirmed my impression from the prior session that we had reached a turning point. I knew, however, from past experience, that although we had gone many laps, the road to the finish line still had some bumps along the way. There is always a need for a period of time to consolidate the gains. Unfortunately, just as the patient begins to feel more confident and independent, that self-confidence often threatens some significant person in the patient's life who needs the patient to feel helpless and dependent. The threat to losing that control often leads the other significant "caretaker" to try to upset the newfound independent functioning before it has become firmly established. This drama is often played out beyond the conscious awareness of the participants. Correct understanding and management of this phase is crucial to the success of the treatment. The treatment focus shifts more to the mind side of the mind-body interaction.

"I'm planning to go back home in a couple of weeks," Susan said. "I've already made plane reservations. I feel I'm really going to be OK now. My mother, however, keeps telling me that there is no security from stress. But I guess I could delay my return home if I slip back."

"Your mother is exacerbating your fears," I responded. "She is projecting her own insecurity."

"You're right," Susan retorted. "And I'm trying not to do my own projecting. I'm beginning to let myself see the difference between Mike and my mother. I invited Mike up for this weekend, since my mother and her husband were going out of town. Mike said that he felt I was progressing really well and he didn't want to interfere with that. He said he was afraid that if we argued, it might lead to a setback. He told me that if I really insisted, he would come up. The 'old me' would have talked him into coming. The 'new me' gave him the option to choose."

I said, "It sounds like Mike is saying to you that you're really doing well and letting you take the credit for that. I think he's trying to help you avoid having your dependency conflicts with him interfere with your progress. If he came up and the two of you argued, it would create tension. If things went well, you might erroneously ascribe some of your progress to his being here."

"I hadn't seen things so clearly, but what you're saying makes sense," Susan replied. "I did have a good weekend totally on my own, without Mike or my mother around. I ate well and felt good. I played golf and enjoyed it. Of course, I had the potential to panic being by myself, but didn't."

"You successfully dealt with your dependency issues this weekend," I replied. "In the past, you had this negative cycle of feeling sick, then being scared and fearing that you couldn't stand on your own two feet. This weekend you created a healthy, virtuous cycle of autonomy, feeling good and self-confident."

"I'm really pleased," Susan said. "But with my plans to go home soon, there's another thing I'd like to discuss with you—my fear of flying."

"Sure," I replied. "I can teach you a quick self-hypnosis technique to assist in conquering your flying fears. Let's plan to do that next time."

Susan maintained the prior biofeedback session's breakthrough level of relaxation response. The ability to repeat at a new level is crucial to firmly establish the gain. Susan was clearly in the homestretch now. My main concern was that some obstacle not be thrown in her path to the finish line.

A Phone Call Creates a Crisis

A few days later when I picked up my ringing phone, I heard a woman's voice say, "Hello, I'm Susan's mother."

"How can I help you?" I inquired.

"I need your advice," she said. "I don't know if my daughter should stay longer or return to where she lives. It is an inconvenience having her here, but, of course, I want to do what's best for her health. I'm really worried about her."

"Susan and I have discussed this," I replied. "We are in agreement as to how long she needs to be here and when she is ready to go."

"But," she responded, "I'm really concerned about her being away from her practice for so long. I know she'll be hit with a lot of stress on her return. I just felt I should warn her."

"Our goal is for Susan to be back functioning as soon as possible," I replied. "When she is to return is her decision. Susan is a wonderful, capable woman and she will leave when she is ready."

"Whatever you say, Doctor," she replied icily. "But please, don't tell her I called. She'll be furious about my interfering, but I'm just trying to be a good mother and help my daughter."

"I understand your intentions are good," I replied. "However, I must inform her of our talk. It is of utmost importance that Susan and I maintain our honest relationship."

"As you wish, Doctor! Good-bye," she said, and the phone disconnected.

As I hung up the phone I thought to myself, *Well, I had been waiting for the other shoe to drop*. I was wondering what mischief would result from her version to Susan of our discussion. I knew I had to begin the next session with a discussion of this phone call and its ramifications.

So I started our eighth session by talking about the phone call, instead of my usual procedure of letting the patient initiate the talk. I presented, in a factual manner, the phone dialogue without embellishment or interpretation. I did this for two reasons. First, I wanted Susan to get an "unedited transcript" capturing the tone and nuance of the phone conversation. More important, I wanted to hear from her how the version I assumed her mother gave her diverged from our actual conversation. This could yield useful information about distortions and misperceptions.

Susan's first comment after hearing my report was, "Before she called you, I had told her about my plans to conclude treatment soon and that I had even bought a ticket to fly home. Yet, she never mentioned that to you."

My response to this new fact was, "The impression she gave me was that her call was prompted solely by her own concerns and not primed by your telling her you were planning to leave soon. It's apparent that she's having trouble letting go of you. Specifically, she can't seem to let go of your needing her."

"Well, I have some good things to report that indicate I can live without her," Susan said. "This morning, I was able to eat my first fried egg without difficulty. I prepared myself for the tunnel traffic jam today by buying a newspaper beforehand, and calmly perused it while I was bumper-to-bumper."

"Living well is the best revenge," I rejoined. We both laughed.

"Now, let me tell you about my mother's version of her talk with you," Susan said. "The other evening she asked me, 'How are your sessions?' I replied, 'Just fine.' She responded, 'That's good. I spoke to your doctor the other day.' I immediately felt annoyed and she must have picked that up in my facial expression because she made the comment, 'It seems like you suddenly don't want to talk to me.' I lost it and yelled that she had a lot of nerve calling my doctor! She said, 'I called for two reasons—to find out how you were doing, and when you would be leaving.' I replied, 'I told you about my decision to go soon and that I bought a ticket.' She replied, 'As your mother, I felt a burden on my shoulders about whether you're ready to go.' I retorted, 'That didn't give you the right to go behind my back to call my doctor!' "

"Did you feel any changes in your body during your exchange with your mother?" I asked.

"When I was annoyed, I felt a tightness in my throat," Susan replied. "After I got my feelings out with her, I felt OK."

"You didn't have to swallow your anger," I said.

"You know, Mike said something similar when I called him to relate the incident with mother," Susan replied. "Mike said it was the first time he could remember my speaking up to my mother. Mike even suggested that I not go too far with my anger at my mother at this time," Susan continued.

"I agree," I said. "You don't want to trigger your guilt feelings about hurting your mother by being too angry with her. It's important to strike the right balance in your response. Your ability to swallow is a sensitive barometer of that balance."

Susan said, "I feel good that I can appreciate the connection between my feelings, like annoyance and anger, and the tightness in my throat. I really understand how expressing myself to my mother is correlated with the relaxation of my swallowing musculature and ease of eating. I feel much more confident now about going home."

"Yes, you have turned a crisis precipitated by your mother's intervention into an opportunity to solidify your gains, rather than falling apart. Let's see if we can help you with your fear of flying next time," I concluded.

Separation Anxiety

Once again, Susan maintained her prior breakthrough level of degree of relaxation response. The threat from her mother had been successfully handled. The path to the finish line was clearly in sight now.

Unfortunately, Susan reported at the start of our ninth session that she had been doing terribly since our last visit. "Last weekend was a mess," she said. "Friday night I went out for a light dinner by myself. I was sitting in this restaurant and all around me I saw couples laughing and having a good time together. I was feeling alone and isolated. I guess I had too much to drink. I was totally hung over in the morning. I also was feeling horribly anxious and light-headed. I did two things that helped me to get a grip on myself. I had ginger ale to calm my stomach and I called Mike. I told him, 'You're going to be upset with me,' but he wasn't. He was understanding and supportive as he always is."

"Sounds like you were feeling disappointed with yourself and expected Mike to be just as critical of you," I said. "You're experiencing how Mike continues to be supportive, which he really is."

"Am I never really going to be cured?" Susan asked. "Is this like being a recovered alcoholic?"

"It's more like golf," I replied. "The more you practice, the better your game becomes. It's human to need people. You were feeling lonely and drowned your sorrows in too much booze. That threw your system off, but you bounced back the next morning by having a soda to calm your system and by calling Mike to reconnect to love."

"I'm still in a lousy mood. I had a bad day: too many errands, too many phone calls, too many traffic jams," Susan replied.

"I can see you're tense. You're sitting on the edge of your chair for the first time that I can remember," I said. "You're focusing on the negative. It could be expected that you would be feeling anxious about finishing your treatment here and returning home."

"I associate being here with regaining my health, and I associate going home with the stress and the symptoms," Susan replied.

Dreams: Pictures from Our Unconscious

"I had a dream the other night that bothered me," Susan began. "But it may be beneficial if you can help me to understand it. In the dream, Dad came back. Mother, however, was remarried to her current husband. Dad didn't want to interfere. He stayed in the background. He told me that he was available if I needed him. Then I had another dream in which Dad said to me that he realized I had been having a difficult time, but that I was getting better. He said he thought that he could go now." Susan was visibly upset as she said that last sentence. I could hear her voice catch in her throat, and see the tears welling up in her eyes. "These dreams seem bizarre to me," Susan continued. "I just don't understand them. What do you think they mean?" she asked plaintively.

"I believe your dreams dramatically portray the inner conflicts you feel," I replied. "You want to hold on to your father. By being sick, in one sense you accomplish this. It's similar to your holding on to your grandmother by identifying with her symptoms of difficulty swallowing when she was dying. You're scared to let go of them concretely. Because death is so final to you, you're experiencing terror at the thought of being eternally cut off from them. Even the anxiety you've been feeling these last few days is part of this fear of separation. By believing your father and grandmother are spirits who live on forever, you can reframe your loss. Their spirits are always available for you to reach out to. You can begin to connect to them through your warm, loving memories of experiences you shared with them. Death isn't finality. It is a transition from the physical to the eternal spiritual world. The timing of this dream occurring near the end of our work together also indicates how you've transferred to me some of the positive feelings you felt toward your father. Now you fear that I will be lost to you too, when you leave."

"Well, I won't be seeing you anymore," Susan said.

"Yes, that's literally true in a concrete way," I replied. "I will, however, both continue to be with you in your remembrances of our work together, as well as quite literally still being here in this place on earth physically."

"Well, I never called you between sessions," Susan said.

"Yes, I know," I replied. "In your case, your fear of depending on a caring figure determined that. However, former patients do call me every now and then just to let me know how they are doing. And, in the unlikely event that it is necessary, I am here for us to work on any problems that might crop up in the future."

I could see the tension melting away in Susan's face and body as I spoke. "Maybe I can begin to let them go," she said. "If I think I can still feel them spiritually. I know I need to go on now with my own life."

"Yes, you have been starving for love," I said, "because you wouldn't let yourself connect spiritually, and have been terrified of intimacy. Now you can partake of the feast of love that your past with your father and grandmother prepared and that Mike is looking to share with you."

As Susan left for her biofeedback training, I was able to feel confident that the last hurdle had been negotiated successfully. Now all that remained was a session of hypnosis to overcome her fear of flying—and a final session to sum up what we accomplished.

As I expected, Susan broke through to new personal levels of physiological relaxation. She was clearly within the normal range of functioning. The cure was in place. Time was now on our side. I felt like a surgeon who had successfully completed a long and delicate operation to restore normal functioning. I had faith that I could rely on nature's God-given healing processes to continue the cure over time.

Overcoming the Fear of Flying with Hypnosis

As Susan sat down to begin our next session, she said, "Well, I'm ready for my hypnosis lesson to conquer my fear of flying. My plane reservations are set for the end of next week. I'm feeling great. Our last session really helped me put things in a new perspective."

"I'm glad to hear that," I said. "We will have the time for one final summation session before you go home, so let's indeed use today for helping you to overcome your flying fears. What do you know about hypnosis?" (It's helpful to ask patients what they know about a technique first, so I can respond concretely to increase their understanding and correct any misperceptions they may have.)

"Not much," Susan laughed. "I always thought of hypnosis as a game to play at a party. Something that's more fun than therapeutic."

"As a matter of fact, hypnosis is a misnomer," I began. "It implies loss of self-control, being under someone else's power. Hypnosis is really a form of focused concentration. In fact, what happens is the individual narrows his mental focus just on to what he wants to accomplish, and screens out everything else. It increases the ability to shift gears from the stress response to the relaxation response."

I continued giving Susan an overview of the subject. "There is a bell-shaped curve of hypnotizability in the general population. At one extreme, about twenty percent of people do not have any capacity for hypnotic states. In the middle range of mild-to-moderate capacity for focused concentration are the sixty percent majority of the population. At the other extreme, about twenty percent of people have such a high capacity for focused concentration that they can perform such feats as 'picture memory' in which they can look at a page and literally have a photocopy of it in their minds. In medical school, I was envious of those students who had picture memories. They had a lot more free time than I did," I said with a smile.

"I know what you mean," Susan agreed, and we laughed together.

"Getting back to hypnosis," I said, "I show people a quick, effective induction technique that they can use themselves. This avoids any fear they may have of being under the control of the hypnotist."

"OK," Susan said. "What do I do?"

"The chair you're sitting in repositions as a recliner," I explained. "Hold on to the sides and push backward." As Susan did so, I said, "That's right. Now, rest your feet comfortably on the elevated extended footrest. Keep your head steady and look forward. Without moving your head, roll your eyes up to the ceiling, look up as high as you can. That's it. Now, while you continue to look up, slowly close your eyelids. Close—close—that's good. Now, take a deep breath and let your body relax down into the chair. As you relax, let your body feel a pleasant sensation of floating. Good. Now visualize in your mind that you are enjoying this calm, serene, safe sense of floating as you picture yourself going through the stages of boarding the plane; takeoff; flight, including turbulence; and finally, a safe landing. When you've completed this trip mentally, slowly open your eyes and let your focus return to its usual state of recognition of your surroundings."

I could see that Susan had a good, natural capacity for hypnotic concentration. The clue was in her eye roll. As she was maintaining her upward gaze and began closing her eyelids, I could see mostly the whites of her eyes. This sign correlates with a high degree of hypnotizability. In the most hypnotizable people, all you see is the whites of their eyes. At the other extreme, unhypnotizable people have their eyeballs shift downward as they close their eyelids. You don't see any whites of their eyes. The middle range has varying degrees of ability to maintain their upward gaze as they close their eyelids.

After about ten minutes, Susan gradually opened her eyes. "How was your trip?" I asked.

"Very relaxing," Susan said. "I was able to remain calm and experience that peaceful sensation of floating, even through a period of bad air turbulence."

"Good," I said. "You have a God-given gift that you hadn't known about. You can also use self-hypnosis in other situations. You can help shift your focus to a relaxed state when you're feeling anxious."

"I'm continually amazed at what I'm learning about the powers of the mind. I never heard about this in my medical training," Susan said.

"Experience is the best teacher," I responded. "You are following the highest code of our profession in following the dictum, 'Physician heal thyself.' From your healing experience, you will be better able to help others."

As I anticipated, Susan maintained her normal range of physiological parameters during the biofeedback training part of the session. All that remained was a summing-up session and Susan could return home with her health restored.

Summing Up

Susan's final session was to have her review her understanding of how her problems had come about and, more important, what she knew about herself and her Achilles' heels. For a cure to be lasting, and not just temporarily working while the treating physician is present, the individual must gain a personal understanding. Like a detective solving a mystery, the patient must discover the *who, what, where, when, why,* and *how.*

The *who,* as in, *Who are you?* In Susan's case, an intelligent professional who was out of touch with her innermost feelings. The *what,* meaning, *What went wrong?* Here, an overintrusive, guilt-provoking mother resulted in Susan feeling terrified of intimacy. *Where,* as in, *Where does it hurt?* Literally, she could not swallow the nourishment (love) she needed to live. *When* asks, *When did events in a precariously balanced life turn sour?* In Susan's life, it was when both her father and beloved grandmother died. *Why* means, *Why did it happen?* Susan couldn't trust loving anyone after her father and grandmother died. She began starving to death. *How,* as in, *How can you change for the better?* This mind-body treatment enabled Susan to go viscerally inside herself, not just intellectually. The physiological retraining enabled Susan to learn how to monitor and control her physiology. She learned how to regain self-control.

With all these questions answered, Susan could go on with her life and meet the stresses and challenges of daily living. Her coping skills were now ready for the task of living and loving.

As Susan walked into our final session with a smile on her face, I took the opportunity to greet her in a light mood.

"What's up, Doc," I said with a smile.

"I am!" Susan replied and we laughed together. "I'm feeling great and I'm ready to go home," she continued.

"I'm glad to hear that," I responded. "I agree with you. So tell me, I want to hear your understanding of what went wrong and how you've learned to set things right."

In addition to discussing the detective's sextet of questions I mentioned before, Susan had some particular points of her own to emphasize.

"Understanding the underlying meaning of the dream I had about my father was crucial for me," she said. "It was like a revelation. For the first time, I can clearly see my need to love and be loved, and how I have been holding on to the past in a sick way, rather than letting myself love in the present. I need to let myself feel my spiritual link to my grandmother and father. My difficulties with closeness with my mother have left me terrified of intimacy with the man I love. I'm tired of starving despite the nourishment of Mike's love available to me. I'm determined to work out my intimacy problems with him."

I replied, "Well, our work has been successfully completed. Your swallowing has returned to normal. More important, you know the hows and whys and what you need to do for yourself to stay healthy. You're in touch now with your basic human need to share love. You have your work cut out for yourself to build on intimacy with Mike, but you're growing daily. Please feel free to call and let me know how you are doing. It's always a pleasure for me to hear from people I have helped. Good luck and God Bless You!"

Postscript

There's a brief and happy follow-up to this successful treatment. A few months later, I got a phone call from Susan. She said, "I just called to let you know that things are going very well. I'm eating normally. I'm handling problems when they occur, before they get blown up out of proportion. I feel more relaxed than ever before. Most significant, Mike and I are getting along better than ever before. Remember that nervous laughter I had about a ring? Well, I took the plunge. I'm wearing Mike's engagement ring and our wedding date is set for a few months from now."

"Congratulations!" I said. "It sounds like you've found your love and inner peace."

"I couldn't have done it without you," Susan said with gratitude in her voice.

"We worked well together," I said. "A good coach needs a good player to create a winning combination."

Epilogue: Future Directions

The mind-body treatment approach described in this book is being applied to more disorders as our understanding grows about the links connecting our emotions, thoughts, and our bodily functioning. A whole new field known as behavioral medicine is developing from our expanding experience in helping people take a more active role in their healing.

New Healing Partnerships

The future holds great promise for further development of new healing partnerships between doctors and patients. Advances in health will result from combining our ever-increasing ability to help people mobilize their own inner powers of renewal with the latest breakthroughs in medical technology. This powerful combination is already creating new successes in the prevention and treatment of heart disease and hypertension, as discussed in this book.

The new frontier is the treatment of cancer. The combination of the latest wonder drugs and mind-body methods of mobilizing inner healing resources is already yielding dramatic results. Doctors have long observed that some of their patients could beat the odds and conquer cancer by marshaling their inner healing powers to work together with traditional medical treatment. The value of using mind techniques such as psychotherapy, imagery, dreams, and visualization to battle cancer has been documented by such doctors as Larry LeShan, Carl Simonton, M.D., and Stephanie Matthews Simonton, and Bernie Siegel.

Recently, a major breakthrough study has proven in a solid, scientific way that you can significantly prolong your life by using mind-body methods even in the face of advanced cancer. As I noted earlier in the book, the "gold standard" of scientific research is a prospective study. As the name indicates, in a prospective study, researchers set up the variables before the study begins. This avoids some of the pitfalls of a retrospective study in which researchers look back at already existing findings to try to figure out what accounted for the differences in outcome.

Living Longer, Despite Advanced Cancer

David Spiegel, M.D., of Stanford's Medical School, is the main researcher of this breakthrough prospective study. He found that the mind can influence how long cancer patients live. He studied women with metastatic breast cancer. The women who attended group psychotherapy sessions for ninety minutes, once a week, for a year, lived twice as long as those women who did not attend the group sessions. Not only did the women attending group live, on average, for over three years after joining the study, but the three women who were still alive ten years later all had been in the psychotherapy group.

Spiegel's research methods were more rigorous than that of previous studies. The assignment of women to the psychotherapy group or control group (that didn't have group psychotherapy) was totally random. In addition, all the patients in the study received the highest standard of medical treatment including chemotherapy, radiation, or surgery. This is particularly significant in demonstrating that the combination of mind-body methods and the latest advances in traditional medicine were responsible for the surprising results.

The results even surprised Dr. Spiegel. In the introduction to his study in *Lancet*, October 14, 1989, he notes that he started out with the belief that no life extension would result from the mind-body methods. As a matter of fact, he decided to do the study to prove that survival could not be altered by these methods.

What Went On in Those Weekly Ninety-Minute Sessions?

Spiegel reports in *Lancet*:

The groups were structured to encourage discussion of how to cope with cancer, but at no time were patients led to believe that participation would affect the course of disease. Group therapy patients were encouraged to come regularly and express their feelings about the illness and its effect on their lives. Physical problems, including side effects of chemotherapy or radiotherapy, were discussed and a self-hypnosis strategy was taught for pain control. Social isolation was countered by developing strong relations among members. Members encouraged one another to be more assertive with doctors. Patients focused on how to extract meaning from tragedy by using their experience to help other patients and their families. One major function of the leaders was to keep the groups directed toward facing and grieving losses.

As Spiegel himself admits, in an article in *Science,* October 27, 1989: "The whole point of the original study was that we could make them feel better. We didn't in any way imply you were going to wash away your illness. In fact, we were saying 'face your mortality.' "

So a study designed to disprove any effect on longevity by mind-body techniques did just the opposite! In his discussion of the results in *Lancet,* Spiegel says that "indeed the only variable to affect survival time significantly was our complex psychosocial intervention."

He notes:

The emphasis in our program was on living as fully as possible, improving communications with family members and doctors, facing and mastering fears about death and dying, and controlling pain and other symptoms. To the extent that this intervention influenced the course of the disease, it did not do so because of any intention on the part of the therapists or the patients that their participation would affect survival time.

What Accounts For the Longevity

Spiegel gives his views in *Lancet* as to what accounts for the differences observed. He notes a number of factors:

Social support is important in how individuals cope with stress. . . . One role of the group might have been to provide a place to belong and to express feelings. Clearly, the patients in these groups felt an intense bonding with one another and a sense of acceptance through sharing a common dilemma . . . the therapy group patients visited each other in the hospital, wrote poems . . . involvement in the group may have allowed patients to mobilize their resources better. . . . Neuroendocrine and immune systems may be a major link between emotional processes and cancer course.

The reporter in *Science* adds, "The result was that patients who received therapy became less anxious, fearful, and depressed and learned to reduce their pain through self-hypnosis."

I have chosen to do a lot of direct quoting to make the point that both Spiegel in *Lancet* and the *Science* reporter describe the healing process in much the same way as my experience with my patients is described throughout this book. Once again, we see that mind-body methods—in this instance, group psychotherapy and self-hypnosis for pain control—can improve both longevity and quality of life even in advanced-cancer patients.

In such illness as cancer, the point is not whether patients can control the disease process by mind-body methods alone. The point is that combining the marshaling of our own inner healing powers with the most advanced techniques of traditional medical care yields the best possible results.

Direct Links Between Our Brain and Body

We now know there are direct biochemical links between the brain and the immune system. Until recently, the accepted notion had been that the immune system functioned totally independently. The new scientific understanding of the complex communication system between our mind and our immune system helps to explain how such well-established techniques as psychotherapy, hypnosis, imagery, and visualization can help us improve our immune functioning. For example, psychotherapy can help us to resolve emotional conflicts and decrease our stress. With a new sense of well-being, we have energy freed up for healing, which can be channeled to aid our immune functioning via techniques such as self-hypnosis, imagery, and visualization. While the specific links between mind and immune system still need to be discovered, we now have proven scientifically that direct biochemical messages are sent back and forth between our brain and our immune system.

Even more far-reaching has been the discovery that information from the brain can go to and from all parts of the body by means of molecules called peptides. Thus, all the bodily systems, including the hormone system and the central nervous system, are capable of direct communication with the brain and the immune system and one another.

We now know of over fifty different molecules that the body naturally produces to carry messages back and forth throughout all our systems. Among the earliest of these substances to be discovered are the endorphins, which we know have potent pain-killing abilities.

Researchers are discovering more and more substances that our mind and body naturally create. Some of these self-generated molecules are responsible for such well-known phenomena as feeling good after exercising and the natural "high" that runners experience.

We are at the beginning of a truly revolutionary advance in scientific knowledge. Remember that we were all taught in high school biology that the only way that information could be communicated in the body was from one nerve cell to the next. We now realize that the need for such direct wiring only is necessary for some kinds of information flow, especially muscle contraction. But the largest amount of information between the brain and the body does not require a network of nerves in close physical contact with one another. Instead, a much broader and more complex system of communication exists in which information is carried by these peptide molecules. These peptide messengers travel throughout the body until they reach specific receptor molecules. These receptor molecules are designed to enable a specific peptide to attach, much like a specific lock is designed to accept a specific key. Thus, the receptors are now recognized as the mechanism that sorts out information exchange in the body.

Brain "Hot Spots": A Molecular Map of Our Emotions

We now also have a scientific basis for understanding how emotions are biochemically interconnected with the mind and body. Scientists have known for a long time that we have specific centers in the brain that mediate emotions and that these centers are linked to other parts of the brain that involve our thoughts, perceptions, judgment, and memory. In addition, in the brain, the emotional centers are adjacent to the pituitary gland, which regulates the hormones in the body.

Recently PNI researchers have demonstrated that a high concentration of receptors (which they call hot spots) for the peptide messenger molecules are located in the brain areas involved with emotions. Equally important, throughout the body there are receptors for messenger molecules, which are also able to produce messages that go back to the brain. Thus, a very complex feedback system exists for sending and receiving information involving our emotions, mind, and body.

One of the leading PNI researchers who has been in the forefront of developing this molecular map of our emotions is Dr. Candace Pert, former chief of the Brain Biochemistry section of the National Institutes of Mental Health. An early pioneer in the PNI field, in 1973, Dr. Pert discovered an important biological landmark known as the opiate receptor. More recently, she has been a leader in developing the concept that biochemical substances with functional aspects of "mind" can be found traveling throughout the body. For example, Dr. Pert has found biochemical and anatomical bases for the common experience of having a "gut feeling" or intuitive hunch that we "feel" in our abdomen.

The Future Looks Bright

In summary, we have a biochemical means of virtual instant communication between the mind and emotions and any part of the body. These kinds of connections between brain and body explain why the mind has power over the body and therefore why the mental techniques described in this book are able to effect bodily changes.

Since the biochemical connections also enable information to go from various parts of the body to the brain, we have a mechanism for understanding why "body" techniques such as abdominal breathing can be used to help restore peace of mind.

The future looks bright for science to develop a fuller understanding of how our complex networks of brain, mind, and body communicate. Right now we can enjoy the benefits of mind-body approaches that have proven to promote healing, bring health and happiness, and enhance the process of self-renewal.

REED C. MOSKOWITZ, M.D., is a clinical assistant professor of psychiatry at New York University Medical Center. He is also the founder and medical director of NYU's Stress Disorders Medical Services Program. Dr. Moskowitz lives in New York City with his wife and daughter.